CHRIST'S HOSPITAL
IN THE YEAR 2000

CHRIST'S HOSPITAL IN THE YEAR 2000

BY
PETER BLOOMFIELD
ROSIE HOWARD & PAM LEGATE
with drawings by
KEITH MACKNESS

Illustrations
Front of jacket: The Head Master, the Senior Grecian and the Second Monitors with some of the Second Form in the Quad.
Back of jacket: Full School Chapel.

Endpapers, drawn by Keith Mackness
Front: The Quad: Chapel and cloister.
Back: The Quad: Science School and cloister.

First page: Statue of Edward VI on the south facing wall of Big School, drawn by Keith Mackness.

Previous pages: Deputy Head Elizabeth Cairncross teaches a Deputy Grecians English class in the Library. Clockwise from the left: Guy Vesey, Jane Mitchell, George Allen, William Owen, Alice Wheeler, Annabel Ward and Tom Webster. Also present, but hidden behind Jane Mitchell, was Zachary Walsh.

© 2001 CHRIST'S HOSPITAL

First published 2001 by
CHRIST'S HOSPITAL
Horsham, West Sussex RH13 7YP

ISBN 0-9507843-4-6

Designed by John Mitchell
Produced by John and Susan Mitchell
with the support of The Sue Thomson Foundation
Typeset by Bexhill Phototypesetters
Printed in Hong Kong by South East Asia Press

Dedicated to
PAM LEGATE
Born 23 April 1944
Died 16 March 2001

A pupil at
Christ's Hospital, Hertford
Ward 2, 1955–1962

*A true Blue, without whose
enthusiasm, commitment
and professionalism
this book would not have seen
the light of day.*

The East Gate and East Lodge.

CONTENTS

His Royal Highness Richard, Duke of Gloucester, President of Christ's Hospital.

<u>CHRIST'S HOSPITAL IN THE YEAR 2000</u>

As Christ's Hospital enters a new millennium it has every reason to offer thanks to its forefathers of a hundreds years ago who had the wisdom and foresight to establish at Horsham a great school campus in unparalleled surroundings of peace and tranquillity. Between the years 1897 and 1902, and after three hundred and fifty years in London, the twelve hundred acre estate was transformed into the school that we enjoy now.

So in 2002 we celebrate two great anniversaries in the long and distinguished history of Housey: four hundred and fifty years since our foundation by Edward VI and one hundred years at Horsham.

It is therefore appropriate that, in addition to a series of celebratory events we should publish a record of life at Horsham in the Millennium Year – a very different life from that which the boys in London and the girls in Hertford lived a hundred years ago.

There has been momentous change in this period and two cataclysmic world wars, which took the lives of two hundred and seventy-six Old Blues. However, what has not changed are the values and ethos of Christ's Hospital which stand as a beacon of hope for children who are fortunate enough to be received into the great family of "Blues", regardless of personal circumstances or social standing.

These celebrations gave everyone associated with Christ's Hospital an opportunity to reflect on the values that have brought and kept Old Blues together for four and a half centuries.

I have said before and I wish to repeat that one cannot help being impressed by all that this most special place has done for so many, the huge contribution they give collectively and the pride they have in being part of it.

May it be so in perpetuity.

President

PREFACE

BY

THE HEAD MASTER
DR PETER SOUTHERN

The year 2000, anticipated world-wide with a mixture of apocalyptic gloom and naïve euphoria, unwound in this corner of West Sussex as a delightfully ordinary year. As such, this annal of Christ's Hospital takes on a special importance. It provides a portrait of the community at Horsham free from the distortion of a very 'special' year and presents a pretty accurate picture of the place, its inhabitants and the life they lead, which many generations from either side of the millennial moment will recognise. Like any good portrait, there are character-revealing wrinkles and warts and the true likeness comes across, not through a flat 'photographic' image, but through an appreciation of the many interconnected strands which make up the fullness of this remarkable and complex place.

Dr Peter Southern, Head Master, teaching Norman history to (left to right) Sandra Bamfo, Sam Curtin, Joe Grant, Ben Goodwin-Self, Tola Ogudipe, Olivia Laband, Liz Pannell and Lyndsey Cambridge.

I am delighted that the Treasurer's initiative has brought forth such an excellent book, admirably written by a number of distinguished hands and wonderfully punctuated with pictures, whose shafts illuminate the text splendidly. I am sure that this volume will be much enjoyed by those with a special interest in Christ's Hospital and, in years to come, will be pored over by historians who will value the remarkable insights and details it provides of this unique microcosm.

Peter Southern
Horsham, March 2001

EDITOR'S PREFACE

The idea for this book was hatched by Susan Mitchell with encouragement from John Gale in 1996, in the early stages of considering ways in which Christ's Hospital could celebrate, in 2002, the two great landmarks in its history: the original foundation in 1552 and the move from London to Horsham in 1902.

It is not intended to be a history of Christ's Hospital although we hope it may provide useful insights for future historians. It is a record of life at the School in the academic year 1999–2000, as we enter a new millennium. A little history has been included to help explain some of the rich traditions – some may say eccentricities – which have survived for nearly half a millennium. Quite an achievement during times of great change but, as we hope the book shows, Christ's Hospital is a modern school capable of embracing change without sacrificing tradition. This, together with its unique ethos of providing education for children in need, is what makes Housie special.

There need to be a few words of acknowledgement before you become involved in what the authors hope you will find to be an absorbing story.

The first are to my co-authors. The late Pam Legate, a Hertford Old Blue and professional journalist, spent a great deal of her time until the Summer term interviewing pupils and members of staff and writing many cogent pieces about aspects of current School life. To our great distress, she fell seriously ill during the Summer term and so was unable to complete the task that she had so ably begun. However, the publishing team was unanimous in its wish to dedicate this book to her name, an intention that she was made aware of before her untimely death in March 2001.

Rosie Howard comes from a background of marketing at Esso Petroleum and academic publishing at Cambridge University Press, and has also worked for the Christian charity Tear Fund. Married to Ian Howard, House Master of Peele B, she is a Lay Reader licensed to the School and has a son, Jonathan, on the LE in Maine A. Rosie learnt about Christ's Hospital's distinguished history while working in the School's Museum and took over writing about current events after Pam became ill. In addition, she continued to research deeply into many of the customs and aspects of the history of the School. Such is her enthusiasm and ability as an historian that the pages which we had allotted her were not nearly enough. What we had imagined would be brief notes on, for instance, the history of St Matthew's Day, became full length essays of considerable substance. Some have been incorporated within the text; others appear in the Appendices.

Another Old Blue, Keith Mackness, Donation Governor and architect, has provided a bonus for the book. We wanted to include a few sketches to give variety to the photographs and were delighted by Keith's great enthusiasm for the project and by his aptitude with the pencil on subjects which do not readily lend themselves to photography. The 'sketches' became drawings of considerable quality which give an added value to the book.

Neil Fleming, now House Master of Grecians' West, is well known around the School for his photographic expertise and he has provided many of the photographs; others, from a number of sources, are individually acknowledged on page 226. We are grateful to all those who have kindly responded to our requests for photographs.

I have to thank the Head Master and the Clerk for their support and encouragement for our efforts and for reviewing and commenting most helpfully on the text of the book. Particular thanks are due to the Head Master for providing his invaluable overview of the academic curriculum in 2000. Thanks are also due to many others, regrettably too numerous for me to name them all but including Bernard Atkinson, Derek Baker, Bob Betson, John Cullen, Jane Hitchcock, Howard Holdsworth, Ian Hoskins, Wendy Killner, Richard March, James Maxwell, Jeffrey Mayhew, Richard McGregor, David O'Meara, Rhona Mitchell, Susan Mitchell, Frank Pattison, Kim Platfoot, Nick Plumley, Dennis Quinn, Bob Sillett, Kerren Simmonds and Steve Webb, all of whom have made special contributions – and the late Jack Watt for the history of the OBRFC.

Finally, I have to mention the major contribution of John Mitchell, Donation Governor, who has worked ceaselessly to 'put it all together'. Photographer, designer, sub-editor, production manager – you name it and John has done it. As a mere amateur in the field of book publishing, I desperately needed a 'senior professional' by my side and I don't know what I would have done without John in this rôle. He has my deepest gratitude.

Peter Bloomfield
June 2001

THE FOUNDING OF CHRIST'S HOSPITAL

ALTHOUGH THIS IS NOT A HISTORY BOOK it is important to know about the beginnings of Christ's Hospital to understand the traditions and ethos of the Foundation and the School. The source for much of what follows is *A Contemporaneous Account in Dialogue-Form of the Foundation and Early History of Christ's Hospital, and of Bridewell and St Thomas' Hospitals* by John Howes (1582 and 1587), printed for the Governors of Christ's Hospital, London, in January 1889.

The beginning of January 1552 marks the first point of our history. On 21 January Edward VI, then aged fourteen, had moved to Whitehall Palace at Westminster for the opening of Parliament, having enjoyed Christmas and its festivities at Greenwich and Deptford. On 22 January Edward recorded in his diary without emotion that his uncle Edward Seymour, Duke of Somerset and Lord Protector of the Realm 'had his head cut off upon Tower Hill between eight and nine o'clock in the morning.'

The next day the young King heard a stirring sermon on the needs of London's poor, and speedily summoned the preacher, Nicholas Ridley, Bishop of London, to talk more about these pressing needs. In his sermon Ridley had called upon 'such as were in authority to travail in some charitable way and mean to comfort and relieve them', and it was on this point that Edward sought to draw him. For he said, 'ye willed such as are in authoritie to be carefull thereof and to devise some order for their relief, wherein I think ye meant me, for I am in the highest place, and am the first that must make answer to God for my negligence if I should not be careful therein, knowing it to be the express commandment of Almightie God to have compassion for his poor and needy members, for whom we must make an account unto him.'

The Bishop was amazed at this swift and positive response, and in reply to his further questions – as to how a work of charity could be started – suggested that Edward write a letter to Sir Richard Dobbs, the Lord Mayor of London, setting in motion measures to help the poor. Edward immediately complied with this suggestion and his letter was taken by Ridley to Dobbs, who in turn responded directly. Ten or twelve of the 'wisest citizens' then conferred with other Aldermen of the City of London to agree upon a course of action.

To begin they undertook a survey of the poor and classified them under six headings:

> Fatherless children and other poor men's children; babes in arms; the lame, aged and homeless; idle and lusty rogues; lepers (lazars); decayed poor citizens.

It was agreed that these should be helped in the following ways:

KING EDWARD VI, *from the portrait which hangs in the Court Room. Although very much in the style of Holbein, this portrait is attributed to Guillim Scrots.*

1

The fatherless children were to be housed in the former premises of the Grey Friars in Newgate Street, which had been owned by the City for thirteen years after its dissolution as a monastery, and which had become run down and filthy. The monastries had been a major means of support for the poor until their dissolution in 1536 which had led to high numbers of distressed folk wandering and begging in the streets and alleys of London.

The babes in arms were to be sent to the country for basic nursing – to Hertford, St Albans, Thaxted and Dunmow – from which provision the Hertford School originated for the Prep boys and for girls.

The lame, aged and homeless were to be cared for at the Hospital of St Thomas the Apostle; the lepers removed from the streets and given a monthly pension, and the 'decayed poor citizens' were to receive a weekly pension in accordance with their needs. That only left the 'idle and lusty rogues' to be found 'some house'. In addition, the number of beadles was to be increased and patrols set up at the City's gates to restrict the influx of 'foreign' poor. The number of people estimated to need help under these categories totalled 2,160 or, by another reckoning, 2,100.

St Matthew's Day orations in the Great Hall in Newgate Street in the late eighteenth or early nineteenth century. From an engraving by Rowlandson, 1808.

The financial implications of the vast programme of social reform were considered by a committee of thirty who felt that in such a work of charity it was 'good to begin with themselves' and each gave according to their means, some £20, some £10, some less. Sheriffs also handed over fines of £200 per annum, and so the total collected at that stage was £748.

The thirty then divided into two groups of fifteen, and also divided the City of London between them, raising money in their respective parts. Ministers, churchwardens and sidesmen were invited to consider their long-term support for the poor, including the provision of weekly pensions.

The appeal then went wider. Every householder in London was presented with a bill in which a window had been left for his name and the sum of money to be donated. Through these divers and ingenious means £2,476 (over £700,000 in today's figures) was raised and the thirty agreed that work should begin on the premises – that they should be 'repaired and made sweet' – for the arrival of their charges: Christ His Hospital needed to accommodate 500; St Thomas's Hospital, 300. Prodigious acts of charity continued: Mr Callthroppe, one of the thirty, gave 500 feather beds and 500 pads of straw, blankets and 1,000 pairs of sheets. The total expenditure in setting up the Hospitals was £2,479 10s 10d, which left a deficit of just £3 10s 10d.

On 6 October 1552 the Governors – who were elected from Guild members of good character and whose appointment had to be ratified by the Court of Aldermen – met to appoint officers to serve the children at Christ's Hospital. At the outset the intention was to provide 'food, clothing, lodging and a little learning', so that the pupils were not only cared for but, more specifically, prepared for the job market. Key skills at that stage were 'reading, writing, siphering and singing', with the ability to play a musical instrument also considered a great asset. The only surviving evidence of a full-time music master working at a school at that time is of the one employed at Christ's Hospital.

The curriculum for the girls was simple: they were to develop skills in handwork which would enable them to find employment in service which would, hopefully, lead them to husbands, their best means of survival. Handwork of the nobler sort – 'sewing in silk, silver and gold, and working in sundry kinds of lace', was encouraged, rather than just spinning, which was considered an inferior form of employment.

In November 1552, almost ten months after Ridley preached to such good effect, Christ's Hospital opened its door to 380 pupils, 100 of whom were soon put out to nurse. Within a year the number had increased to 540.

Consideration was also given to the needs of those thought to be in need of correction and, hearing that Edward VI was preparing to sell his newly-built palace at Bridewell, the Governors thought that this would be a suitable house. Ridley was summoned to make another Godly exhortation to the King for charity and again Edward responded with generosity, granting the palace at Bridewell, and also conveying the Savoie, which had been used as a hostel for the homeless and wayfarers, and its lands, with the provision of £450 per annum in rents from them.

He also agreed to become the patron and founder of these Hospitals, and it is the Charter for these conveyances, signed by Edward on 26 June

1553, as he lay desperately ill, that hangs in the School Museum. The so-called 'Charter Picture' which hangs in the School Library is symbolic rather than factual. Edward was eleven days from death when he signed the Charter and had to be propped up in bed to do so. His brief prayer of thankfulness to God for having been granted life thus far, to complete this work to the glory of His name, takes on real meaning in this context.

It was agreed from the outset that Bridewell and Christ's Hospital should work in tandem: if a child taken to Christ's Hospital was deemed to be in need of correction, he or she would spend time at Bridewell; equally, if inmates of Bridewell proved themselves to be reformed and hard-working they could be removed to Christ's Hospital. The close relationship between the two institutions continues to this day. Bridewell Royal Hospital ceased to be a penal institution in 1855 and became known as King Edward's School from 1860, moving to its present site near Witley, Surrey in 1867.

Still the Governors were not satisfied that the quality of their care was of the highest standard for they continued to express concern that these children, though well educated and raised virtuously, would yet be unable to compete on equal terms in the job market with children of privileged backgrounds: there was no-one who could put them about in society and bring their hard-won talents to the attention of potential employers. So schemes were devised which would display the children in society, and so attract 'preferment'. These schemes included high-profile attendance at the Spital Sermons, at St Matthew's Day celebrations, and – perhaps most audacious of all – arranging for a senior pupil to deliver an oration to a new monarch-elect on her or his first entry into the City of London, a right exercised to this day.

The Treasurers of Christ's Hospital and King Edward's Witley, Mrs Susan Mitchell and Mr Richard Abbott.

The Livery Companies were another channel of support for the children: they not only provided employment, they also gave generously. Through their munificence £1,540 – a princely sum, well over £400,000 at today's rates – was raised for the Hospitals. Edward himself, seeing how the vast work of charity was progressing, gave a charge that all the linen belonging to the London churches, apart from that in daily use, should be brought to the Governors of the Hospitals. Tools were bought 'to set the idle to work'. Rooms were built or partitioned to create accommodation and teaching space. A porter, cook, and steward were employed, with a matron to look after the single women.

By 1587 Howse reports that of the 540 children being cared for at Christ's Hospital, 150 left each year either to enter into some employment or go to university; £4,300 was paid out each year in pensions.

One Governor in particular, Sir Richard Grafton, Treasurer of Christ's Hospital in 1553, and also the King's Printer, gave generously of his time, skills, money and experience to take the good work forward; a commitment which almost brought him to financial ruin.

It would be good to think that from this point onwards, continuous progress was made. But that was not so. Edward's tragic early death on 6 July 1553 brought about major changes in political and religious life. In 1554 Christ's Hospital faced real opposition when Queen Mary appointed Spanish friars to inspect the children with a view to shutting down the Hospital. But one of the persecutors became so moved by the love and hospitality shown to the children, that he remarked famously that he

Big School under construction, 1901.

would rather be a scullion in the kitchens at Christ's Hospital than a courtier to the King of Spain. Trouble again confronted the Hospital in the Plague of 1665, and the Great Fire of 1666, and there was the continual need for new buildings, for more teachers, for support for those going into employment or to the universities, and for the pensioners.

But help always came and, indeed it could be said that the trials served to strengthen and deepen the character and achievements of both pupils and staff.

THE MOVE TO HORSHAM

Any consideration of the factors that contributed to the momentous decision to move the School from its original site in the centre of the City of London must take account of the broader social and political life of the City and of the country at that time. From 1868–80 Gladstone and Disraeli created a climate in which the living conditions of the poor and vulnerable were considered with a new compassion.

In 1869 the Endowed Schools Act empowered Commissioners 'to alter and add to any existing trust, and to make new trusts, directions, and provisions which affect such endowment and the education promoted thereby.' Christ's Hospital was an obvious target for investigation.

One of the Commissioners appointed to examine the School was a Mr Fearon, who became a renowned critic of the School. The Commission's report stated that he: 'has found much that calls for amendment in the methods and practice of the School teaching. . . . . But the most important practical suggestion with which he concludes is that the School should be almost wholly removed from its present site.'

This conclusion was drawn in the light of the conditions currently prevailing in London, where environmental health was very poor. The water supply had become polluted by sewage, which commonly led to death from cholera. Food supply was also beyond regulation and one parent, a Mr Thomson, complained to the Treasurer that poor quality meat had been the cause of 200 boys being sick one night. The Treasurer rejected this claim, asserting that it was the bread, or the fruit, or the excessively hot weather, that had made them sick. The Dining Hall regularly swarmed with rats, fleas and other vermin, against which the use of yellow-dyed garments was an uncertain defence.

The Commissioners also suggested that the school at Hertford be disposed of, that the rôle of Donation Governor should be abolished, that the uniform should be changed and brought into line with contemporary styles, and that the number of girls should be increased from the current minimum required by the Wests' Foundation of eighteen. Christ's Hospital immediately lodged a complaint against these shocking proposals, and nothing further was done until the sad incident of William Arthur Gibbs, which occurred on 4 July 1877.

Gibbs, nearly thirteen, had been a difficult pupil, and had twice run away from the School. On the second occasion he was brought back by his enraged father, whereupon he expected to be birched for his offence. The night before this was due he was kept in the Infirmary and, on the day itself, appears to have been quite cheerful. But during the morning he hanged himself on a ventilator cord. A Royal Commission was set up to investigate the affair and it was found that Gibbs had been regularly bullied by his Ward monitors, two boys both under the age of sixteen.

The Commission discovered that the care of the pupils outside the classroom was left to the beadles, the warden, the matrons, and the older boys, who frequently used force to gain control. The masters simply arrived in the morning, taught, and went home at 4.15 pm. Occasionally a master or a Grecian would visit a ward, but there was no element of a personal relationship between pupil and master. All these matters the Commission attacked and insisted that 'as soon as conveniently may be after the date of this Scheme, the Council of Almoners shall provide for the Schools, upon convenient sites, buildings suitable, in the case of the Boys' School for 700 boarders, in the case of the Girls' School for 350 boarders, in the case of the Preparatory School for 120 boarders.' They also stipulated that the schools were 'to be maintained within a convenient distance from the City of London.'

These proposals were vigorously opposed by Christ's Hospital, not least by its President, the Duke of Cambridge, but the Commissioners

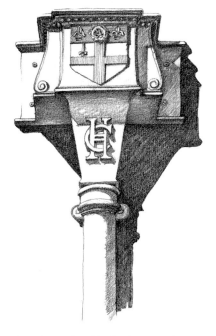

Attention to detail in the design and building of the new School.
Left: a rainwater hopper head; above right: a window latch; below: carving on the arm of the Head Master's chair in Dining Hall.

were adamant and even recourse to the High Court could not deflect a defeat for the School. Move they must, but what and where was a 'convenient distance' from London? Several sites were considered, including a very enthusiastic offer from Sir Henry Peek to sell a portion of his land at Wimbledon, but this was rejected in favour of an unexpected location – the 1,200-acre site of the Aylesbury Dairy Farm, three miles south of Horsham, in Sussex.

Objections were raised that it would be too far, and too costly, for parents to visit their sons; but the London and South Coast Railway agreed to provide a new station close to the School, and to issue cheap return tickets to visitors for half-a-crown. The farmer had recently been declared bankrupt, and the School was therefore able to purchase the estate at a very favourable price: just under £50,000 in total. The Council of Almoners invited architects to submit designs for the new School and the contract was won by Aston Webb and Ingress Bell, a notable London partnership.

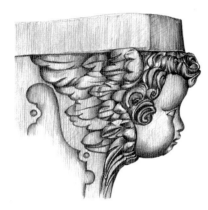

After the pruning of many embellishments and artistic features by the Charity Commissioners, their plans were approved, and the Foundation Stone was laid at Horsham on a singularly cold, bleak and windy day on 23 October 1897.

Longleys of Crawley were the builders, and they produced work of the highest standard, as often as possible incorporating original details from the London site – including the Wren portico, the clock tower and the cupolas, which now adorn Big School, and the Grecians' Arch. Local workmen dug the unwieldy clay soil to lay foundations and set out the labyrinth of underground passages which criss-cross the site and become known as 'the Tube'. The heaviness of the soil and the lack of a sufficient fresh water supply had led the consulting engineer to assert that never, in any circumstances, could the Horsham site be a desirable one for a school. In the event a deep bore hole was sunk down by the station which was able to draw on what was believed to be the fresh, pure water of the Tunbridge Wells basin. This was stored in a reservoir on the top of Sharpenhurst, and in two large water tanks in the tower above the Dining Hall. It was then piped through the Tube around the School.

It was not only the buildings which the architects addressed; everything – from door handles and keyholes, desks and tables, chairs and cupboards – was designed by the team. The total cost of building and equipment was approximately £400,000. Other buildings were added later, including the New Science Schools in 1930 and classrooms for the Prep boys in 1931.

The move from London was an emotional one. Once the artefacts had been removed, including transportation by horse drawn cart of the monumental Verrio painting, parts of the old School were transferred to St Bartholomew's Hospital; others were demolished for a new Post Office depot. On 16 April 1902 the Right Revd William Temple, Archbishop of Canterbury, preached at the Farewell Service in St Paul's Cathedral, and on 29 May 1902 the pupils assembled for the first time at their brand new, red-brick, purpose-built premises at Horsham.

The portly but astute the Revd Richard Lee, Head Master in London, had declined to follow the migration south, and so the mantle of leadership fell on his successor, Dr Arthur William Upcott. His was the vision of everyone having a Charge setting out their duties and responsibilities; his was the Foundation Hymn. He moulded together a School very different from the one that left London, the one described by Mr Fearon as 'a middle school of the third grade.'

Boys learnt how to play, and succeed in, field sports, so that no-one could ever again say, as Mr Fearon had, that 'Christ's Hospital boys don't know how to play.' They had fresh air, good food, including fruit and vegetables and home-produced milk; they had light and airy dormitories and a day-room in which to work, and adequate toilet and bath facilities, (though not by today's standards); they could learn about the countryside and, perhaps most importantly, they had masters actually living with them, who could take a keen, personal interest in their charges. For it was at Horsham that the named house system was developed, in which a house master lived, (perhaps even with a wife), together with an assistant; and where some attempt was made, however tenuous, to get to know the pupils.

The next twelve years were a golden era, as pupils and staff adapted and flourished in their new setting. The pupils' height and weight was recorded: they grew taller and stronger; parents were still able to visit; and Grecians still won Exhibitions to Oxford and Cambridge. But, in 1914, the smooth progression was interrupted by the first World War, which would claim many Housey lives, and cause Dr Upcott untold anxiety.

The exodus had been safely accomplished; the fears of the Duke of Cambridge had been confounded; the land was, indeed, flowing with milk and honey – if mixed with a little Wealden clay. Within these idyllic surroundings – 'ringed with downs and woodland fair' – the pupils would flourish, the girls would, in due course, come to regard it as their home too, and the Prep, which was housed separately on the same site, would be integrated into the main corpus of the School. An exciting century lay ahead, even if not entirely peaceful: storm clouds were gathering both internally and externally, and the School would survive the rigours of a second World War, as well as some painful domestic conflict, before the next hundred years were through.

THE NAMES OF THE BOARDING HOUSES

It has become so commonplace to say 'Mid A', or 'Col B', that one rarely stops to think why the names were chosen to distinguish the eight great boarding blocks on the Horsham site. In London there had been wards, which were numbered, or the King's Ward – for the Mathemats. But the boarding houses of Horsham were planned to be more than just dormitories: they were to be homes, where masters and pupils lived and worked together, developing a sense of shared identity which would, in some way, reflect family life.

Hence it was to famous Old Blues that the Almoners turned when choosing the names of the houses situated on the Avenue, facing south and running from west to east:

PEELE: is named after George Peele, (1558–97) whose father was the first full time Clerk of Christ's Hospital. He joined the School in 1565 and left in 1571 to go to Oxford, where he remained until 1579. He was an author

Thomas Fanshawe Middleton. Engraving by H Mayer from an original drawing by J Jackson.

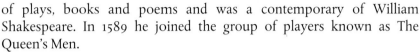

A montage showing one of the many styles of lettering used in the architecture.

of plays, books and poems and was a contemporary of William Shakespeare. In 1589 he joined the group of players known as The Queen's Men.

THORNTON: Sir Edward Thornton, PC, GCB, MA, (1766–1852) at Christ's Hospital 1773–85; in 1798, became a Fellow of Pembroke College, Cambridge. A distinguished diplomatic career followed: in 1807, to Sweden as Envoy Extraordinary; in 1816 he became a Privy Councillor. As a diplomat he served in Lower Saxony, Brazil and in Portugal.

MIDDLETON: Thomas Fanshawe Middleton MA, DD, FRS, (1769–1822), at Christ's Hospital 1779–88. In 1792 he gained his BA at Pembroke College, Cambridge, and in 1809, acquired a prebendal stall in Lincoln Cathedral. In 1812 he became Archdeacon of Huntingdon. Through involvement with the SPCK in 1814 he became the first Anglican Bishop of Calcutta where, in 1820, he founded the Bishops' Mission College. He wrote numerous theological books. His statue stands in St Paul's Cathedral.

COLERIDGE: Samuel Taylor Coleridge, (1772–1834), at Christ's Hospital 1782–91. A gifted and highly-strung child he was, in turns, bullied and praised by the volatile Upper Grammar Master, James Boyer. He proceeded to Jesus College, Cambridge (1791–94), but his studies were not completed. He was a gifted poet, philosopher and metaphysician, his most prominent works being the *Lyrical Ballads*, which he wrote with his

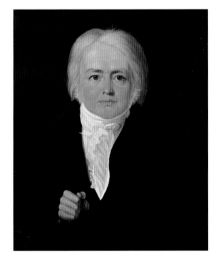

Samuel Taylor Coleridge. From a portrait attributed to Moses Haughton.

lifelong friend Charles Lamb (1798); and his literary criticisms, the best of which are found in *Biographia Literaria* (1817). His statue stands in Westminster Abbey.

LAMB: Charles Lamb, (1775–1834), at Christ's Hospital 1782–89 and was a contemporary of Coleridge. Renowned for his wise and gentle disposition, as well as for his essays and literary works, the most notable of which are, *Recollections*, and *The Essays of Elia*. His stutter precluded him from becoming a Grecian – ie able to recite Greek and Latin. His statue is one of those on the fountain in the Quad.

Charles Lamb. A drawing by A B Wyon, 1876.

BARNES: Joshua Barnes MA, BD, FRS, (1654–1712), at Christ's Hospital 1656–71. Fellow of Emmanuel College, Cambridge 1678–1701. Considered to be an eccentric, he is best known for his editions of *Euripides, Anacreon* and *Homer*. Of himself he wrote, 'I have lived in the University above thirty years fellow of a college, now above forty years standing and 58 years of age; I am a bachelor of divinity and have preached before Kings.'

MAINE: Sir Henry James Sumner Maine, (1822–88), at Christ's Hospital 1829–40, entered Pembroke College, Cambridge where he became Regius Professor of Civil Law in 1847. In 1861 he published his great works on Ancient and International Law. In 1862 appointed Legal Member of the Supreme Council of the Governor General in India, and later Chancellor of the University of Calcutta. Returning to England in 1869 he was elected Corpus Professor of Jurisprudence at Oxford University. He later became Secretary of State for India and, in 1877, became Master of Trinity Hall, Cambridge. In 1887 he was elected Whewell Professor of International Law at Cambridge and Honorary Fellow of Pembroke College. His motto was: 'Success and glory are the children of hard work and God's favour.'

James Henry Leigh Hunt. From a portrait by John Jackson, RA.

LEIGH HUNT: James Henry Leigh Hunt, (1784–1859), essayist, poet and critic, at Christ's Hospital 1791–99. A man of great versatility, he was considered practically a genius in literary circles. He was a friend of Shelley and Byron, and his motto, from his poem *Abou ben Adhem* runs, 'Write me as one who loves his fellow men'. Of a mixed race, sometimes described as American or Creole, he was probably excluded from the original list of house names because of his two year sojourn at His Majesty's pleasure for criticising the Prince Regent. This was corrected in 1966 when the Prep was integrated within the main School and the block was given his name.

The two new Grecians' residences are the first to be built for the accommodation of pupils since 1902. After much discussion about whether other distinguished Old Blues should be commemorated in their names it has been decided, for the time being, that they should be called simply 'Grecians' East' and 'Grecians' West'. The Grecians will have the benefit of more spacious living conditions to aid them in their studies and prepare them for the next stage in their lives. They remain integrated with their 'Avenue Houses' through sport, music, drama and their monitorial duties.

Some of the first girls at Horsham, 1985, marching on the Avenue before the trees were destroyed by the storm of October 1987.

THE GIRLS ARRIVE FROM HERTFORD

The early history of the Hertford School, which also dates back to 1552, is described in Historical Appendix III. By 1980 a possible merger between the two Schools was being quietly discussed. Even in 1902 there had been a suggestion that a new School should be built for the girls, too, at the Horsham site, but this was dismissed on moral and behavioural grounds. In the 'seventies, major schools were making the decision to become co-educational and Christ's Hospital had to face the issue again. Again it was hotly rejected, but a new and powerful ally was emerging in the favour of the co-educationalists: the matter of the Foundation's finances.

In just over fifty years, from 1914 to 1970, the cost of educating a pupil had risen almost tenfold, and income from benefactions had not kept pace. The suggestion that Christ's Hospital become a fee-paying School was unanimously rejected. Even creating the new category of New Foundationer for a limited number of pupils who paid full cost did not meet the shortfall. The harsh facts needed to be faced, and the co-educationalist lobby was not slow in putting forward its views.

Eventually, on 2 April 1980, the Council of Almoners accepted a resolution, described in 1984 by Jack Morpurgo in *Christ's Hospital*, 'as momentous and brave as anything in its history: "This Council resolves to bring together the boys and girls of the Foundation on one site at Horsham".'

Over the next five years intense preparations were made at Horsham. To accommodate all the pupils on one site the numbers of both boys and girls would have to be reduced: from a total of 820 pupils, 620 would be boys and 200 girls – a ratio the Foundation would balance when finances

Last days at Hertford, 1985. The uniform at Hertford changed frequently but the iron bedsteads served for generations.

permitted. The first day of the Michaelmas term 1985 was set as the date of the merger, and the Ways and Means Committee set to work, supported by committtees of Almoners, staff, and professional advisers.

There were many issues to be clarified. There was the disparity in the School year between the two Schools. Hertford had four terms; Horsham had three. They used different examination boards for O and A levels. There could be only one Head. In the event a new interim Head Master, John Hansford, was appointed and Miss Morrison, Head Mistress at Hertford, became Senior Mistress. Could a girl be Senior Grecian? How would sporting fixtures be organised when the girls traditionally played matches mid-week and the boys on Saturdays? Could the different teaching syllabuses be integrated? And what of the girls' privileges – their Leave Days in which they could see parents or even visit London? There was a great deal to be clarified as Coleridge and Barnes houses were refurbished to accommodate girls.

Unified in the Housey uniform. Kerrie Downing Robertson and John Nwatu on Speech Day.

Peter Rice, a theatrical designer, was asked, with the Committee of Women, to design a uniform for the girls which was sympathetic to that of the boys. He produced what is essentially the current design of pleated skirt, jacket, lace jabot, blouse and tights, with a dark blue yellow-lined, gabardine cape. The cape was universally unpopular, as were the blouses, for which a boy's shirt is often preferred, and the jabot was quickly limited to ceremonial wear.

Those early days were exciting, and shocking. The girls had quickly to adjust to a whole new way of life, and to prove themselves equal to their new colleagues. Jean Morrison is believed to have exhorted her girls, just prior to the move, 'Don't let them brush you under the carpet'. To which, some weeks later, the reply came, 'We haven't let them sweep us under the carpet. In fact, we've nailed the carpet down!' Most Hertford mistresses declined to make the move to Horsham, and so the girls had to adjust to a new approach to teaching. But they coped famously and soon proved themselves to be equal and valued members, not only of the Marching Band and the Orchestra, but of the whole community.

When male Horsham Old Blues return for reunions, or Old Blues' Day, they may look strangely at the unaccustomed presence of girls in Housey life. But they have come to relax, as they note the grace and precision with which the girls march; and acknowledge the positive influence they exercise in the life of the School. In the academic year 1999–2000 there are 328 girls living and working alongside 472 boys and it is almost inconceivable that they were ever separated. Their achievement in every sphere has taken them far beyond the narrow confines of diarist John Evelyn's definition of a Hertford girl – that they 'should be good wives and a blessing to their generation.' They are surely that and far, far more. The merger, though not without its problems, has been a great success.

A GENUINELY PUBLIC SCHOOL

It is an anomaly that Christ's Hospital is not a 'public school' at all, in so far as that expression is generally understood to apply to fee-paying schools for the children of mainly wealthy parents in the United Kingdom at the turn of the century. Christ's Hospital is an independent school, proud to be an educational charity which has remained true to the intentions of its sixteenth-century founders.

For 450 years Christ's Hospital has enjoyed the financial support of the City of London, Old Blues and countless other benefactors who have believed passionately in its principles and purposes. The accumulation of these benefactions in endowment funds and their wise investment and rigorous management have resulted in Christ's Hospital, in the year 2000, being not only the wealthiest school in the United Kingdom, but also the most philanthropic: all of the income from its endowments contributes to the outstanding, broadly based boarding education within a Christian environment provided to children regardless of means. And so Christ's Hospital remains a genuinely 'public' school – open to any child with need of an academic boarding education, and the intellectual capacity to benefit from it, and which the parents cannot afford to pay for.

GOVERNANCE AND MANAGEMENT OF CHRIST'S HOSPITAL

It comes as a surprise to many people to discover that Christ's Hospital has two distinct aspects with a shared purpose: the School – a co-educational boarding school known as Christ's Hospital – and also a substantial charitable Foundation, registered by the Charity Commissioners under Articles of Governance, the most recent of which are dated 28 January 1990. The two form an indivisible educational charity: the Foundation supports the School, and both give expression to the Charity. Understanding this principle clarifies the position regarding the management of the School – for the successful governance of Christ's Hospital depends on the inter-relationship between these two facets.

The charitable Foundation is led by the Clerk of Christ's Hospital, Michael Simpkin. He is supported by a team of officers whose work is described in Chapter Nine.

Bust of Thomas Lockington, Treasurer 1707–16, from his tomb in the church of St Mary Magdalen, Old Fish Street, London, which was destroyed by fire in 1886. Now in the corner of the East Cloister, adjacent to the Court Room.

The School is run by the Head Master, Dr Peter Southern, supported by two Deputy Heads. The Head Master is, of course, responsible for the education of the pupils and for their welfare, as well as that of the teaching staff. Through the Bursar he is also responsible for all the support staff: matrons, groundsmen, cleaners and catering staff, as well as those running the Infirmary, Wardrobe and Laundry.

Christ's Hospital is extremely fortunate that the relationship between these two key people – the Head Master and the Clerk – is so open and amicable, for it enables complex issues to be discussed and handled in a warm and supportive atmosphere. That was not ever so, and it is not a factor to be taken for granted.

'The Worshipful the Treasurer' is the formal title of the post currently held by Mrs Susan Mitchell, an Old Blue from Hertford, and the first lady Treasurer in Christ's Hospital's history. That position sits atop of those of the Head Master and the Clerk and forms the apex of the triumvirate pyramid under which both School and charitable Foundation are governed. As Treasurer Susan is Chairman of the Council of Almoners.

The Council of Almoners is the Trustee body of the charitable Foundation and the governing body of the School. Its rôle is described on page 216.

Including the President and Vice-President (always the current Lord Mayor of the City of London), the Council of Almoners is made up of twenty-five members of diverse disciplines. Their appointment is historical, as can be seen from the Council's constitution and membership on pages 216–7.

Originally 'Governors' governed the School, as is the case in most others. But the need to form a finite body of Trustees of the charitable Foundation caused the creation of the Council of Almoners. Ten of the

The Council of Almoners meets in the Court Room, 28 June 2000.

A ceremony performed at every summer Court Meeting is the reading, by the Clerk, of that portion of the Will of St James Amand, a good benefactor, whose monetary bequest to Christ's Hospital in 1754 was conditional upon the production of this miniature portrait of his grandfather annually to the Governors. Vicky Haigh, Protocol Officer and secretary to the Clerk, performs the honours on this occasion.

Formal meetings of the Court of Governors are held twice a year, in December in London at the Mansion House under the Chairmanship of the Vice President, the Lord Mayor, and, in the summer, at the School. Here the Head Master, Peter Southern, the Deputy Chairman, Chris Bruce-Jones, the Treasurer and Chairman, Susan Mitchell and the Clerk, Michael Simpkin, preside over the Court meeting in Big School on 28 June 2000.

Below: Two leaving senior members of staff receive presentations. On the left, Elizabeth Cairncross, Deputy Head, from Almoner Peter Attenborough; on the right, Rachel Adams, retiring Bursar, from former Lord Mayor of London and Almoner Sir Alan Traill.

Almoners are elected by the Court of Governors, now numbering over 600. Its composition and rôle is described on page 218. The School has long had connections with three major Universities, so each is represented on the Council.

The Wests' Gift was a major donation from John and Frances West in 1720, which gained them a position in the governance of the School. It provides places in the School for as many pupils as the income from the Wests' Gift can support. In the academic year 1999–2000 there were forty Wests' Foundationers in the School. They come from the families of John and Frances West and from Reading, Newbury and Twickenham. The Wests' Gift Almoner is appointed by each of these areas in rotation.

The representation from the City goes back to Christ's Hospital's foundation, which has resulted in four senior members of the City governing bodies being appointed. The Ministry of Defence representative has always been from the naval side, continuing the link with the Royal Mathematical School instigated by Samuel Pepys. The Head of the Mathematics Department is still known as the Master of the Royal Mathematical School. The appointment of a member from the Royal Society dates from the revised Christ's Hospital Scheme of 1891, although the School's connections with the Society can be traced back to the seventeenth century. The London schools' representation recognises the high proportion of pupils from the London boroughs, as was to be expected from the School's City connections.

The Almoners are supported by the Court of Governors which,

New Donation Governors are elected by the Court of Governors on the recommendation of the Council of Almoners. They are then invited to a Governors' Induction Day at the School, when they are given guidance on their rôle by the Clerk (left) and other senior staff before watching Band Parade and taking lunch with some of the senior pupils. Those present at this meeting, on 8 March 2000, include (centre) Richard Poulton, Head Master 1987–96.

THE MISSION STATEMENT OF CHRIST'S HOSPITAL

It is and shall be the mission of Christ's Hospital in perpetuity:

• To offer to boys and girls of suitable age an education of such breadth and excellence as will fit them pre-eminently for work and service in society in their generation and in particular to enable them to compete confidently with their peers for opportunities in further education and careers;

• In so doing to develop first the skills, learning habits, independence of mind and spiritual awareness that will enable and motivate them to continue to educate themselves throughout their lives; and second, a high sense of responsibility towards themselves, their families, their associates and to society at large, such as to form a permanent foundation of their training and character;

• To present to its pupils the Christian faith in all its mystery and splendour;

• To have regard especially to children of families in social, financial or other need, in the choice of pupils, that choice to remain the prerogative of the Foundation;

• To maintain and further the close connection between the Foundation and the City of London so successfully nurtured since 1552.

although quite limited in its powers, remains another fundamental part of the structure of Christ's Hospital. The Court has two meetings each year, one at the School, chaired by the Treasurer, and the other at the Mansion House in the City, presided over by the Lord Mayor and followed by a short reception which he hosts. The meetings are formal and quite brief, if there are no 'Matters of Emergency', which is the last item on the Agenda to which Governors may address themselves.

The meeting at the School is usually followed by more open discussion on matters which are of interest to the Governors – such as the new Grecians' residences and the possibility of some of the Foundation's land surplus to the School's requirements being sold for development, discussed in June 2000.

An important current function of most Donation Governors is more fully described in the section on Admission to Christ's Hospital on page 81.

CHAPTER ONE
AN ACADEMIC SCHOOL

THE ACHIEVEMENT OF HIGH ACADEMIC STANDARDS are at the heart of Christ's Hospital and the School gives all pupils unrivalled opportunities to realise their full academic potential. There are 117 full time members of the teaching staff who are chosen not only for their intellectual skills but also for their ability and enthusiasm in communicating them to boys and girls of all ages. The teachers are well supported by technicians and other ancillary and administrative staff. The extensive computer network covers all boarding houses, libraries, laboratories and many classrooms, allowing pupils to log on at any site to access a variety of up-to-date software, including CD Roms and their own files. Increasing use is made of the internet.

Teachers are encouraged to be flexible and individual in their approach. In the first two years classes of about twenty are the norm and, at the top of the School, A Level sets usually number less than ten to allow an emphasis on group discussions and individual response. Because all the pupils have reached the qualifying entry level academically, much of the teaching takes place in unstreamed groups. However, where there is a benefit in learning in more specialised groups, setting is sensitively employed. In this way everyone can enjoy the social and academic advantages of mixing in a variety of groups and much of the intellectual energy of the School springs from the opportunity for outstanding individuals to strike academic sparks from those around them.

Every pupil is encouraged to advance as rapidly as possible, but no great store is set upon taking examinations early, in the belief that sound education is best served in the long term by stimulating pupils to stretch themselves more deeply and broadly rather than simply by leaping over examination hurdles as fast as possible. The Head Master and his staff do not believe that a child benefits from being accelerated in an unnatural fashion to premature development in a narrowly academic sense.

Pupils of all ages are able to benefit from an extraordinary range of educational trips and visits. In many cases, the Foundation is able to contribute towards the cost. Some departments organise overseas expeditions, including Russian language courses in Kiev, geography fieldwork in Morocco, exchanges with schools in Pléneuf-Val-André, Rennes and Boulogne, visits to Munich and Nuremburg, work experience in Eschwege, Ansbach, Bamberg and Boulogne, study visits to Toulouse and adventure expeditions with scouts and cadets to mountains, moors and lakes at home and abroad.

The Head Master with some of the Second Form and (on his right) Kate Atkinson, Senior Grecian, and (on his left) Second Monitors Sophie Naish and George Busby.

THE ACADEMIC CURRICULUM 2000
BY THE HEAD MASTER

The pupils of Christ's Hospital come with a wide variety of educational experiences, with the majority coming from state primary schools. Thanks to the National Curriculum there is more common ground among them than was once the case, but there is an immediate need to weld them into a coherent group. The Second Form curriculum is an interesting balancing act. The principal task is to reinforce basic skills so that all may advance with full confidence as the pace of academic life quickens. However, it is also important to ensure that those who arrive at the School with relatively sophisticated skills continue to be challenged. Rather than becoming competitive, in a narrow 'doing-down-the-others' way, each individual is taught to challenge him or herself and to recognize that coming top is not as important as keeping progress moving ahead in a way which brings fulfillment, enjoyment and a sense of achievement. Teachers contribute to this aim by adjusting the tasks and targets for each pupil and rewarding positive attitude and individual progress with commendations and other less formal expressions of approval.

In the senior school nearly all pupils are prepared for nine GCSE subjects, and take some other classes which may, or may not, lead to examinations. In order to guarantee the solidity of the GCSE core experienced by all, there are only two fully free choices and another which requires pupils to select History or Geography. English Language and Literature, a balanced Science course (in which Biology, Chemistry and Physics are taught separately and count as a double GCSE), Mathematics, French and another language make up the core. Among the more recent additions to the subjects available at GCSE are PE and Classical Civilization. Every pupil takes a course in Religious Studies, which can lead them to GCSE if they wish. Great encouragement is given to give every pupil an experience of a technical or practical subject, such as Information or Design Technology, Art, Music or Drama.

The year 2000 is a curricular watershed in all English schools and is making its mark on Christ's Hospital too. For many years observers of (and participants in) the English post-16 educational set-up have been struck by the narrowness and degree of specialization. Some have seen these characteristics as strengths in that the mature enthusiast has been allowed to experience remarkable depth and sophistication in a few areas of study. A more blinkered handful has relished the opportunity given by the A Level system to duck out of unwelcome challenges. Despite these benefits, a growing body of opinion has come to see the problem of narrowness as more significant than the opportunity of depth. Recent government thinking had also been faltering in this direction until a new policy was finally adopted for the academic year, starting in 2000, to encourage most sixth formers to study four subjects to AS level for one year, reducing to three for a further year leading to an examination known as A2. The AS is a free-standing qualification bridging between GCSE and A Level and the final A2 assessments are intended to match the rigour of A Level. The transition was accompanied by a great deal of doubt and confusion which arose chiefly from the fact that as the academic year started, much of the detail of the new syllabuses remained in flux with government assessment gurus, examination boards and subject

*Bob Sillett, Second Deputy Head,
Elizabeth Cairncross, Deputy Head and
the Head Master, Dr Peter Southern.*

specialists pulling in opposite directions. Those who were charged with wearing a confident expression as they introduced the new AS courses in September 2000 had a difficult task.

Christ's Hospital, in common with many other independent schools, took the opportunity provided by the inevitability of some change, to evaluate a number of alternatives. A prominent contender was the International Baccalaureate, which has become a growing force world-wide in the last ten years. Its supporters have chiefly been attracted by its clear commitment to breadth, insisting on a number of elements which might be considered essential building blocks for a well-educated young person. Its opponents have found these same requirements unduly prescriptive. Christ's Hospital finally decided to stay with the new model A Levels, attracted by their capacity to allow more breadth and by the flexibility to encourage specialization where appropriate.

By the end of 2000, the new courses had been in operation for only one term and it would be unfair to rush to premature judgment. It is clear, however, that the new pattern is significantly changing the rhythms of sixth form life with a heavier diet of exams. Each AS and each A2 qualification is composed of three modules, each of which may be taken twice. There is now a clear risk that the three years from the GE to the Grecians may turn into a relentless cycle of examinations dominating all other activity. The notion of a Deputy Grecians year with reduced pressure from formal assessments, allowing actors, musicians and cricketers to develop their skills relatively free from immediate academic demands, is already seeming a quaint anachronism.

Christ's Hospital's home-grown, unexamined General Studies programme, which has offered Deputy Grecians opportunities to share their teachers' enthusiasms for modern art, contemporary film, Buddhism, recreational Italian and Spanish or classical music or the like, is in danger of being squeezed out by a content-heavy, examination-focused curriculum. Those post-war Grecians (historians especially, if the tales are true) who were encouraged to develop their skills independently but in the company of teachers whose priority was intellectual rigour rather than syllabus coverage, and who never had what would nowadays be regarded as a lesson, would not know what has hit them (though they would be able to detect our envious admiration for a system which allowed such fruitful indulgence for the very few). All systems have their strengths and weaknesses and, as the dust settles and the reality of the new approach becomes clearer, Christ's Hospital will be able adjust the mix and to preserve the values which have underpinned sixth form education at Horsham.

Among the other developments affecting the provision offered by Christ's Hospital in 2000 is the increasing rarity of the skilled, sports enthusiast teacher. Universities no longer put a premium on sporting ability, which has reduced the flow of teachers who can share an experience of sport at a high level, and has also undermined a part of the motivation of school sportsmen and women. The emphasis on safety in sport has, quite rightly but nevertheless sadly, reduced the opportunity for the good-willed amateur to help with the U14 B XV.

Sue LaPlain, the Head Master's Executive Assistant.

Despite these facts, Christ's Hospital in 2000 continues to make sport a prominent part of its mainstream provision. Many of the qualities we most wish to see developed in the young, such as teamwork, dedication, resilience, dignity and self-control, are stimulated most effectively through the sports programme. The accent is placed on team games for the younger children and, at all levels, the benefits and joys of participation are emphasized to all, as well as a proper fostering of the enjoyment of winning and developing high-class skills. On many afternoons through the year thirty-five teams may be found representing the School. On most evenings less formal games of indoor mixed hockey, basketball, soccer, fives or squash provide a last flurry of post prep exercise.

All courses are regularly reviewed to ensure that they play their part fully within a curriculum which is challenging, broad and varied enough to give satisfaction and a sense of achievement. From time to time changes are made to reflect syllabus revisions, to meet the educational needs of pupils and to keep all courses fresh and enjoyable. At all stages the precise tasks given to children may vary from one individual to another to ensure that the teaching stretches the most able pupils and fully supports those making slower progress. Members of the teaching staff are encouraged to approach subjects in individual ways which communicate their personal enthusiasm. Departments see the National Curriculum as an essential baseline, but we seek to offer more wherever possible and constantly to improve our academic provision and pupils' performance and enjoyment.

Each year the working life of three year groups is put under the microscope by a team of teachers who visit each class, observe prep and other activities and consider what improvements might be made. The Board of Studies meets to develop new thinking on academic issues on topics (in 2000) such as challenging the most able, making the most effective use of prep and the ICT strategy. In this way the School curriculum is kept fresh and those with new ideas can be heard.

The descriptions which follow, extracted from the School Prospectus, provide a snapshot of departments' approaches to their work in the year 2000.

Neil Fleming, Head of Archaeology, teaching Grecians.

DEPARTMENTS AND COURSES

ARCHAEOLOGY

The Archaeology Department is open to all pupils in their sixth form years, as an AS or A level course. The subject requires no special background or experience. The Department seeks to inspire a thirst for knowledge, especially in the form of an open-minded and open-ended 'backward-looking curiosity' which leads pupils to test evidence and theories against their own experience and their observations gleaned from practical involvement and a huge range of exciting sources. Original work and initiative are required of all pupils.

The Department provides a wonderfully stimulating environment full of images and objects that will intrigue and fascinate, believing it much better to be presented with a Palaeolithic flint, to test against your thumb, feeling the weight and balance, imagining the edge gliding through raw flesh to provide a meal, than simply to be told that this is what an 'Acheulean hand axe' from a 'Hoxnian horizon' looks like from a picture.

Above all the subject seeks to uncover the people behind the stones and bones; the static remains in themselves can be as dry as dust without imagination but it is the dynamic processes, the behaviour that they betoken, that is the core of the fascination of the subject.

ART AND HISTORY OF ART

Art is neither solely an intellectual nor an expressive medium, but a combination of the two. Effective guided discovery can produce disciplined modes of enquiry and expression through which feeling and concepts about experience may be organised. A balance between intellectual pur-

Third formers in the Art School: (left to right) Natalie Smith, Bart Chan and Alice Hattrick designing a mosaic for a swimming pool.

suits and emotional expression must be maintained and Art provides one of the most natural vehicles for this. Our feelings are inextricably bound up with values. Art helps pupils to investigate their own values through practical involvement, stimulating constant re-evaluation.

The Department makes the fullest use of its unique staffing arrangement, whereby the three full time teachers are supplemented by five artists-in-residence. These are young professionals, looking to launch their creative careers. They work directly with pupils part time and, just as important, pupils are able to observe them tackling their own artistic enthusiasms and crises.

Learning takes place in a multiplicity of ways and situations. The Department's aim is to work pupils across as many disparate and diverse situations and working practices as possible. At no time are pupils permitted to specialise. It is felt that this is restrictive and severely limits artistic and experimental understandings. We are not directly seeking to make Artists or Designers but to present pupils with problem solving situations, discovery procedures and, most importantly, opportunities to create and discover how to make sense of a small part of the world and their lives.

Art is taught throughout the School, as a core subject in the first two years and as an option at GCSE and A Level. Specialist facilities allow each pupil to become confident in many mediums, including ceramics, drawing, printmaking, textiles, painting, sculpture, and electronic imagery. The Department has a wonderful resource bank of visual stimuli and an inspiring library. History of Art is offered also as a free-standing A Level exploring the ways in which artists and architects have expressed the feelings of their day. The Department achieves outstanding results and makes its beneficial mark on many young lives, as well as stimulating remarkable creative energies.

CAREERS DEPARTMENT

Christ's Hospital education is designed to be broadly stimulating and to encourage learning for its own sake, but it is also important that thoughts of a productive and fulfilling personal future are stimulated early on, both to inspire a desire to work to the best of one's capacity and also to recognise, nurture and direct individual talents and enthusiasms.

The recognition begins gently in the middle years, with discussion and evaluation of individual strengths and weaknesses. With the employment of computer analysis and the guidance of personal tutors, the exploration of career prospects begins in the two years before the specialisation of A level study commences. The young adults of the Sixth Form are then exposed more specifically to visions of the future through the experience of visiting speakers, many of whom will themselves be only a few years older than their audience.

There are important choices to be made, and expert help is available in identifying and applying for the most appropriate of the seventy thousand courses at our two hundred and eighteen universities, in selecting suitable employment, or the most practical of the GAP Year opportunities. Financial provision, interview technique and the presentation of a Curriculum Vitae are among the many subjects upon which advice and guidance are given. Special attention is given to preparing candidates for the university of their choice.

The Department keeps abreast of the latest developments, using ICT in many forms: videos, visits and personal contacts. Pupils gain awareness of what the future can hold in time for them to take the necessary active steps to realise it.

CLASSICS

It is difficult for English speakers not to speak Latin every time they open their mouth. The Department lays bare the roots of literature and civilization for all, not just the select few. All human life is here. Classics is about people, their feelings, thoughts and emotions, whether in the thick of battle, on the lover's couch or in the cut and thrust of the law-courts. The subject provides a detailed insight into the Ancient World and its rich traditions in literature, politics, philosophy, drama and art.

The experience of understanding how language works comes most

Marlene Fleming, Head of Classics, teaching the LE Latin Set 1.

easily to many through learning the words and structures of Latin. Sadly, this chance to study a fundamental part of our heritage is now denied to pupils in many schools but at Christ's Hospital it is much enjoyed.

Everyone has the chance to learn Latin in Year 7, either beginning from scratch or building on earlier experience. Most continue in Year 8, but there is a more general option of Classical Civilization for those for whom a language based course is not so suitable. A healthy number continue with Latin to GCSE, A Level and beyond – several pupils each year go on to follow classics courses at university.

Paul Edwards (right) with Belinda Faulkner (standing, to his right) in the Design and Technology School. A group of French exchange students are working with members of the UF on making a plastic case for a radio. The group began the project in France and completed it at CH.

DESIGN AND TECHNOLOGY

A major new building which will reinforce contacts between Design and Technology, art, ICT and science is a central part of the School's development plan. The Department introduces all pupils to a problem-solving approach to learning. Emphasis is placed on design, the use of the most appropriate materials and design technologies, and an insistence on high-quality products. Pupils develop their critical and communication skills, allowing them to record and explain their thinking effectively with due attention to technical, environmental and aesthetic aspects. In doing so they learn to apply expertise, knowledge and understanding from other subjects where appropriate, including those mentioned above. At all stages pupils are taught the central importance of health and safety issues for both their design projects and practical activities.

Design and Technology is a part of the core curriculum of the Second and Third Forms (Years 7 and 8) and everyone is encouraged, though not required, to pursue a practical subject as part of their GCSE option package. The Department offers a number of courses with different points of emphasis at GCSE and A Level.

DRAMA

The Christ's Hospital Theatre is at the heart of the School's artistic and recreational life and all aspects of Drama and Theatre Studies enjoy a high profile and enthusiastic support. Professor Howell's magical building,

Members of the junior school in a production of Ernie's Incredible Hallucinations, *a Junior Play performed on 26 May.*

acknowledged to be among the finest theatres built in the last fifty years, challenges our pupils to be creative and adventurous, to fill its welcoming, multi-directional space with every kind of theatrical presentation. It also allows all members of the Christ's Hospital community to enjoy regular visiting performances from fine professional artists.

Drama requires an athletic as well as an intellectual response and marries bodily action with spiritual aspiration. It explores the whole range of human imagination and experience but in a special way that demands specific skills, complex areas of sensitivity and awareness and the ability and courage to communicate thoughts and feeling through physical expression. For some pupils, such a study may be a preparation for a life in the theatre but for all it is a powerful education medium, sharpening perception and deepening understanding. We want our children to act 'to the very life' and, in the process, to discover themselves.

Drama exists both inside and outside the official curriculum. It is a firmly-rooted academic subject, forming part of the core for everyone on the first two years and proceeding to well-supported courses in Drama at GCSE and in Theatre Studies at A Level. It is also a popular leisure activity with frequent opportunities for participation in plays, musicals, operas, dance and physical theatre. Thus all Christ's Hospital children can discover the magic of theatre for themselves through a programme of vigorous and enjoyable theatrical action and, through Drama, open themselves to greater personal and social awareness, creative energy and freedom matched by discipline – a road into the world.

ECONOMICS AND BUSINESS STUDIES

Economics and Business Studies are offered at A Level only. They do not require specific preparatory groundwork to be undertaken, but build on the skills and understanding developed through the core GCSE subjects.

Economics aims to enable pupils to apply economic principles and theories to explain and try to resolve the economic problems facing contemporary society. The course is problem-led and current issues are studied. The subject helps pupils to develop lively, inquiring minds and the ability to question and argue rationally. It may be seen as a basis for understanding and participating in the popular and political debate on economic policy, as providing pupils with particular vocational skills, or as an introduction to economic theory for an audience who might at least consider studying economics at university.

Business Studies fosters a critical understanding of business through a consideration of the internal workings of firms and their management and, in particular, how decisions are made in the face of an ever-changing external environment. Business behaviour is studied from the viewpoints of all stake holders, drawing on a variety of disciplines. Emphasis is placed on 'doing' rather than 'learning' Business Studies by both the A Level assignment and the Young Enterprise Programme. Pupils are fortunate to have a thriving business on their doorstep, Christ's Hospital Enterprises, which provides some of the raw material for the course as problem-solving exercises from a real-life business.

ENGLISH

The Department possesses and encourages a way with, and a relish for, words. It emphasises at all year levels the intimate engagement with, and detailed analysis of, language to promote aesthetic perception, imaginative practice and clarity of thought and argument. Creativity and clarity are the hallmarks of its aims which are to promote in pupils the need to develop listening and speaking skills in formal and informal situations. It encourages the development of pupils as writers by aiming for control over such matters as grammar, spelling and punctuation, structure and organisation of material, complexity and fluency of thought, and an awareness of moods, styles and forms.

In preparing pupils for GCSE, the AQA/NEAB syllabus is followed. This requires a level of competence in three main areas: speaking/ listening, reading and writing. Presentation of handwritten and word-processed work is also taken into account.

At Advanced Level, the OCR syllabus is followed. The Department's aims at this level are to ensure that pupils engage with a wide range of literature in all three main genres. The discipline of close reading of texts is dealt with alongside need to place texts in a wider social and cultural context. The opportunity to write creatively and imaginatively is also dealt with in the framework of this syllabus. In fact, pupils are encouraged to see the craft of writing as an ongoing process, with redrafting of written work a crucial element in the quest for success.

A magazine of original writing, *Outlook*, is published each year by the Department, while from time to time pupil writing appears, in electronic form, on the School network. Visiting speakers, together with theatre and conference trips, form part of the Department's programme.

Tony Adlam, Head of English, teaching a junior class.

A particular strength of the Department lies in the variety of talent and depth of experience of its teaching staff. Each has his or her own specialisms yet, first and foremost, each is a professional teacher who values the close rapport with pupils of all age groups. In acknowledging the diverse nature of its subject area, the Department aims to fulfil rôles that are at once aesthetic, cultural, academic and spiritual.

FOOD TECHNOLOGY

Food Technology is taught to all juniors. Pupils can later opt to study the subject either as a GCSE or as a short course. The subject is offered as a creative minority to Year 12 pupils and cookery actives are also undertaken on two afternoons a week.

Food Technology aims to increase pupils' knowledge of nutrition and healthy eating as well as skill in and enjoyment of cooking. The subject promotes an understanding of human needs and the interdependence of individuals and groups. This is achieved through both practical and theoretical study using a technological approach in the classroom.

Pupils are encouraged to be critical and analytical in their work while developing knowledge and expertise which will ensure safe and effective organisation. Sound dietary information and the ability to prepare food are essential life skills which are needed by all. The success of Old Blues in later life is, in many cases, soundly based on their confident ability to look after themselves and to lead healthy lives, putting into enjoyable practice what they learned in the Food Technology Department!

Sean Davey, Head of Geography, with a Deputy Grecians A Level class.

GEOGRAPHY

Geography is a wide-ranging subject which brings together study of the Earth's places, peoples, environments and societies. At its core lies the understanding of the relationships and impacts between people and the environment. It is unique in bridging the social sciences (human geography) with its understanding of the dynamics of societies, cultures and behaviour, and the earth sciences (physical geography) in the understanding of physical landscapes and the dynamics of environmental processes. Geography puts this understanding of social and physical processes within the context of places and regions, encouraging all pupils to recognise and relish the differences in cultures, political systems, economies, landscapes and environments across the world, and the links between them.

All pupils study Geography for their first three years in the School. For GCSE they choose between Geography and History, but can take either subject up to A Level whether or not they have taken the GCSE examination. This somewhat unusual pattern allows a strong and focused humanities core throughout the curriculum to GCSE.

The Department makes much use of ICT, with a convenient suite of computers, including an automatic weather station with facilities for downloading satellite images. The value of fieldwork and outside education is generally central to the philosophy of the Department. Christ's Hospital's geographers draw great strength from the School's location, with many important forms of habitat, such as forest, lowland agriculture, downland, marine environments and varied gradations of townscape, close at hand. In addition the Department organises field study courses for A Level candidates in the Alps and, most recently, in Morocco. These remarkable opportunities are generally available to pupils on the same subsidised basis as their school costs.

HISTORY

There can be few environments as conducive to the study of history as that which pupils enjoy at Christ's Hospital. The History Department aims to use the unparalleled resources at its disposal to foster an awareness of and enthusiasm for history throughout the school. We believe that an awareness of the past is essential for a humane, civilised and responsible outlook on life, and that history uniquely trains pupils in the skills they will need to operate effectively in a world which demands the ability to master complex material and formulate cogent analytical arguments under pressure – skills which are almost infinitely transferable.

We aim to cover all the topics and skills prescribed in the National Curriculum, but also to go beyond this and take account of the particular needs, interests and abilities of our pupils. All pupils study History in their first three years at Christ's Hospital. In their fourth year (the UF) pupils presently choose to study either History or Geography to GCSE, but on the understanding that they may later study either or both subjects at A level. At A level pupils doing history study one of three courses – Mediaeval, Early Modern or Late Modern – and the Department is committed to maintaining this breadth. All pupils also submit an individual study, which many find the most satisfying and worthwhile aspect of the course. History combines well with a very wide variety of arts and science subjects. It is highly popular at A level and a number of pupils every year choose to study it at university.

Pupils studying History at Christ's Hospital have the benefit of resources of an astonishing range and quality. The teaching staff is unusually highly qualified. The History Library boasts a collection which exceeds what is available to many undergraduates, in addition to the rich collections in the main School Library. There are abundant textbooks, large collections of slides and videos and a growing collection of IT Resources. History Days are arranged for the junior years, the department undertakes major trips abroad, and there are also day visits locally.

There is a long and distinguished tradition of studying history at Christ's Hospital. Our aim is to foster among pupils the enthusiasm and the intellectual edge to carry forward that tradition, in the ultimate belief not just in the usefulness of the skills which it cultivates, but in that deeper sense of our common humanity which the study of history quickens.

INFORMATION AND COMMUNICATIONS TECHNOLOGY

Christ's Hospital believes that skills in Information and Communications Technology are essential to allow all pupils to compete and succeed in the future. ICT is promoted throughout the curriculum and the pupils are encouraged to use the resources effectively by making appropriate choices of software for particular applications in all their academic subjects. A broad range of up to date facilities exists to develop skills in ICT.

A fully integrated computer network operates throughout the School, with PC stations clustered in various locations. This generous provision of equipment allows pupils, whether in class room, library, boarding house, laboratory or workshop, access to an extensive range of software applications and information resources. Each pupil is provided with a secure network account, filtered access to the World Wide Web and a mail box for e-mail.

ICT skills are taught specifically to all pupils on Years 7 and 8, providing an essential base of skills which can be applied to other subjects. There is an optional Short Course in ICT which includes CLAIT assessment of a range of IT skills in Year 9 and the GCSE Short Course examination in ICT in Year 11. In Year 12 there is an AS programme in ICT for pupils wishing to extend their skills and knowledge in this area. In the Sixth form there are minority courses in Word Processing, leading to a range of Pitman qualifications, and there is also a minority course to extend pupils' knowledge and skills in a range of ICT applications.

Alan Smith, Master of the Royal Mathematical School, discusses the excitements of Astronomy with Michael Francis and Lizzy Hawke.

MATHEMATICS

All pupils study Mathematics as a core subject to GCSE. In Years 7 to 9 the emphasis is on developing and practising basic skills, while also applying these in problem-solving contexts. Extended coursework practice takes place at the end of each summer term after the examinations in June. During Years 10 and 11 the course is more focused on GCSE preparation. Teaching is organised within six teaching sets, initially in two bands but fully setted by ability from Year 9 onwards. In the final year of the GCSE course a seventh teaching set is introduced, enabling the class sizes of the lower sets to be as small as possible.

A wide range of ICT skills is used, from a two-week logo course in Year 7 to the use of spreadsheets in GCSE coursework. Pupils also have access to specific mathematical software such as Derive and Omnigraph.

The Department does not prepare GCSE candidates for 'early' exams, but the top set takes an A Level module at the same time as their GCSE at the end of Year 11. As well as reinforcing the Higher Tier work this module provides a useful extra boost to those who go on to A Level in Mathematics and especially Further Mathematics.

The strongest mathematicians benefit from a weekly extension period in which more challenging work is studied, and the more able pupils in each year group take part in the UK Junior, Intermediate or Senior Mathematics Challenges.

A variety of A Level Mathematics syllabuses is offered, with a common core supplemented by optional areas of greater specialisation. Mathematics at A Level combines effectively with a range of other subjects. Further Mathematics allows the best mathematicians to develop their skills to an even higher level and to earn two separate A Level awards. A Minorities Course encourages non specialist mathematicians to promote a wider understanding of modern statistical methods, including elementary hypothesis testing, while also maintaining regular practice of algebraic and numerical skills. It thus provides valuable support for other numerate A Level courses such as Biology, Geography or Economics.

Each in his or her own world in the language laboratory.

MODERN LANGUAGES

French, German and Russian
In a world in which language awareness is an increasingly important asset and in which many pupils are likely to spend part of their working lives in another country, the development of language skills is one of the most vital parts of the School curriculum.

This fact leads the Modern Language Departments to promote pupils' independent use of their language skills to levels which are of practical use and which would enable them to deal with life in France, Germany or Russia. At the same time they acquire a positive attitude towards the culture and inhabitants of the countries whose languages are studied, through contact with native-speaking assistants and through trips abroad. Pupils are also developing general language learning skills which will stand them in good stead should they want to learn another foreign language later in life.

Each Language Department provides suitably stretching programmes of study to keep each pupil advancing in their learning with a sense of achievement and fulfilment. The experience of many years shows the great benefits pupils derive from the School exchanges organised with France (Toulouse) and Germany (Ansbach) and other visits abroad, such as study visits to Bavaria and Paris, visits to Moscow and St Petersburg and work experience programmes in various centres in France and Germany. All pupils currently learn French in Year 7. In Year 8 everyone has the opportunity to take up either German or Russian and, if enjoyed, to continue it, together with French, to GCSE and A Level.

Additional courses are offered in the Sixth Form to maintain the interest and skills of the non-specialist and to give some the opportunity to start a new language, such as Spanish or Italian. In all lessons as much communication as possible takes place in the language being taught. Much use is made of varied and extensive resources, including ICT, tape and video collections, a state-of-the-art language laboratory, and satellite television which receives live programmes from all three countries.

MUSIC

Music plays an integral part in everyday life at Christ's Hospital. The Department has six full time and thirty visiting staff, who teach in a purpose-built Music School offering unrivalled facilities. It aims to develop the skills, creative powers and musical awareness that will equip pupils for adult life, with an appreciation and love of music, the incentive for further artistic development, and the foundation for continuing practical music-making whether as an amateur or professional.

Music is taught as an academic subject in the first two years to all pupils who can then opt for a course which will lead to GCSE in three years. There is also a short course offered which allows the non-specialist to maintain an interest or the specially talented to add a further GCSE without undue pressure on curricular time. The general level of musical expertise at Christ's Hospital results in A Level, which comprises aural, composition, harmony, history and analysis and performance, being within reach of a much greater proportion of the pupil body than at most schools. Every year a number of pupils progress to Music Colleges or to music courses at university, some with choral awards at Oxford or Cambridge colleges. Instrumental tuition is available to all, though there is sometimes a waiting list for popular instruments.

There are extensive opportunities for free instrumental tuition, especially for pupils of exceptional promise; the remainder pay on a graded scale according to family income. Instrumental tuition is free for all studying music as an academic subject at GCSE and A-level. All receiving instrumental and voice tuition are provided with sheet music and accessories and free use of the School's fine collection of string, wind and brass instruments, two Steinway Grand Pianos and four Pipe Organs.

There is a huge variety of large scale ensemble and concert work – Symphony Orchestras, String Orchestras, Chapel Choir, Chamber Choirs, Choral Society, Symphonic Wind Band, Marching Band, Big Band and more.

Beyond this, however, for many the primary focus is on developing their own solo technique and repertoire. The School offers exceptional and generous tuition, frequent concert opportunities including concerto work and South Bank appearances, regular masterclasses and extensive chamber music coaching to ensure that each individual develops his or

Peter Allwood, Director of Music, introduces a lunch time concert in the Court Room.

her talents to the full. Exceptional pupils have successfully combined a full Christ's Hospital life with attendance at a Junior College in London.

PHYSICAL EDUCATION AND GAMES

PE in the timetable is compulsory for Years 7 and 8, and optional thereafter as a GCSE Sports Science course. PE is also taught as an AS on Year 12.

The Physical Education Department aims to provide an enjoyable, satisfying and balanced programme with opportunities for every pupil to develop to the full physically, emotionally, and socially. A comprehensive, balanced and differentiated range of activities and experiences meets the needs of all pupils and encourages active involvement as performers, observers and officials.

The School has remarkable facilities and equipment for PE and games. The centrepiece is an extensive modern Sports Centre with a double sports hall, gymnasium, squash and fives courts, a swimming pool of Caribbean perfection and a state-of-the-art Fitness Centre. It is complemented by an astroturf hockey pitch, all-weather surfaces for tennis and netball and sufficient grassy acres for innumerable rugby, cricket, rounders and hockey pitches.

There are opportunities to play games on most afternoons. The accent is on team games for younger year groups, to establish skills, implant sporting attitudes and to give everyone the opportunity for developing the personal and corporate attributes best learned through games. Later

35

Roger Massey-Hicks, a gap year assistant from South Africa, conducts a hockey training session for a group of Second Formers on a sunny day.

in their career, more optional games activities are added. The School runs representative teams in most sports at all age levels. The top teams play on a highly competitive circuit, but School matches are not only for the stars – we believe that the opportunity to represent the School on a competitive basis is extremely valuable and the chance is offered to all those who can take advantage of it, with 'B' and 'C' teams, on many occasions.

Through this games programme important qualities are developed, including a sane attitude to winning and losing, a constant pride in doing one's best and the vital element of making individual skill serve the communal interest; at all times, however, the process is intended to be enjoyable and acts as a restorative balance to the daily academic pressures of School life.

RELIGIOUS STUDIES

The development of each pupil's spiritual awareness is a vital part of education. Chapel Services are an important element in this process at Christ's Hospital, and in addition express the fundamental values that bind the whole School together as a community. The Religious Studies Department also has a vital part to play within the curriculum in ensuring that the spiritual awareness of pupils is fostered and honed.

The principal aim of the Department is to enable pupils to acquire a knowledge and understanding of religious beliefs and practices, philosophy, and related human experience, and so to be able to build secure foundations for their own spiritual life. It is an important part of this process that pupils learn to respect ways of thought and of action which they do not share. The individual is always supported in whatever beliefs they have been brought up to follow and everyone's views are listened to as everyone's understanding is expanded.

Religious Studies is taught to all pupils during Years 7–11 and is an option available both at GCSE and A Level.

End of Term: Full School Chapel.

The Department makes full use of its opportunities through School trips to introduce pupils in all year groups to different ways of worship. The GCSE sets visit pilgrimage sites and, from time to time, the A Level pupils have had the chance to visit Israel, which always proves an experience of a lifetime whatever their individual persuasion.

SCIENCE

Biology, Chemistry and Physics

We live in a technological age where our every move is channelled and influenced by Science. Young people need a grasp of the principles which guide the modern scientist but also need to have an awareness of the limitations of science so that they can hold informed opinions about science related issues and be critical in their appraisal of the claims of advertisers, politicians and journalists.

In the teaching of science at Christ's Hospital we aim to ensure that these citizens of tomorrow will be scientifically literate as well as to attract, stimulate and equip those who will join the next generation of professional scientists and engineers.

The tradition of learning science by 'discovery' (heurism, which was developed at the School during the early part of the twentieth century and has subsequently been adopted nationally) continues to be our guiding principle in teaching science to all age groups. We encourage pupils to learn scientific principles by experiencing them at work in a

Jenny Williams, Head of Chemistry, with colleagues (left to right) Ian Torkington, Dr Paul Maddren and Dr Chris Lawrence, developing the use of the department laptops in lessons.

practical situation and to answer their own questions by further research in the laboratory and from computer based and library resources. Each teaching laboratory is equipped with video and networked multimedia computer facilities, as well as having access to notebook PCs for class use in recording and processing experimental data and running a wide range of teaching software on CD ROM.

In their first two years pupils are taught aspects of all three sciences in a combined course and from Year 9 onwards all study Biology, Chemistry and Physics as separate disciplines to GCSE, taking the Dual Award examinations which form the foundation for all more advanced syllabuses. All the Science subjects are taught in specialist laboratories, which enable pupils to undertake sophisticated work with up to date equipment in a safe and stimulating environment.

Biology at A level – Biology has proved to be a popular choice by pupils who have a career interest in biological sciences, dentistry, medicine, physiotherapy, psychology, biochemistry and biotechnology or who have found the subject of interest at GCSE and who want to study it further for one or two years, possibly in combination with non scientific subjects. The modular course places a high emphasis on practical investigative work and the majority of the Ecology section of the syllabus is covered during a residential field course in Devon at the end of the first year. The department is staffed by very experienced and well qualified teachers, each of whom has their own specialist field of knowledge in order to help with problems if they occur. Five fully equipped laboratories, a microbiology room and a sixth form project room mean that there is no shortage of spacious facilities for practical work. Collected data can be analysed statistically within the School computer network or immediately upon collection with the use of laptop computers.

Chemistry at A level – Chemistry, being the central science at A level, is necessary for higher education in both biological and physical sciences, as well as medicine. It is therefore a popular choice and record numbers of pupils chose one of two courses. The Nuffield syllabus is favoured

One of many examples of delicate stone carving. This is above the entrance to the Library.

by pupils studying mathematics and physics, as well as those with an interest in pure chemistry. Alternatively, the Salters' Scheme introduces chemical concepts through everyday application and is chosen by pupils with an interest in chemistry in everyday life. Some of the topics studied support and extend work pupils are studying in art, archaeology or geography and the range of A levels taken with chemistry has increased greatly as a result of the Salters' course. A donation from the Salters' Company contributed towards the refurbishment of the five chemistry laboratories in 1993 and they are bright and airy, enjoying space for practical work to be carried out separately from theory.

Physics at A level – Nationally, figures for the uptake of A level physics have shown a general decline over recent years and Christ's Hospital has, to some extent, mirrored this but is now turning the corner and prospective numbers show a healthy increase. With five laboratories, three of which have recently been refurbished, the Department enjoys the space to encourage practical work and projects which may take place over several weeks. There are also full facilities to undertake practical and project work to A level standard in electronics. The A level physics course emphasises the understanding of physics and its applicability to a wide variety of situations. It also expects pupils to develop skills and attitudes that should be useful outside physics, especially those of individual investigation, the gaining of knowledge from a wide variety of sources and communication skills. Without doubt, the problem solving skills and variety of communication techniques developed on the A level physics course stand pupils in very good stead whatever their chosen career.

A summary of the public examination results for 2000 is on pages 129 and 169 and the destinations of Grecians leaving in July 2000 are on pages 169–71.

The day room in a boys' house.

40

CHAPTER TWO
LIVING AT CHRIST'S HOSPITAL

THE BOARDING HOUSES

TIME WAS WHEN, IN LONDON in the seventeenth and eighteenth centuries, eighty children slept, two-to-a-bed, in a sparse open ward, with just a hook for their Housey coat and a small box or settle to store their scant personal belongings. Personal hygiene consisted of washing all together with one bowl of water, one bar of soap and one towel – under the supervision of matron – each morning. The move to Horsham brought relative luxury, with its lav-ends and day rooms, but life was still spartan, in comparison with the facilities available to today's pupils. Now they are allowed to wear their own clothes after lessons. They can have as many showers as hot water permits, and they have wardrobes and drawers in which to keep their personal items. The life of pupils has changed beyond belief in the last hundred years.

In this year there are three boarding blocks for girls – Coleridge, Barnes and Leigh Hunt. They are divided into A and B sides, each with its own house parents: Neil and Marlene Fleming in Coleridge A, Alison Röhrs in Coleridge B; Lois Helyar in Barnes A and Debbie Stamp in Barnes B; Vicky and Stephen Buckman in Leigh Hunt A and Elspeth and Christopher Robinson in Leigh Hunt B. The houses are 'all-through', that is, they cover the age range from 11–18, and a system of 'trades' and duties ensures that each child plays her part in keeping the house neat, tidy and smooth-running. There is also Hertford, a small unit for about twelve Deputy Grecian girls in part of the Infirmary building, who maintain connections with their old houses.

There are five boarding houses for boys: Peele A is run by Howard Holdsworth, Peele B by Ian Howard; Thornton A by Sean O'Boyle, Thornton B by Oliver Marlow; Middleton A by the Revd Gary Dobbie, Middleton B by Simon Reid; Lamb A by Dr Sean Hobson, Lamb B by Frank McKenna; Maine A by Dr Ross Stuart and Maine B by Andrew Phillips. The boys are still divided into junior and senior houses, although this will change in September 2000. Typically, at present, the B side would be the juniors – Second Form, Third Form and LE, and the A side the seniors, although this neat rule of thumb does not apply in Middleton, where both sides are occupied by seniors.

The pastoral team in each house consists of the house parents, their assistant housemaster or housemistress and several tutors. Between them they wake the children up, oversee lunch parade and mealtimes and supervise Prep before the gradual migration to bed. But they are not just supervisors or disciplinarians: they are also friends of the house, supporting inter-house sporting fixtures, arranging Sunday outings and joining in celebrations. Non-teaching wives and matrons can also be tutors, a development of recent years which has proved very successful.

The leave weekends every third week or so and the half-term holiday

Junior boys' day rooms aren't always quite as tidy as Keith Mackness's drawing (previous page) might suggest.

provide welcome breaks. It is a matter of continual amazement how quickly the School empties for those holidays once lessons have ended. Hundreds of cars park around the boarding houses and there is intense activity, ant-like, up and down the staircases. With practised efficiency car boots are filled with dirty washing, musical instruments, or *objets* made in Design and Technology, and the cars quickly file out to the perimeter road, to form a queue at The Boar's Head, before moving onto the A24 and to all points north, south, east and west. Only those who live abroad, or too far away, stay on site for a leave weekend and then they, like the teaching staff, taste the delights of this peaceful setting, for a brief time free of the bustle of School life. Half-term, which is a week – or longer – allows for a more substantial break.

So the terms come and go. Pupils grow and mature, and gradually the man and woman they will become can be seen. Behavioural problems improve, attitudes change, they become calmer and more mellow. The house staff quietly watch and enjoy the miraculous meta-morphosis, hardly believing that the harvest they are witnessing, the fruit that others will enjoy, has been husbanded in large measure through their own patience and toils.

PARENTAL SUPPORT

No survey of pupil support would be complete without a mention of the parents, who continue to play an important rôle in the development of their children, even when they are in the charge of house staff. For house parents want to develop good relationships with parents, so that they can share in feats deserving praise, and can be consulted and involved if need be in discipline. To this end parents and guardians meet with their child's teachers at least once a year to discuss progress and shape the future; they can also meet the house parents and tutors much more frequently to maintain an open dialogue. Parents who live locally will probably make extra weekend visits, bringing welcome tuck or just watching a sporting fixture, offering encouragement from the touch line. Christ's Hospital encourages close links between parents and the School.

John Shippen, a senior geography teacher and Group Scout Leader, is one of many teachers meeting parents to review their children's progress at an LE Parents' Meeting in the Sports Hall.

'On an average day, I take calls from two or three parents,' says Neil Fleming, house parent in Coleridge A and now moving to run a Grecians' residence. 'They call to check if their child is sick, or to discuss her welfare or other issues. We maintain a close partnership with parents from the time each child arrives at the School.'

In the Summer term the Parents' Forum is a regular event at which parents can join in discussion with the Head Master. This is described more fully on page 128.

Good behaviour and discipline does not have to involve glum faces.
Left to right: Nicola McCabe, Louise Wootton, Christina Asafu-Adjaye, Lucinda Hutchins, Catherine Williams, with Eleanor Mitra behind Nicola on the left.

DISCIPLINE

There is, in the School's Museum, a punishment book from the 19th century which cites 'a bad case of shuffling' as grounds for punishment. Times have moved on and there is now a great deal more tolerance towards the mores of adolescent behaviour, but even so it is deemed appropriate to set out in the School's termly calendar the parameters of acceptable behaviour. Failures to live up to these standards are met by a progression of punishments, ranging from relatively minor (though not easy) House Drills, to full School Detentions which must be completed by the pupil on a daily basis, or even yellow or red cards.

In the past, house masters beat troublesome pupils, and indeed some Houses were known for the severity of their house master's cane. House tutors were normally only expected to administer the slipper. The Children Act of 1989 has, mercifully, changed all of that and now more sensitive and, hopefully, more effective methods of punishment and correction are used. Today the senior pupils and the House Captain work with the house pastoral team in applying disciplinary measures. Bullying amongst pupils is certainly much reduced by comparison with earlier times and efforts are continually being made to keep it to the minimum, in any of its manifestations. But human nature is such that it remains a subject for constant vigilance.

As a guideline for what he expects, Dr Southern has set out, in con-

junction with his Deputies and the School Monitors, a Code of Conduct for behaviour which applies to all members of the Christ's Hospital community. Its four-fold aims are:

To master academic subjects and develop useful skills.
To establish effective working habits.
To discipline ourselves to be efficient and reliable.
To learn to live happily with other people.

The Code is reproduced in full on page 196.

THE TUTORIAL SYSTEM

In addition to the support given by the house teams, each pupil on the LE and above has a personal tutor, who will meet them at regular intervals and discuss all aspects of their School career. It may be difficult, in such a

Bob Sillett, Deputy Head, with some of his tutees in the Garden Quad. Left to right, standing: Madeleine Moore, Stephanie Coaten, Annabel Ward, Natalie Rosier; seated: Kerrie Downing Robertson, Hayley Bridgman, Vicky Bell, Brigita Ziferman, Sergiu Panaite, Katie Bannon and Lucy Dunn.

44

busy schedule, for both parties to find time for these meetings, but they are well worth the effort. It is very often a quiet word of encouragement or admonition from a trusted tutor that can transform a troublesome situation.

BUTTONS AND CUFFS

The buttons on Housey coats depict the head of the School's Founder, Edward VI, and have been known to attract a high price from Japanese and American tourists. Indeed, there is a story of an enterprising pupil who, on a school trip to London, sold his entire uniform for profit.

From its earliest times, and still today, the academic focus of Christ's Hospital is signified by the fact that the highest distinction, and the only outwardly distinguishing mark a pupil can earn, is the award of academic 'buttons'. The large silver buttons and the velvet cuffs are the mark of a Grecian who in his or her final year has demonstrated outstanding academic performance in more than one subject. It is a privilege still respected throughout the School community, just as it was when Charles Lamb, over 200 years ago, saluted Samuel Taylor Coleridge as his academic inspiration for the fact that he had been awarded his 'buttons'.

The Button Grecian's or School monitor's coat differs in several respects from the normal Housey coat. Button Grecians may also be

A Scholar of Christ's Hospital, *published in 1816 in R Ackermann's* History of Christ's Hospital. *A history of the boys' uniform is on pages 205–6.*

monitors, but they are chosen primarily on the grounds of academic excellence to wear 'Academic Buttons'. To distinguish this elite, their dress has been modified and, in a sense, codified. In many respects their Housey coat is the same but it does not have the small epaulettes, or shoulder wings, of the normal coat. It is lined in black and not in yellow. The collar has a square opening in front to admit the bands, and is lined with black velvet. The cuffs, too, are turned with black velvet, and they carry three large buttons. The coding lies in the fact that an Academic Button Grecian leaves the top button of the cuff undone, while a School monitor has them all done up. If one is both an Academic Grecian and a School monitor then one cuff is fastened completely, and the other cuff leaves the top button undone.

Pupils admitted to the School under certain historic arrangements, or with the support of certain designated endowments or significant benefactors, wear a distinguishing badge, sewn on to their Housey coats. Clockwise from top left: Royal Mathematical School, Wests' Gift, Oliver Whitby Foundation, Worshipful Company of Ironmongers, 617 Squadron.

An Academic Grecian or a School monitor will have twelve or fourteen large buttons (depending on their height) on the bodice of their Housey coat; a normal Housey coat only has seven buttons, six smaller ones and a large one at the waist. The Academic Grecian or School monitor's coat is made of superior kersey, a finer fabric which drapes and folds well and looks extremely elegant. It also has two side pockets instead of one, and the skirts are fuller. More evidence of status is to be found on the sleeves of the Band Captain and the senior Drum Major. They are both entitled to wear twelve gilt buttons on each arm of their ceremonial coats.

The history of the boys' uniform is recounted on pages 205–6.

THE WARDROBE

Wardrobe manager Marion Parkin and her assistant seamstress, Ann Clifford, look after the storage and distribution of uniforms. Breeches, shirts, skirts and jackets are passed down the generations, as are the famous Housey coats. Children provide their own underwear and nightwear.

Hidden behind a distinctive green door near the kitchens are two huge rooms connected by a spiral iron staircase, with breeches, shirts and stockings piled on shelves.

Newcomers arrive to find ready and waiting a set of uniform items prepared according to their measurements: coat and breeches for boys; coat, jacket, short pleated skirt for daywear and long skirt for special occasions for the girls. Matrons keep a stock of shirts and bands.

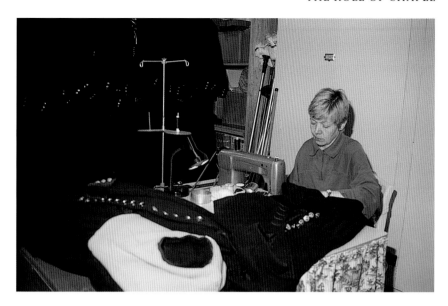

Marion Parkin manages the wardrobe with its vast array of every item of uniform. Her work involves keeping the stock in good repair.

Housey coats and breeches come from a Leeds supplier. They cost £90 each, or £100-plus for Button Grecians' and School Monitors' coats with two pockets, velvet cuffs and collars and extra buttons. The longest Housey coat in stock measures 68 inches and the shortest, seldom needed, is 43 inches long.

The same coats are worn by both boys and girls in winter; from Easter through to Michaelmas half-term the girls wear short belted jackets instead. The children are responsible for ensuring that their coats and skirts or breeches are dry-cleaned in the holidays.

THE RÔLE OF CHAPEL AT CHRIST'S HOSPITAL

The Mission Statement of Christ's Hospital includes the statement that it is and shall be the mission of Christ's Hospital, in perpetuity, to present to its pupils the Christian Faith in all its mystery and splendour. But how does one, in this age of post-modernism, present the Christian faith, with relevance, in all its complexity, to children, few of whom have previous experience of church-going and who are mostly unaware of spiritual matters?

Laura Riley and Nick Bethell talking about revision.

This is the challenge confronting the Chaplaincy team of Christ's Hospital, which comprises the Senior Chaplain, the Revd Munna Mitra; his wife, the Revd Nicola Mitra; the Revd Gary Dobbie; Ian Howard and his wife Rosie, both lay readers.

The members of the Chaplaincy team work closely together and with the Director of Music and organist and each term work around a theme to which they each bring their unique contribution to the life of the Chapel. Thus young minds are stimulated to think about social, moral and ethical issues, and all the time are buoyed up, perhaps obliquely, by scriptural and spiritual solutions. Sometimes songs and drama are used to illustrate a biblical principle; sometimes stories are told, or the lives of the saints and martyrs retold. Guest preachers are invited to address Full School Chapel, and other members of staff offer to speak to Senior or

Interior of the School Chapel.

Junior Chapel. Occasionally the pupils themselves talk about how they have overcome some pain or loss in their lives. It is like a patchwork quilt, where the pattern of the individual pieces combine to produce a much larger work, of intricate beauty, depth, and variety; all of which is supported by the School Choir, which each week, under the expert leadership of Peter Allwood, Director of Music, leads the singing of hymns, provides the sung responses and contributes an often complex anthem.

There are many opportunities to attend Chapel. On Sundays there are two services, one an informal service of Holy Communion, the other a Full School Chapel, when over 800 children fill the banked, collegiate-style pews. There is a Chapel Service for seniors on Tuesdays and for juniors on Wednesdays, when there is also at 8am a service of Holy Communion and at 8.30pm Compline by candlelight for juniors, which is followed by the special treat of hot chocolate.

Seniors have their own service of Compline on Friday evenings when, in the candlelight, the Chaplain and the Cantor create an atmosphere of such peace and tranquillity that the pains and trials of the past week are gently eased. After this service pupils who enjoy Taizé chants gather around the High Altar for perhaps twenty minutes of reflective singing.

There are other services too – All Saints, Harvest Festival, Candlemas, Ascension. These all pass with due observance. At Christmas, even though the pupils have gone home, a Midnight Mass is held on Christmas Eve, when staff, their parents and children, and some Old Blues, join in quiet celebration. Then there is Christmas Day itself when the Chapel, surprisingly full, reverberates with jokes and quizzes, nativity scenes and sweets-for-the-children, but always leaving a serious and thoughtful message as everyone strolls to the Court Room for drinks with the Head Master and his wife afterwards.

Easter is less of a Housey highpoint as many staff take the opportunity of overseas travel at this time, but Easter Day is celebrated with a Family Service, when an Easter garden is set out in Chapel, as are banners and posters, all made by the children of staff. The Chapel, too, is used for services of Thanksgiving and of Remembrance, for Old Blues Day and for House Reunions, for weddings, baptisms and, occasionally, for memorial services and funerals. The exact status of the Chapel in ecclesiastical terms is complex. It is not a parish church nor is it a private chapel. It operates under licence from the Diocese of Chichester and special permission must be sought for services which are not directly related to the life of the School. Its beauty is renowned, and it is viewed each year by hundreds of visitors as they admire the Brangwyn murals, the roof, the reredos and the woodwork, the organ and the pulpit.

The Chapel stands at the heart of the School in every way but it is not the only avenue by which a Christian witness is maintained. There is also the Christian Union which meets – in two groups, for seniors and juniors, – and, in a context of prayer and fellowship, considers key social and ethical issues in the light of biblical revelation. There is the small group from the community which meets fortnightly in the chaplaincy Quiet Room behind the Tuck Shop for a service of Holy Communion. House Communions take place every Tuesday and Thursday when, in a very relaxed atmosphere, pupils are invited to pray – for contemporary world

Nicola Mitra, Rosie Howard and Lizzy Callaghan enjoy a cup of coffee after an informal service of Holy Communion in the Chaplaincy Quiet Room, behind the Tuck Shop. The Quiet Room is also used for individual prayer, as well as by the pupil-led Peer Support Group.

issues, for their families, their house and for one another – and receive the sacraments, or a blessing.

Above all of this there is the quiet, committed Christian witness of so many staff. Some may be overt in their beliefs; others may be quite private, and only give expression to their inner debt to Christ by their many unobtrusive acts of kindness and consideration. It is understood that their time at Christ's Hospital is, for most pupils, a time of exploration and, for some, a little cynicism. Many of them have had to cope with hurt and disappointment, and want to prove for themselves that this Christianity which they are being offered has relevance and value. No one person can convince them of this. It will be a work of grace, brought about by the Holy Spirit through many, different, circumstances.

The Chapel continues its round of services and observances, its prayer and praise, its sacraments and ceremonials; and slowly, 'soul by soul and silently', more and more pupils, and staff, indicate that they too want to be part of the Christian community here.

FOOD GLORIOUS FOOD

Dining Hall, strategically placed in the centre of the avenue of boarding houses, is an important part of communal life in the School. Band Parade takes place every day except Sunday and the School marches in by houses to the stirring rhythm of the Marching Band, the most efficient means of moving the School into dining hall for lunch. In fact the juniors and those travelling to 'away' matches have nowadays already eaten before marching but the unity of the Parade is maintained.

Catering is awarded under a renewable five-year contract to outside caterers. Fairfields' team of thirty four, who hold the current contract, have been in place for several years during which Rachel Adams, the Bursar, and the Catering Manager, Michael Blunden, have introduced a number of changes.

Since 1996 a cafeteria service has speeded up service of lunches and teas and allowed the introduction of a range of dining options, including

GRACE BEFORE MEAT
Give us thankful hearts, O Lord God, for the table which Thou has spread for us; bless Thy good creatures to our use and us to Thy service, for Jesus Christ His sake.

Dining Hall abuzz. Robin Nordgreen, a modern languages teacher, joins some of the pupils for lunch.

hot meals, salads, 'healthy eating' and vegetarian dishes and a variety of desserts, served from counters behind the Dining Hall.

'By introducing a choice, we were able to cut wastage and spend our budget more wisely,' says Mrs Adams. Breakfasts include popular porridge, juices, cooked dishes and croissants. For lunch there is multiplicity

The cafeteria in action. James Gill (left) and Peter Newman make their selections.

of choice. The hot meals include casseroles and stir-fry dishes, roasts and fish, as well as burgers, sausages and pizzas. There is always a vegetarian alternative and the pupils do eat extremely well, augmenting their School diet with toast and pasta, which they can cook in their house kitchens, or with 'tuck', either brought from home or purchased in the Tuck Shop. Later there is a cooked tea, with a choice of ten menu items, which is available within set hours. Tea-time menus are often themed. Italian nights focus on pasta dishes, American nights on pizza and burgers, Chef's Choice concentrates on traditional pies and sausages.

A senior catering manager and the head chef meet regularly with staff and children through the senior and junior food committees. Children are encouraged to express their views on current menus, which are changed and adapted so that dishes are both palatable and nutritious. Croissants and bagels at breakfast, sophisticated Indian and Chinese dishes, more varied vegetarian items, curly chips, and wafers with ice-cream indicate that the days of 'frogspawn' and 'Thames mud' and other gastronomic curiosities described on pages 211–2 are long gone.

Visiting Old Blues are invariably impressed with the improvements in catering since their schooldays. The children enjoy much greater choice and there is less waste.

GRACE AFTER MEAT
Blessed Lord, we yield Thee hearty praise and thanksgiving for our Founder and Benefactors, by whose charitable benevolence Thou has refreshed our bodies at this time. So season and refresh our souls with Thy Heavenly Spirit that we may live to Thy Honour and Glory. Protect Thy Church, the Queen and all the Royal Family, and preserve us in peace and truth through Christ our Saviour.

THE INFIRMARY

Few visitors to the School ever see inside the secluded redbrick building which gives the Infirmary the appearance of being a major asset of the NHS. Nowadays it houses only twelve beds for in-patients and medical surgeries. It is supervised by the Infirmary Manager, Judith Avenell.

In addition to liaising with the sixteen matrons, who provide in-house primary care, Judith Avenell works with four doctors from Horsham's

Yvonne Sheppard-Burgess, Matron in Peele, passes the time with boys from Peele B as they wait for their inoculations in the Infirmary.

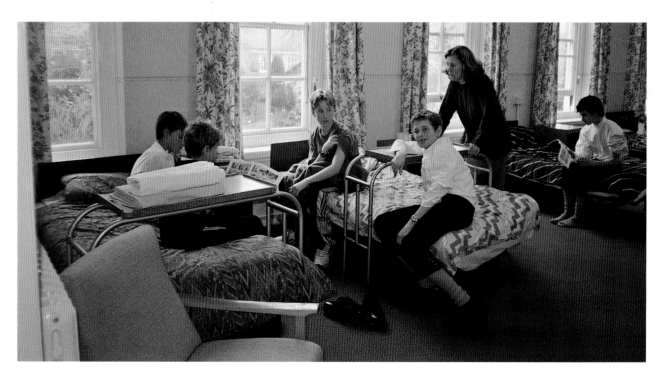

Park Surgery, who visit for daily surgeries. Other 'outside' medical staff include the orthodontist and dentist, a physiotherapist and a counsellor, who each visit twice a week.

The Infirmary-based team includes three staff nurses, a housekeeper and two assistants, a secretary and a driver who organises trips to clinics, hospital appointments and pharmacies, as well as acting as 'ambulance' driver on busy games afternoons.

Morning, lunchtime and evening surgeries are held on weekdays for children referred by their matron or who need treatment during the day.

Judith Avenell, Infirmary Manager.

The principal complaints include colds, headaches, sore throats, a variety of sports injuries and hay fever symptoms in summer. As a preventive measure, the 1999–2000 academic year is marked by the national mass meningitis vaccination programme.

Each child has two dental check-ups a year with the emphasis on preventive dentistry. 'A few years ago, twenty per cent of children needed no dental treatment; now only twenty per cent require attention,' says Mrs Avenell, who has been at the School for twenty years, first as housemistress for Coleridge B, welcoming the first girls in 1985, later at Leigh Hunt B, and for the past two years as infirmary manager. 'We are very well-served in our medical care,' she adds. 'Other schools are amazed at our set-up.'

CHAPTER THREE
OPPORTUNITIES AT CHRIST'S HOSPITAL

CREATIVE AND PERFORMING ARTS

THE FIRST COURTYARD THEATRE

CRITICALLY ACCLAIMED as the country's first modern courtyard auditorium, Christ's Hospital Theatre was designed by the distinguished theatre architect Bill Howell and developed with Duncan Noel-Paton, who later joined the School as Director of Drama. Money for a major building project had been donated by Old Blues and Dr David Newsome, then Head Master, saw the need for a professional theatre.

The theatre opened in 1974 and in 1999 it was the focal point of a major international touring exhibition: 'Making Space for the Theatre'. The theatre's design reflects the New Inn Yard in Southwark. A factor in its great success were the dramatic moving towers, making it possible to stage a performance in the round, then transform into a traditional proscenium arch. The 500-seat courtyard design won a regional award from the Royal Institute of British Architects.

The professionally-equipped theatre is a unique asset for the drama department. At any one time, more than 120 children are studying for GCSE with around 25 proceeding to A-level, and the School has produced several renowned performers.

But teaching is only a part of the School's dramatic activities. The drama department stages around thirty three performances a year, open to the School community and the public, and has toured in the UK and overseas. The department also runs at least three different voluntary activity sessions every week and an increasing number of pupils are taking up and participating in dance work.

The theatre is also a commercial enterprise. Over the years it has attracted Kent Opera, London Contemporary Dance Theatre, Ballet Rambert, English National Opera and Ballet, and the Royal Shakespeare Company. Trevor Nunn acknowledged the influence of the theatre on his development of The Swan theatre at Stratford-upon-Avon. This year's public programme, arranged by Director of Drama Jeffrey Mayhew and drama teacher Paul Ward, includes drama and musical events, as well as Sunday morning workshops for children aged from four to ten.

Bookings are made through box office manager Jackie Davies, and Barbara Wolstenholme is responsible for the patrons and supporters group Christ's Hospital Arts. Productions are co-ordinated by an Arts Committee led by Elizabeth Cairncross.

Key performances in the Michaelmas term are *Titus Andronicus* by the English Shakespeare Company; *The Crucible,* performed by Middleton B and Coleridge A, and the London press night of George Bernard Shaw's

The Theatre

A scene from A View from the Bridge, *CH Drama Department, 2 and 3 December 1999, with (left to right) Toby Davies, Gemma Brown, Ed Marland and John Jukes.*

Widowers' Houses by the Royal National Theatre Mobile.

This play, reviewed in the national press, is directed by distinguished actress Fiona Shaw who comments: 'This is the kind of theatre that performs itself. It's great to have a wide stage, and to be able to enthuse about the architecture. It's a beautiful theatre and a beautiful School, and I would love to come back.' 'The visit by Fiona Shaw and the Royal National is a highlight of the year,' says Jeffrey Mayhew. 'The production was more successful here than at any other venue on their tour.'

Lent term brings the Edinburgh Festival's sell-out, Gypsy band Loyko, and Snap Theatre Company with *Sense and Sensibility*, a stylish take on the wit of Jane Austen, as well as unrivalled opportunities to discover new talent in a School which has produced such successful performers as conductors Sir Colin Davis and Charles Hazelwood, actors Michael Wilding, Tenniel Evans, Roger Allam and Jason Flemyng and comedian Mark Thomas.

Students throughout the School have a chance to shine, with Peele B's rousing production of *Oliver*, Middleton A's *The Long and the Short and the Tall* by Keith Waterhouse and Willis Hall, and Thornton A bringing the Wild West to life in *Gunslinger*.

The School staff and community launch the musical programme with *The Mikado*. The Robert Louis Stevenson School, on tour from California, perform *Oklahoma!*, and Summer term at the theatre includes a performance of David Mamet's controversial *Oleanna* by the London Classic Theatre Company. The Friends of Christ's Hospital Arts annual buffet is linked to the first of two performances of Agatha Christie's *Murder at the Vicarage*, performed by the Christ's Hospital Community.

Young visitors are encouraged to take part in a regular Children's Theatre Workshop on Sunday 7 May; the Second Form Drama Festival takes place on 14 May and a series of short plays and dances are given by junior performers on 25 and 26 June.

Meanwhile by Easter, Paul Ward has finalised the programme for the coming Michaelmas term 2000 and is confirming bookings for the Lent term 2001.

Professor Hugh Bean demonstrates a phrase for Zheni Kanani during a music master class in the Court Room.

MUSIC AT CHRIST'S HOSPITAL

It is almost impossible to escape the sound of music at Christ's Hospital. More than half of all pupils learn at least one instrument, and Director of Music Peter Allwood oversees the organisation of a wide range of orchestras, bands, ensembles, rock and jazz groups, quartets, combos and choirs operating around the campus.

The School timetable includes more than 500 music lessons a week. Instrument tuition is free to pupils who have passed Grade V practical exams, and to those taking GCSE or A-level in music. Awards are also given to new entrants who show strong musical potential. Parents of other children pay according to their means.

The School has six full-time music teachers; thirty who teach part-time, many of whom enjoy a considerable professional reputation; and visiting distinguished musicians who offer masterclasses and workshops.

During the Lent and Summer terms international concert pianist Stephen Kovacevich, who has a son at the School, holds piano master-classes, and choral conductor Sir David Willcocks leads a day-long workshop for singers participating in *Belshazzar's Feast*: a part of the annual Angus Ross Memorial concert at the end of the Lent term.

Piano students participate in a workshop with John Thwaites and Ronan O'Hora, head of keyboard at the Guildhall School of Music and Drama, and a Piano Day gives opportunity to almost 150 students, with an evening recital by seniors.

In the second and third forms, pupils are taught to listen to and understand music, to perform and create their own sounds. The Chapel Choir, currently topping 100 singers, is open to any child who has an accurate sense of pitch and shows commitment.

Instrumentalists and singers with talent benefit from the School's annual concert at the Purcell Room on London's South Bank, as well as a concert at St John's, Smith Square in London and numerous concerts at venues in the South of England.

This year the Concert Band is booked to perform at a millennium garden party in Hampshire, and the Musicians Group have been invited to

A lunch-time concert in the Music Library. Katy Ayling, clarinet, accompanied by Adrian West, piano.

play at a garden party in May for Sir Alan Traill, former Lord Mayor of London and an Almoner.

Both the Chapel Choir and the School bands have featured on recent CD recordings. Recording expenses are high and CDs do not make great profits, but they do provide remarkable experience for children, and encourage them to perform at their best.

Children of all ages gain experience of public performance to a regular and enthusiastic audience at the Tuesday lunchtime concerts in the Court Room, now furnished with a new Steinway piano. Musical instruments, accessories and sheet music are loaned free of charge to students. With 160 piano students in the School, plans are underway to provide each house with a practice room and an acoustic piano with electronic pedal.

The School's tradition of musical excellence has spread around the world, and the children of the Mathieson Music School, Calcutta, visit in the Summer term. This year's students in Christ's Hospital include pupils from Romania, Albania and Lithuania, and requests for places for musical children have been received from as far afield as Russia and Finland.

STRIKE UP THE BAND

Each year, thousands of Londoners and tourists watch the Band marching with the School through the City on St Matthew's Day and leading the Lord Mayor's Show every November.

Over the years, the Band has played at Twickenham rugby internationals, Test Matches at Lord's and taken part in overseas tours. In the Summer term 2000 the Band perform at Lord's when England play the West Indies, and at the American Ambassador's official residence in London's Regent's Park for Beating Retreat on the Fourth of July.

But most important of all, the Band is the focus of the School's lunch parade, with the full Band playing three marches as the School parades into Dining Hall on Mondays, Wednesdays, Thursdays and Saturdays, and the Bugle Band doing the honours on Tuesdays and Fridays.

After rehearsal in the Music School, the Band assembles for lunch time Band Parade – the quickest way of getting the School into Dining Hall.

The Band playing in the lunch interval for the England vs. West Indies Test Match at Lord's on 1 July 2000.

Bandmaster Terry Whittingham, a former bandmaster with the Grenadier Guards and the Queen's Own Highlanders, also teaches bassoon, clarinet, saxophone and music theory. He joined the School in September 1999 and was immediately faced with the task of producing a 76-strong Band capable of immaculate marching and musicianship on the St Matthew's Day parade. For two weeks the Band drilled and rehearsed ten different marches; then they tackled ten more for the Lord Mayor's Show.

Band Captain, Lucy Morgan (Barnes B/Hertford), is a tenor saxophonist in her fifth year with the Band. She acts as administrator, takes the register, assembles musicians into line, conducts, works out placings for big occasions and co-ordinates daily rehearsals. Her deputy Ben Allwood, a Grecian from Middleton A and a trumpeter since he was nine, shares Band duties, with special responsibility for the twenty-strong Bugle Band.

This year's senior drum major is James Busby from Middleton A, the house which traditionally provides the Grecian who leads the Band. Four years ago, James was recruited by a predecessor and learned to build up his strength with a metal pole, before progressing to a small mace for Bugle Band parades. He took part in his first Band parade a year later, progressing to the full-size mace which he proudly claims he has never dropped in public. His seconds are two fellow Grecians, with a Deputy Grecian and two boys from Great Erasmus. He says that he enjoys the privilege of leading the Band, even if he is the centre of attention at public events.

For musicians in their last year the focus in the Summer term is Beating Retreat, which follows their Leavers' Service at the end of term. Work on the marches and display marching starts in the autumn. It's an emotional moment for Grecians in particular, so nothing is left to chance.

Terry Whittingham, Bandmaster.

59

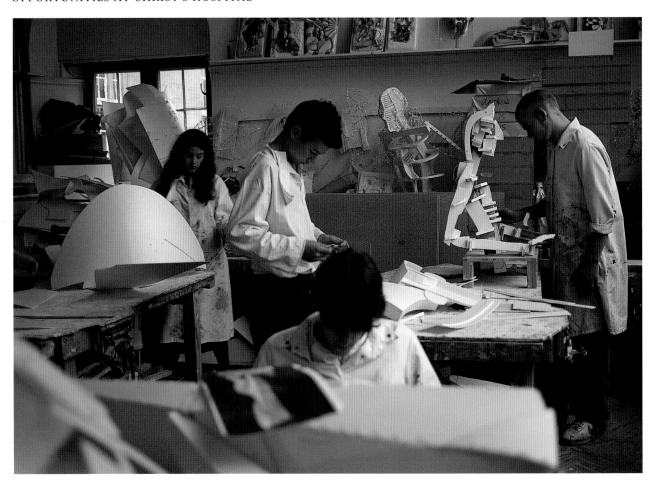

FINE ARTS AT CHRIST'S HOSPITAL

The Art School may be celebrating its centenary, but lessons and tutorials delivered by Head of Art Mike O'Connor and his team are at the cutting edge of creativity. Around thirty six GCSE and twenty A-level candidates sit art exams each year, with everyone achieving astonishingly high standards in their exams and project work.

Art lessons are compulsory for the first two years at the School, and it is a subject in which nobody fails. All children are challenged to realise how good they can be, using paints, ceramics, textiles, sculpture materials and computers and benefiting from imaginative tuition.

They are taught to define colour by context, to re-examine their drawing skills by switching hands, and to consider texture by painting with fingers or a piece of plastic, often on large scale projects.

'We are challenging their perceptions all the time,' says Mike O'Connor, who gives some of his time to every class. The Art School has three full-time staff, including an art historian, and five artists-in-residence, each of whom has a studio.

Opportunities for pupils to explore their creativity and develop their techniques in the Art School extends well beyond the curriculum and the demands of public examinations. The Art School is open seven days and eighty hours a week and was memorably described by the HMC inspectors in November 1997 as '. . . a centre of unquestionable excellence, a

Pupils are also creative in the Design and Technology School. Georgia Bell and David Newman join with other Second Formers in honing their woodworking skills.

refuge for some who have no other natural habitat . . . a vehicle for self-discovery . . . a jewel in the crown.'

Visitors and parents invited to the School's art exhibitions are constantly amazed at the high standards achieved in a wide variety of media.

GRECIANS' LECTURES

During their last year in the School, the Grecians have the opportunity to hear a variety of outside lecturers talking on a wide range of subjects. Lecturers speak of the warm and lively reception they enjoy at the School, and the perceptive questions and eagerness to engage the issues. The Grecians appreciate the change of focus from the confines of the A-level syllabus.

Grecians and staff welcome twenty one speakers in millennium year. Their topics range from 'The Dangers of Cults' to 'Writing for Children', from 'I fought for Hitler' to 'Doctors playing God', and from the 'Northern Ireland Peace Process' to 'All that Jazz'.

At the end of the series, Grecians are required to complete evaluation forms, to give their considered approval and reasoned criticisms. From the comments it appears that future speakers should be fluent, enthusiastic, concise, controversial, confident, knowledgeable and capable of providing a real insight into their subject – a position perhaps of aspiration more than total achievement.

Asked to suggest topics for future lectures, Philip Firmin (Peele A) suggests practical life studies talks on mortgages, finance, house-buying and starting a business. Other proposals range from the monarchy to the mafia and topics unlikely to be aired in the Riches Lecture Theatre in the near future!

The netball squad in action during their tour of Barbados in the summer.

SPORT

The School has 16 rugby pitches, 16 soccer pitches, 6 grass and 2 all-weather hockey pitches, 16 tennis courts convertible for netball in winter, 10 cricket squares with 2 artificial wickets and 12 artificial nets, an athletics track and a cross-country course spread across 100 acres of the campus.

The Sports and Social Centre, opened in 1990, provides a 25-metre six-lane swimming pool, two sports halls marked out for badminton, hockey, netball, tennis and volleyball, basketball, a gym for judo, fencing, table tennis, aerobics, keep fit and circuit training, six squash courts, and two fitness suites equipped with rowing machines, exercise bikes, weight stations, joggers and treadmills, and multi-gym stations. Four fives courts are located in a separate building nearby.

Small wonder that Muir-John Potter, the Director of Physical Education and Chairman of the Games Committee, is faced with a challenging task co-ordinating PE timetables, team and non-team games, indoor and outdoor activities, and girls' and boys' sports. He is supported by four physical education specialists, around 40 academic staff who coach various sports and 25 part-time coaches from outside the School.

All pupils have a double period of PE in their the first two years, with a short optional course in the following three years. In 2002, physical education will be examined at GCSE level as a sports science course. A dozen students have opted to take the course, with 18 taking the subject as one of the new AS exams for 2001.

Games are organised on three afternoons a week, with matches on Saturdays. On typical Wednesdays or Saturdays midway through the School year, two dozen teams will be involved in four or five sporting activities, participating in home and away fixtures. Every week, around 500 children each day will be involved in 50 sporting and non-sporting activities.

Over the years the School has produced under-15 and under-18 county-level players in rugby, netball, hockey and cricket, with talented Grecians going on to play at national level, or to follow sports studies courses at university. This year's netball players have proved particularly strong, winning 18 out of 21 fixtures. The under-14s have shown greatest success at rugby, with the under-12s showing considerable promise.

Sporting success against other schools is particularly rewarding, as most eleven-year-olds arrive at CH with no experience of team games, unlike rival schools' teams who have had several years' prep school experience.

'Our aim is to develop the children's abilities and experiences of team and individual sports so that they can compete here, then continue to enjoy sports by joining university or other sports clubs,' says Muir-John Potter.

One sporting event in which the whole school participates is the annual Steeplechase run in the Lent Term over distances of 1.5 to 4 miles.

Members of the cycle touring group stopping at Shrewsbury, half-way between John O'Groats and Lands End. Frank Pattison, left, is heading south, while Ed Lebon, centre, and Theo Usherwood are about to pedal in the opposite direction.

CYCLE TOURING CLUB

The Cycle Touring Club is run by Frank Pattison, Head of German and President of the Common Room, who shares his enthusiasm for cycling with each succeeding generation of pupils. This year the Club has organised four major tours. During the Easter holiday five members spend three days in the Cotswolds. In the summer half-term holiday a group of five spend four days in the Lake District, climbing Hardknott, Wynrose, Honister, Whinlatter and Kirkstone passes.

The major tour is to Krakow and Southern Poland. At the beginning of August a group of nine present pupils and Old Blues cycle 570 miles from Krakow to the south-eastern tip of Poland, where it borders the Ukraine and Slovakia, before returning via the Carpathian mountains, the Dujanec gorge, Zakopane and Auschwitz back to Krakow. A few days

later Theo Usherwood and Ed Lebon become the first members of the cycletouring club to cycle from Lands End to John O'Groats, covering 1,036 miles in 13 days and meeting Frank Pattison, cycling the route in the opposite direction, half-way.

Fives is a popular sport – this group includes about half of those who play the game at Christ's Hospital.

SCHOOL CLUB OPTIONS

Clubs and 'actives' are available to all pupils not involved in School teams on Monday (juniors) and Thursday afternoons (juniors and seniors).

Options include a wide range of sporting activities, including aerobics, golf, archery, fencing, squash and fives. Around a dozen girls are coached

Pony riding by courtesy of the Passmore family, who have had four children at Christ's Hospital. Six Welsh cobs and ponies are loaned to the School during the winter months. The riding is organised by the Passmore children, assisted by Jenny Williams, Head of Chemistry. Muddy but fun, this activity is open to all from Michaelmas half term until the Easter holidays, when the ponies return to Wales for summer trekking.
From the front: Catherine Williams, Lucy Foster, Niki Williams, Heidi Durnford, Meera Singh and Jenny Williams.

in soccer, rugby and cricket. Others participate in voice and instrument ensembles; and technology workshops in the Design and Technology School, open seven days a week. There are, too, a wide variety of other activities, clubs and societies, including astronomy, bell-ringing, bicycle repair, bridge, chess, Christian Union, creative writing, debating, history, human rights, learning sign language, scenery design, Shakespeare, and much more.

For those with aspirations towards publishing, the annual *Outlook* magazine publishes a selection of pupils' creative writing and graphic art and *The Blue*, each term, financed by the Christ's Hospital Club, gives extensive coverage of School activities, with pupils making up the majority of the editorial and design team for the School section.

COMMUNITY SERVICE

On Thursday afternoons, pupils in the UF and GE participate in a 'service' activity such as Combined Cadet Force, Duke of Edinburgh Award, Community Service, Scouts and Ecology. Community Service is now available to all pupils at every age level throughout the week.

This year, around 100 boys and girls are involved in sixteen community activities each week. In addition, there are regular visits to work with the homeless at the Aldgate Advice café, part of the St Botolph's homeless project in London, reinforcing the School's charitable links with the City. At the School pupils work at a day centre for the disabled, help run a sports club for them, and offer respite to the carers of special needs children through the Grasshoppers Club run at the Sports and Social Centre.

Some volunteers work with a local school for special needs children, others teach Latin at a nearby primary school, or work in a local charity shop with the elderly, or at St Barnabas Hospice in Worthing. They provide music and sports coaching, comfort, companionship and practical help to a variety of communities. The School's community projects are singled out for special praise by the Lord Mayor on Speech Day.

All participants in community service ventures are given initial training and advice, and a comprehensive handbook, the *Guide for Volunteers*, with practical information and reminders.

THE ROMANIA PROJECT

Since 1990, the School community service co-ordinator has been Muir-John Potter, whose work here and in Romania was recognised with an

MBE in 1997. The School's most challenging community work has been in Romania, and 2001 marks the tenth anniversary of its links there.

Each year, a group of staff and pupils has spent two weeks there, undertaking a community service project involving integration between able-bodied and disabled children, and working with local students and officials to ensure that the momentum continues after the School contingent has left.

In the first eight years of the project, around 150 volunteers have visited Romania, learning to work in an unfamiliar environment with deprived, disabled and abandoned children. Former Head Master Richard Poulton has undertaken the rôle of 'special envoy' on fact-finding trips to the country.

On the first visit to Sighisoara in July 1992, the community service team set out to restore a school sports centre, taking with them more than 100 boxes of decorating materials and equipment. They returned to the same school in October 1993 and in 1994. In that year a party of local inspectors and staff from Romania were hosted by the School on a return trip to Britain, when they visited a school for children with learning difficulties, and the club for the disabled at the Sports and Social Centre.

Since 1995 School groups have undertaken community service work in Craiova, Onesti and Iasi, motivating local students and voluntary workers who were often unaware of the situation in institutions such as the School for the Deaf and the Children's Day Centre for handicapped youngsters in Craiova. Working with local authorities has presented its own challenges, requiring considerable tact and diplomacy.

This year, as on previous visits, Housey pupils share their skills in drama and music, arts and crafts, sports and information technology with young Romanians. They use aromatherapy to help disabled children relax, and they show Romanian staff and students how to maintain the same levels of care.

In return, the volunteers learn to use their initiative, assume responsibility, and commit themselves to unpredictable challenges in a strange environment. They learn the importance of thorough planning and preparation; they work with children of varying levels of disability, and with their parents; and they learn to appreciate a basic lifestyle and the lack of material advantages.

Alice Holdsworth and two children with learning difficulties at the Bless the Children Day Centre in Onesti, Romania.

THE COMBINED CADET FORCE

Some 200 pupils are enrolled in the CCF at Christ's Hospital. In the war years, the whole of the Quad would have been filled with members of the Youth Training Corps, previously known as the Officer Training Corps. But school militias have followed the trend of the modern armed forces and are now reduced, streamlined, and trained to a high degree of operational efficiency. Pupils at the School are allowed to join the CCF on the UF, (at the age of fourteen), and many join the Army, though the Navy and the Air Force have their devotees. They are led by trained staff members and former professional servicemen.

Squadron Leader Ian Stannard, a master at the School, underwent an Officer Training course at Cranwell before taking on the rôle of Contingent Commander of the CCF. He is enthusiastic about the influ-

C/Sgt. Laurie Cooke, flanked by Sgt. Nicola Whitley and Cpl. Alex Woodbridge, leads the Army section onto the parade ground for the CCF Inspection on 18 May 2000. This parade is the culmination of weeks of training and preparation. The School Band provides a musical accompaniment under the direction of the Band Master.

ence of military training in the lives of the pupils. 'It is about leadership, discipline, teamwork and taking responsibility', he says, and feels that – whether pupils pursue a military career after School or not – it provides a vital foundation for every walk of life. He adds, 'More recently the CCF has become involved in adventure training and the Duke of Edinburgh's Award Scheme, with overseas postings and travel.' Ten per cent of pupils who have trained in the School's CCF go on to take up careers in the armed services, and last year Paul Stephenson was successful in gaining a coveted Flying Scholarship.

There is no gender bias in the CCF and all pupils work on equal terms. The CCF is an officially Government-sponsored organisation, receiving over £3,000 each year to support its activities. The day-to-day administration and liaison rôles are undertaken by Sgt Major Rick Smith who, at other times, is the School Marshal, bringing a trained military eye to the maintenance of good discipline and smartness of dress.

The CCF is under the control of the Ministry of Defence and visits to military camps, in which they are subject to military law, form part of their training. Ian hopes that one day one of his pupils will come back as a senior officer and inspect the CCF, as has happened in the past. Previous members of the CCF who have achieved senior military rank in recent years include: General Sir Garry Johnson, who became C-in-C NATO Forces Northern Europe; Lt General Sir Michael Gray, who was concurrently Lieutenant HM Tower of London and Colonel Commandant of the Parachute Regiment; Rear Admiral David Bawtree, Rear Admiral Ian Pirnie, Maj General John St J Grey and Maj General Dick Gerrard-Wright.

Solo watches Band Parade with her boss, Rick Smith, and sets a good example of neatness of dress.

DUKE OF EDINBURGH AWARD SCHEME

The Duke of Edinburgh's Award scheme is much more that just another activity to be fitted into a busy schedule. Introduced at Christ's Hospital thirty-five years ago during the Head Mastership of Clarence Seaman, the scheme is a measure of personal initiative and achievement across many spheres and, for those who take it to its highest Gold Award level, it almost becomes a way of life.

The scheme was founded to develop human potential across a range of disciplines and within different contexts. 'Its intention', says Mike Overend, Head of French, who runs the scheme at Christ's Hospital, 'is to challenge participants to do things they otherwise wouldn't do.' There are, therefore, elements of public performance as well as community service and pupils face perhaps their greatest challenge in planning and carrying out expeditions to different locations within the UK and beyond, putting their navigational, logistical and cooking skills to the test.

The Award scheme is open to all pupils from the UF (year 10) and above. As well as the sixty candidates whom Mike, mathematician Lois Helyar and modern linguist Kate Biggs guide through the programme, many more Christ's Hospital pupils take part under the aegis of the CCF or Scouts. Some candidates complete their Gold Award only after they have left the School and possibly completed a gap year. Certificates for the Gold Award are presented at Buckingham Palace or St James's Palace, when the Duke of Edinburgh himself will, whenever possible, be present. It is an achievement to be proud of: it represents dedication, commitment and team work and will be highly regarded by future employers.

SCOUTING AT CHRIST'S HOSPITAL

The Christ's Hospital Scout Group was founded in 1925. The first Grecian to act as assistant scoutmaster was Michael Stewart, who became Lord Stewart of Fulham after a distinguished career in politics. The movement's founder, Lord Baden-Powell, opened the School's Scout headquarters in 1930 and, in 1949, Kingfisher patrol included Derek Baker, later Head Master of the School.

Today's Scout Leader John Shippen arrived at the School in 1966 and re-organised the Group into a Scout troop for 11–15 year-olds (girls were admitted from 1990); and a mixed Venture Scout unit for over-15s. There are now 60 Scouts and leaders, and 30 Venture Scouts and leaders in the School.

Senior Patrol Leader Eleanor Brade and Patrol Leader Richard Ashley-Smith conduct a patrol camp inspection in Shelley's Wood.

The millennium, coinciding with the 75th anniversary of School Scouting, sees a variety of activities. On 1 January Old Blue Scouts greet the new century on Coniston Old Man, based at John Shippen's nearby cottage. Back at School, Scouts enjoy night hikes, survival exercises, canoeing, family camps, district quiz and soccer contests, and weekend or week-long trips. More than fifty Scouts and Venture Scouts take part in the annual expedition to the Norfolk Broads at Easter and, during the summer holidays, Venture Scouts join the West Sussex expedition to Poland for Duke of Edinburgh Gold Award and Queen's Scout candidates.

The following is an extract from Kate Atkinson's Oration on Speech Day, in which she makes special mention of the Scouts' successes:

We would also like to congratulate Mr Shippen on completing one hundred terms here at Christ's Hospital.

The group who will be most affected by this year's staff departures will be the Scouts. This year we lose our Chairman in Mrs Cairncross, our Treasurer in Dr Wolstenholme, our Auditor Rachel Adams, and Mrs Jeffers also steps down as Venture Scout Unit leader after ten years. Over those ten years the Scouts have produced: 70 Queen's Scout Awards; 4 Explorer Belts and 42 of the 116 Duke of Edinburgh Gold Awards that have been obtained by the School.

The current Venture Scouts take an active part in or lead many different activities, groups or teams within the School. The impact that we have can only be achieved with the encouragement and support of dedicated and committed staff. Recent adventures have included the invasion of an Austrian alpine hut by a party of twenty two Venture Scouts and their eight adult helpers, and the ascent of Silver Howe in the Lake District by a Venture Scout in full Housey. Holiday makers in the Norfolk Broads were also seen to disperse rapidly as a flotilla of yachts, cruisers and dinghies containing fifty Scouts and Venture Scouts hove into view this Easter! The unit also hope to join other Scouts from our district camping in Poland this summer. Therefore it is only right to show our appreciation to those who have made it possible. Thanks must be given to Mr Shippen and other staff helpers and Old Blues who give their time so willingly to help both with the Scout troop and the Venture unit.

The Scout Group publishes an annual account of its activities in its magazine *The Schout*.

CHAPTER FOUR
LOOKING FORWARD TO THE NEW SCHOOL YEAR

THE PEACE THAT DESCENDS on the Quad after Beating Retreat, when all pupils and parents have gone, and the formalities are finally over, seems to herald an endless period of holidays and stress-free living for the resident teaching staff, although not for the administrative staff and officers in the Counting House, nor for the support staff who maintain the buildings and grounds. Defying any known laws of physics, it can seem to the teachers that the approaching eight weeks represent a boundless ocean of time and space, in which distant countries can be visited, hobbies pursued, friends visited: all those things which are simply impossible in the bustle of term.

But the prospect is deceptive. The pupils will return, and sooner than one thinks. Suddenly there is just a week to go, and house parents begin to wear that busy, distracted look which spouses have learned to recognise: they are now thinking about house affairs, and no longer 'open' to normal family activities. Is the punishment book up-to-date? And house accounts? Who will be sharing with whom, in which 'cubi' or study? Has this or that problem been addressed and overcome? Is the house in good physical repair: has that hole or that broken table been repaired? Perhaps a trip to IKEA can be fitted in, when plants, lamps, rugs and pictures can be loaded into a minibus, to revitalise a common room?

Matrons and their assistants will be sorting, mending and allocating School clothes to their respective pigeonholes, so that every pupil begins the year with the approved number of shirts or blouses, bands, and pairs of stockings. Pressed and starched sheets will be returned in heavy bags from the laundry, to be stored in their cupboard, before being used to make up beds for the returning pupils. Blankets are folded and counted; towels stacked; breeches or Housey coats returned from the dry cleaners are recorded on meticulously kept lists. Any pupil with a particular medical condition is noted and appropriate drugs or equipment checked.

While the matrons are busy in their quarters, the groundsmen and estate staff are equally busy in theirs. For grass needs to be cut, hedges trimmed, pitches for hockey and rugby marked and goal posts set in place. Very often at this time special street-cleaning vehicles with brushes and hoses will visit the site from Horsham and clean and sweep all the gutters so that, by the time the first arrivals return, the grounds are in sparkling and pristine condition.

The first pupils to come back are the sportsmen and women – the rugby and hockey players – who have returned early for pre-season training. Displaying fast-fading tans, they train and jog, discovering just how unfit they have become during the long break. Gradually teachers return

Shaun Castle mows the lawns of the Quad in readiness for the new School year, with the south-facing façade of Dining Hall and the water tower in the background.

Dr Roger Hackett, Director of Studies, chairing a heads of department meeting. Left to right: Jeffrey Mayhew, Jenny Williams, Steve Eason, Peter Allwood, Roger Hackett, and Kevin McArtney.

to site, slipping quietly back into their School accommodation and, apart from forays into Sainsbury's or Tesco's, lying low. House and departmental meetings are held to discuss strategies for the new School Year and, on the last day, a Staff Training Day is held, when various aspects of educational practice are considered and discussed. Heads of Departments are engaged with their staff in establishing the syllabus for the coming year, having already ordered textbooks and considered what practical involvement their courses will require.

Dr Roger Hackett, the Director of Studies, is particularly busy. Among his other duties it is his responsibility to plan and oversee the timetable, and the sheer complexity of it can cause him many hours of detailed manoeuvres – something between a crossword puzzle and a game of solitaire – as he attempts to balance the needs and expectations of both staff and pupils. It is a process which he will have started the previous November, when a straw poll of the GE was taken to assess their preferences for A-level subjects. By December he had allocated the subjects to 'blocks', his building blocks from which the timetable is constructed. In January and February the A-level prospectus will have been drawn up and presentations made to interested groups; and by March the GE will have made their choices. Also in February the GCSE option choice prospectus will be available, and in March and April the III Form will have made their GCSE option choices. In March the Heads of Department give their staff allocations for all forms; and the stage is set for the main activity of the Easter holidays, which is – using pencil, rubber and computer-generated proformas – the construction of a draft timetable for the LE, UF, GE, Deps and Grecians.

By the end of May any changes have been agreed with Heads of Department and the II and III Form timetables have been added. By June the entire timetable is complete and ready for inspection by all staff. It remains for rooms to be allocated and any late changes incorporated. Only then, just before the beginning of the Michaelmas Term, the final full

YEAR GROUPS AT
CHRIST'S HOSPITAL

Second Form	Year Seven
Third Form	Year Eight
Little Erasmus	Year Nine
Upper Fourth	Year Ten
Great Erasmus	Year Eleven
Deputy Grecians	Year Twelve
Grecians	Year Thirteen

timetable is published. The normal teaching week for an assistant teacher is about thirty of the forty 'teaching periods'; but house parents and heads of department have a remit of about six periods to allow them time for their other duties. Other senior members of staff – the Deputy Heads, the Director of Studies and the Head Master – are also entitled to reduced timetables. The Heads of many schools are no longer able to teach at all but Peter Southern insists on 'keeping his hand in', as he puts it, with six lessons a week.

It is a Herculean labour, the construction of the timetable, and one in which Roger Hackett cannot please all of the people all of the time; but he makes a brave attempt, and is largely successful, in achieving a working compromise for all.

While this is going on intense activity can be noted in staff accommodation, for there are frequently seventeen or more moves taking place in School property, as new staff move in or existing staff move around. Sometimes the estate staff take the opportunity of refurbishing a house,

Mike Blunden, Catering Manager.

and ancient piping and wiring is ripped out so that safe modern equipment can be installed. It is a necessary task to maintain these beautiful old houses, but considerable costs can be incurred by the new occupant as carpets, curtains and fittings have to be bought. It is a complicated business living in staff accommodation: who pays for what: and what happens when the houses change hands? Despite the existence of clear guidelines, this is a time of year fraught with tense negotiations.

Fairfield Catering are busy too, planning their menus and ordering giant bags of pasta, crates of milk and mountains of bread, tubs of yogurt, and vast quantities of vegetables, pizzas, frozen chips and baked beans. During the term over 3,000 meals are served each day: fruit, vegetables and meat are ordered the day before they are needed; frozen food is delivered three times a week, and dry food twice a week. It is an extraordinary feat of planning and organisation to ensure that the pupils are

Left: Modern kitchens lie behind the Dining Hall.
Above: Washing up is not the chore it used to be.

well fed, and that the kitchens are maintained to the impeccably high standard required by the Environmental Health Inspectors.

It just remains for the Chaplains to plan their service for the beginning of term before all is ready. In ones and twos, and then in droves, the pupils return to their houses. Some have grown and changed almost unrecognisably in those eight weeks. Some are full of news of visits to Disneyland or camps or overseas trips. Others maintain a low profile and are just glad to be back in the safe and predictable routine of Christ's Hospital. With extraordinary speed the rhythm of term begins to beat – of Chapel and lessons, of sport and actives, of relationships and quiet walks. It is almost impossible to recall any other kind of life; but it is right to set out just how much hard work and preparation is done by so many to make this School, uniquely, what it is.

THE BURSAR'S TALE

So much of life at Christ's Hospital revolves around classrooms and teaching that it is easy to forget that a whole army of people are at work behind the scenes, providing the all-important 'food, clothing and lodging' that, with a 'little learning', were the essential elements in the early provision for the children.

Pat Taylor, Banqueting Manager.

At the start of the Michaelmas term, Bursar Rachel Adams looks back on seventeen years' service with the School, starting as Finance Officer in the London office at Great Tower Street, then at Horsham, and glances forward to her retirement at the end of the academic year.

Before taking the step into a more leisured lifestyle, Rachel faces a typically busy year. Her responsibilities range from catering, cleaning, wardrobe and laundry to house matrons and infirmary, the furnishing of the houses, and the condition of the School grounds, which includes the estate and tenanted farms.

She and her Assistant Bursar Jan Sargent supervise a workforce of 158.

To care for the physical needs of the pupils there are sixteen matrons – two for each block – who are supported by twenty-seven part-time matrons' assistants. The matrons work very closely with the School Infirmary to provide excellent healthcare, as well as overseeing the

Rose Hunt, left, and Joan Ingram, matrons in Lamb.

tidiness of the bedrooms and study areas, and providing clean linen. The new Grecians' residences will have housekeepers, instead of matrons, who will live out, rather than in the houses as present matrons do.

The matrons work on a shift basis, so that there is 24-hour cover for the pupils. The matrons' offices occupy 'the middle' between the two houses of the blocks. They are places of welcome and comfort as well as of practical care; and the matrons, with their assistants, provide an essential and much-valued link in the overall welfare of the pupils.

As well as the matrons and their staffs there is an army – the largest department in the School, as they proudly assert – of cleaners. Led and managed by Bob Barker, forty cleaners work a complex system to keep all the buildings of the School clean and tidy. It can be difficult and dispiriting, bearing in mind the personal habits of some teenagers, but they carry out their work with extraordinary good humour and patience. Some become more actively involved, and there is certainly one instance where a cleaner has instituted her own league table for cleanliness, providing a bar of chocolate to the tidiest pupils. Holidays give no respite to the clean-

Julia Watson, left, has been Middle Lady in Lamb for fourteen years and Rita Upton, right, sorts and darns countless stockings and other garments, guarded by a faithful companion.

Bob Barker, Cleaning Manager, with members of his army of forty cleaners enjoying a coffee break.

ing staff, who keep everywhere immaculate for the organisations who use the School facilities.

The School has its own laundry, managed by Ann Fuller who has logged twenty years' service, and each house has a set day for sending in bed linen, sportswear and other items.

Richard Churchman, Grounds and Estates manager, is responsible to the Bursar for the efficient running of the 1,200-acre Christ's Hospital estate – both the grounds inside the 'ring fence' and for liaising with the tenant farmers outside it. He ensures, too, that all is in order for School events such as Speech Day, Parents Day and Royal visits, and that the correct flag is flying at the right times. Martin Bowyer, with thirty-four years' service, leads the Estate Grounds team; the Playing Fields team is led by Peter Sands, and between them they ensure that the lawns, hedges, trees and playing fields of the School are always in good order.

Top: Andrew Dickinson mowing the 1st XI square in front of the pavilion.

Centre: Three ground staff on perennial clearing up.

Left: The sports field team, left to right: Peter Sands, Dave Capewell, Andrew Dickinson and John Wait with the Grounds and Estate Manager, Richard Churchman.

The Common Room sitting room and library.

COMMON ROOM

Common Room, linked to Dining Hall through a doorway at the back of the dais, comprises a dining room and bar, a snooker room, and a spacious library lounge: a particularly cosy refuge with a roaring fire in winter, where members can relax in comfort.

Frank Pattison, head of German, is the current President of Common Room, re-elected in 1999 for his second four-year term. He has an elected committee of six and a membership of 140, two-thirds of whom are academic staff. Senior administrative staff, non-academic house parents and the house matrons are also eligible for membership.

President of Common Room Frank Pattison shares bartender duties with Jackie Jeffers and John Denison, Secretary and Treasurer of Common Room respectively.

'We also have a lively group of honorary members, many of them retired members of staff, who have given good service to the School,' says Frank.

Until 1985, Common Room existed principally for the use of bachelor masters who had only basic accommodation and gathered on six days a week for formal dinners. With the arrival of more female staff and co-education, the barriers were broken and women were welcomed to the inner sanctum.

Today, Common Room enjoys two formal dinners and a couple of dozen smaller gatherings each year, as well as theatre trips and talks by members, such as Thornton A House Master Sean O'Boyle, who sets crosswords for a national publication.

'Common Room offers a mutual support system, as well as a place to meet socially and informally and enjoy some very jolly occasions,' says Frank.

THE MASTER PLAN

A hundred years ago, while the pupils remained in London, builders were on site – churning up the ground with picks and shovels and battling against the frustrations of water-laden ground – to dig foundations and carry out the major excavation work needed to accommodate the Tube. A century later more builders, this time with mechanical diggers, turn over the heavy sodden soil to excavate foundations for the Grecians' residences, for new piping, for car parks and, eventually, for new classrooms. In the 1890s they had the problem of delivering building materials by

Construction of the Grecians' residences started in July 1999 but exceptionally wet weather through to summer 2000 slowed progress. The Grecians moved in at the beginning of the Lent Term 2001, about one year after this photograph was taken.

A sketch of a study bedroom in the new Grecians' residences.

Architect of the Master Plan, Nick Thompson, right, a Peele B Old Blue, enjoys a joke with the Head Master and Mrs Southern.

horse-drawn carts along the narrow winding roads of Tower Hill. Today's contractors experience similar frustrations as they negotiate those same roads with their seventy-ton cranes and articulated lorries.

The urgent necessity to upgrade the pupils' facilities – both domestic and academic – and the decision to provide two new residences for the Grecians, thus enabling the pupil numbers to rise again to 850, cause the conception of the Master Plan. After wide-ranging consultation it came to include the refurbishment and redevelopment of the whole site. Just as the Summer term of 1999 came to an end, all the accoutrements of a massive building programme began to arrive on site.

New car parks on Little Side, one on the site of the previous running track, have been begun, and progress continues to be made on them during the summer. At the same time trees – as few as possible – on Big Side are felled, and foundations dug for the new Grecians' residences which are to be sited precisely at each end of the Quarter Mile, abutting East Gun Copse and West Gun Copse. The work continues all through winter; through the brief snow of Christmas and, haltingly, through the heavy rains of New Year. Gradually, almost imperceptibly, the sky-line changes as scaffolding is erected and the first red-bricked gable completed.

Nick Thompson, Old Blue and Donation Governor, and now a distinguished architect, is responsible for the Master Plan. He freely admits that the design of these residences is complex and unusual, requiring a high degree of skill and proficiency from all the trades involved. His intention, and that of the Head Master, Clerk and Almoners, is that the concept of the original buildings should be retained, although the actual design of the new ones is modified to reflect the spirit and needs of the present age. As the shape and complexity of the buildings have emerged it is clear that he has been spectacularly successful in achieving both those aims.

But the scope of the refurbishment and redevelopment does not stop there, for the Master Plan is breathtaking in its scope and complexity. New classrooms are being considered, contiguous with the East and West Classrooms, with new accompanying cloisters.

The Art School and the Library are to be extended, and a new

CHRIST'S HOSPITAL
AERIAL VIEW

© COPYRIGHT 2000 ARCHITECTS DESIGN PARTNERSHIP

Technology Centre developed, all around the area formerly known as the Arts Quad, which housed little more than cycle racks and some dilapidated lavatories. The Theatre is to have a costume store and a larger foyer and, to the north of the site, the Counting House may be extended, to provide more office space and a Visitors' Centre. In due course, if circumstances permit, the Museum will be moved to a more central location.

All this is for the future: it is part of a ten-year plan, at least, estimated to cost about £60 million at 1999 prices. The Council of Almoners has earmarked some £29 million of reserves for the first, most urgent phases, and launched The 100 Years On Appeal for £5 million, described on page 192, commemorating the move from London one hundred years ago. Meanwhile, each new project within the Masterplan is commissioned according to its priority for the School and the availability of funds to see it through to completion.

The Prep classroom block, meanwhile, will be turned into a residential block in the summer holiday 2000, which will act as the 'decanting' house for pupils while each of the boarding houses in turn is being refurbished. This will, of course, mean that alternative locations have to be found for the subjects taught there, which include Archaeology, Business Studies and Religious Studies, Food and Nutrition, and Classics. These subjects will be relocated, either to other classrooms within the main body of the teaching blocks, or moved to the new double-storey modular classrooms which will arrive in the Arts Quad in summer 2000 and remain until the time comes for its re-development.

The scope of this programme of refurbishment and redevelopment –

The Architects Design Partnership are the architects of the refurbishments and extensions of the Avenue boarding houses. This is their concept drawing of the appearance of the back asphalts after the addition of the new house parents' houses and new landscaping. It comes from an extensive document considered by the Estates Committee in April 2000.

and the vision behind it – is vast, and will require a cool nerve, flexibility, and sheer determination to see it accomplished. But in the Head Master, the Treasurer, the Clerk and the Steward we have all these qualities, and more. There is a realisation that Christ's Hospital has always been in the process of growth, change and adjustment, and that this present phase of our corporate life is simply a continuation of the remarkable story which began in 1552.

In the Annual Report for 1999 the Treasurer observes that, 'Many challenges, both practical and financial, lie ahead in the realisation of the vision for the School and the Foundation in the twenty-first century. But we are most fortunate in having a highly dedicated team of Trustees, staff and professional advisers working enthusiastically and in harmony to take the plans forward and – unique to Christ's Hospital – in having a Court of Governors, many of whom actively provide encouragement, constructive criticism and help or expertise when appropriate.'

THE WAY IN: ADMISSION TO CHRIST'S HOSPITAL

The methods of entry into Christ's Hospital are several, varied, and at first, or even second sight, complex. All are under the control of Mrs Patricia Gilbert, the Admissions Officer, who works from the Counting House under the authority of the Clerk. The explanation for this lies in the Mission Statement '. . . to have regard especially to children of families in social, financial or other need in the choice of pupils, that choice to remain the prerogative of the Foundation.'

A method of entry which distinguishes Christ's Hospital from all other schools is its 'presentation' system, under which individuals or corporate bodies subscribe for and take on the mantle of Donation Governorship and in doing so accept a duty to identify a child or children who have a need for the academic boarding education which Christ's Hospital provides, and the

Patricia Gilbert, right, with Vicky Haigh, the Clerk's secretary, advising parents on Open Day.

potential capacity to benefit from it. There are currently over 550 Donation Governors who, either individually or on behalf of the organisations they represent, have each made a qualifying donation to the Foundation, entitling them to present one foundationer pupil to the School. A child who is 'presented' has only to reach the required standard academically, and to show his or her suitability for boarding, to be offered a place in the School.

There are over twenty-five categories, both individual and corporate, under this ancient system of presentation, all detailed in the Scheme of

Administration (Trust Deed). The largest is that of the Wests' Gift, an endowment dating back to the eighteenth century, the income from which funds places in the School for descendants of John and Frances West and for children of parents employed in the City of London, or living in Reading, Newbury or Twickenham.

Historic privileges of presentation are available to the President, the Vice-President, eight City Livery Companies and the President and Governors of Guy's Hospital. The Council of Almoners has a general duty of presentation. Others are in the gift of the Council of Almoners with specific criteria attaching to them, including up to forty for children of serving or retired naval personnel as members of the Royal Mathematical School, up to ten for orphan girls and those in memory of John Lock, Edmund Tew and John Stock. More recently, the establishment of the Royal Air Force Foundation has provided for the presentation of the sons and daughters of serving or former RAF personnel.

The process of linking Donation Governors who have a presentation available with potential candidates is complex and involves a great deal of thought and effort by the Governor, the parents, and the Admissions Officer.

'For entry into the Second Form (Year Seven), we like to see an application when a child reaches age nine, so that we can advise parents which methods of entry are open to them,' says Patricia Gilbert. She is expert on giving assistance to Governors, too, and has a data base of potential entrants from which she provides details of possible presentees which match the Governors' aspirations of the sort of pupil they would like to see in the School.

Aside from the presentation categories, there are two principal competitive entries. First, in recognition of the School's historic links with the

Open Days, held twice a year, are an important prelude to admission. Pupils, suitably briefed and equipped with answers to the most commonly asked questions, conduct prospective entrants and their parents on tours of the School and tell them what life at Housie is really like. Assembled and ready to go are (right to left) Kade Amoo, Sam Bass, Danielle Scott, Paul Fosker, Emma Halden, Geoffrey Jones, Constance Usherwood, Krishan Singh-Gill and Joshua Gimenez. The Open Day on 1 April 2000 is described on page 117.

On Open Day Big School is thronged with visitors. Here Alan Smith, right, Master of the Royal Mathematical School, discusses his subject with aspiring pupils and their parents.

City of London, the Scheme provides for up to 150 places to be competed for by children from London primary schools. Secondly, the Council of Almoners, through the Clerk, nominates children who do not have a presentation for the entrance examination but whose family income brings them within the limits laid down at the time of their application.

The Scheme also provides for the Council of Almoners to admit, on the basis of competitive examination, children who are not 'in need' as full cost paying pupils. They are known as New Foundationers and the Council's policy is that not more than three per cent of the pupil population may fall into this category.

Subject to certain limits on overall numbers and approval of the Council of Almoners, all staff of the School can enter their own children for the entrance examination; on entry they become 'non-Foundationers' and there are thirty five in the School in the academic year 1999–2000.

The School also has an expanding Sixth Form. In recent years about thirty-five pupils have arrived as Deputy Grecians each September. Such is the absorbent quality of the School that they find themselves welcomed, integrated and quickly Housiefied. They also contribute much both in terms of freshness of approach and specific skills. Last year's Senior Grecian, Joel Jardine, exemplifies this particularly well, transferring from a Sussex comprehensive to be quickly recognised as an outstanding leader at Christ's Hospital.

For over 450 years, through war and peace, through prosperity and hardship, Christ's Hospital has been able to sustain and develop its extraordinary provision of support and education of the highest quality for children whose parents could not possibly afford it elsewhere. This has been possible through the generosity and altruism of so many individuals and through the prudent management of endowments and resources by generations of Governors and Almoners. It is perhaps through the unique system of Donation Governorship and Presentation that this beneficence can most clearly be seen.

Broadly, forty per cent of pupils at the School have been presented; the other sixty per cent have gained admission through competitive entry or

as non-Foundationers. In January 1999 the number of candidates of every variety number over 300 for only 120 places available in September.

All candidates trying for admission at age eleven or twelve visit the School early in January and stay overnight to experience the boarding lifestyle. They take part in art, sporting and musical activities, undergo a one-to-one interview with a senior member of the academic staff, sit examinations in English, maths, verbal and non-verbal reasoning and cognitive abilities, and their academic and social skills are assessed.

Selection involves both the School and the charitable Foundation. The School looks, of course, for a sufficient level of academic knowledge and potential to cope with the demanding curriculum, as well as the capacity to live in, enjoy, and benefit from a boarding school environment. The Foundation is concerned to ensure that the criteria of need are fully met.

Making the final choice is a full day's work for the Head Master, who chairs the Admissions Panel, his Deputies, the Head of English, the Head of Maths, other staff involved in the recent examinations, the Clerk, the Admissions Officer, and with two or three Almoners as non-participating observers. Starting with the presentees, every candidate's case is individually considered with the results of their examination papers, reports on the interviews they have had with staff, and the assessment of their attitude and behaviour in the day and a half which they spent in the School.

Of course some will fail on academic or social grounds. This is especially difficult with Donation Governors' presentees, and emphasises the need for Governors to be as sure as they can that their candidate has the necessary qualities. Governors can, and usually do, make an alterna-

Grandmothers are especially good at asking searching questions during tours of the School. Ishaan Chauhan supplies the answers while Joshua Gimenez and Krishan Singh-Gill lead the way.

A symbol of the City connection: the City of London flag flys on Speech Day when the Lord Mayor attends in state.

tive presentation in a later year if their first or a subsequent presentee fails to be offered a place. If, for any reason, a Donation Governor's presentee leaves the School within the first two years, he or she may make a further presentation without making any further donation. Under a recently introduced scheme celebrating the Centenary of the School's move to Horsham in 1902, existing Donation Governors can, for a limited period, make a second presentation after another donation of just £5,000 under Gift Aid (which enables the Foundation to recover the basic rate tax). Any Donation Governor may renew his or her presenting privilege at any time upon payment of a further donation at the current rate, but Governors may not normally have more than two presentees in the School at a time.

By the end of January places will have been offered to the successful candidates and parents will be sent the New Entrant Pack, a comprehensive package of information covering almost every aspect of School life.

The question of financial contribution will also have been addressed. This is assessed annually, according to family income, on a sliding scale. In 2000 forty per cent of families paid nothing at all, and only three per cent paid the full costs of educating their child.

In preparation for their arrival in September, all new entrants are asked to attend a New Entrants' Day in May, so that parents and children can see their new house, and meet the house parents and pupils. Finally, during the summer holidays, the new entrants will receive details of arrival time and parking arrangements for the first day of term.

The Housey uniform of long blue coat and yellow stockings is provided free of charge, funds are available to help the most needy families with travel costs, and the Benevolent Society of Blues exists to help needy pupils, as well as Old Blues throughout their lives.

THE CITY CONNECTION

Christ's Hospital's connection with the City of London goes back, of course, to its foundation. The ties with it are still strong despite the passing of the centuries, and they remain important. When the School was at Newgate Street it was common for the Masters of City companies to visit the School to select new apprentices and clerks. At one time an Old Blue could get anything he needed in the City: every company employed at least one Old Blue who could be of assistance.

The connections now include having the Lord Mayor as Vice-President and the historic events such as St Matthew's Day, as well as the continuing and much-valued financial support of the Corporation.

There is a close affinity with many of the City Livery Companies, several of whom present pupils to the School. At a reception for The 100 Years On Appeal, hosted by the Master of the Worshipful Company of Vinters, no less than nineteen Livery Companies were represented by their Masters or Clerks. It has become a tradition, too, that the Head Master, the Treasurer and the Clerk are invited annually to the City Dinner of the Worshipful Company of Ironmongers, who also have several presentees in the School.

The late Mr Roger Parker, Master of the Worshipful Society of Apothecaries, wrote that 'For the first time in recent history there are

Hats are popular but vulnerable to the gusting wind on Speech Day. Left to right: Mrs Weston leads Lady and Alderman Sir Richard Nichols, with the Rt. Reverend Frank Weston in front of Dining Hall. Sir Richard and Frank Weston are Old Blues and Almoners influential in maintaining the City connections.

Three Masters of City Livery Companies in 2000, all Old Blues: left to right, Leslie Kemp, Master Founder, Roger Parker, Master Apothecary and Michael Pickard, Master Insurer.

three Old Blue Masters of City Livery Companies in post at the same time. They are the Master Founder, Leslie Kemp, the Master Insurer, Michael Pickard, and myself as Master Apothecary. We each head our Livery Companies for the year and meet on numerous occasions at City functions with or without the Lord Mayor.'

Roger Parker's millennium fund-raising effort on behalf of the Society of Apothecaries acquired funding from its members and from the Society itself to present three sixth-form entrants who are proposing to study medicine. Sixth-form entry is quite new to the School, and the Society of Apothecaries claim the distinction of being the first City Livery Company to support this form of entry. They join several other Livery Companies who have supported presentations to the School over many years, even centuries.

Historically the Society of Apothecaries, just down the road from Newgate Street, had a regular business and professional arrangement with Christ's Hospital, at least in the eighteenth and nineteenth centuries, providing both the Apothecary and medicines for the School. The Society's last presentation to the School was in the 1850s and so the connection with the School is being renewed for the first time in 150 years, with an Old Blue and Master Apothecary playing a key rôle.

The Head Master congratulates Kate Atkinson on her appointment as Senior Grecian for 1999–2000.

The Second Monitors: Sophie Naish and George Busby.

SENIOR GRECIAN AND SECOND MONITORS
1999–2000

Senior Grecian for the Millennium year is Kate Atkinson of Coleridge B, the daughter of a vicar in charge of five parishes in North Oxfordshire. She was presented in 1993 by Donation Governor John Bacon.

'My parents heard about the School and sent for a prospectus,' she says.' I read about the sports centre and music and the band and it seemed exciting, too good to refuse.' Kate has flourished, playing tennis and being vice-captain of hockey for the School, as well as an oboeist in the Band. She amassed six A* and three A passes at GCSE, and is spending her final year studying maths, economics and French at A-level. She plans to read economics with French at university.

Kate is the fourth girl to be appointed Senior Grecian since the girls' school merged with the boys' campus in 1985. 'I was invited to become Senior Grecian half way through the summer term,' she says. 'The Head Master called me into his office and told me then. It was quite a shock. He gave me time to think about it, so I went to find my tutor and we discussed it, and I accepted that evening. The official announcement was made at end of term assembly.'

THE SECOND MONITORS

The Second Monitors help the Senior Grecian with general duties. 'We provide a link between the pupils and senior management team, we attend a variety of functions and represent the School to different bodies,' explains George Busby, one of this year's two office holders.

George is in Middleton A, together with his twin brother James who is House Captain and Drum Major. A West Gift presentee from Hungerford, George heard of the School through family friends and his teachers.

He achieved two A* and seven A grades in his GCSEs, and is taking geography, biology and chemistry at A-level, with a conditional offer to read zoology at Bristol. He is vice-captain of the 1st XV rugby team with under-18 representative honours for Sussex, a member of the School Choir, singing a bass part in Brahms' 'Liebeslieder' at the School's Purcell Room concert in London, and plays the trumpet in the Marching Band.

George shares Second Monitor duties with Sophie Naish of Leigh Hunt A, who was admitted to the School from Cosham near Portsmouth as a member of the Royal Mathematical School as a result of her father's service as a Lieutenant in Royal Navy submarines, 1969–77. Sophie is the youngest of three sisters to benefit from the School's education.

Sophie achieved eight A* grades and a A grade in her GCSEs, is taking A-levels in German, Latin and history and hopes to read German and Latin at Oxford. She is captain of netball, plays tennis for the School, is a senior Royal Navy cadet in the Combined Cadet Force, and teaches Latin to primary school children as her community service project.

The Second Monitors supervise the team of School monitors, organising events such as School balls and the Remembrance Sunday service, attending major School and outside events, liaising with the Head Master and the deputy heads, and helping generally with the smooth running of the School.

CHAPTER FIVE

THE MICHAELMAS TERM

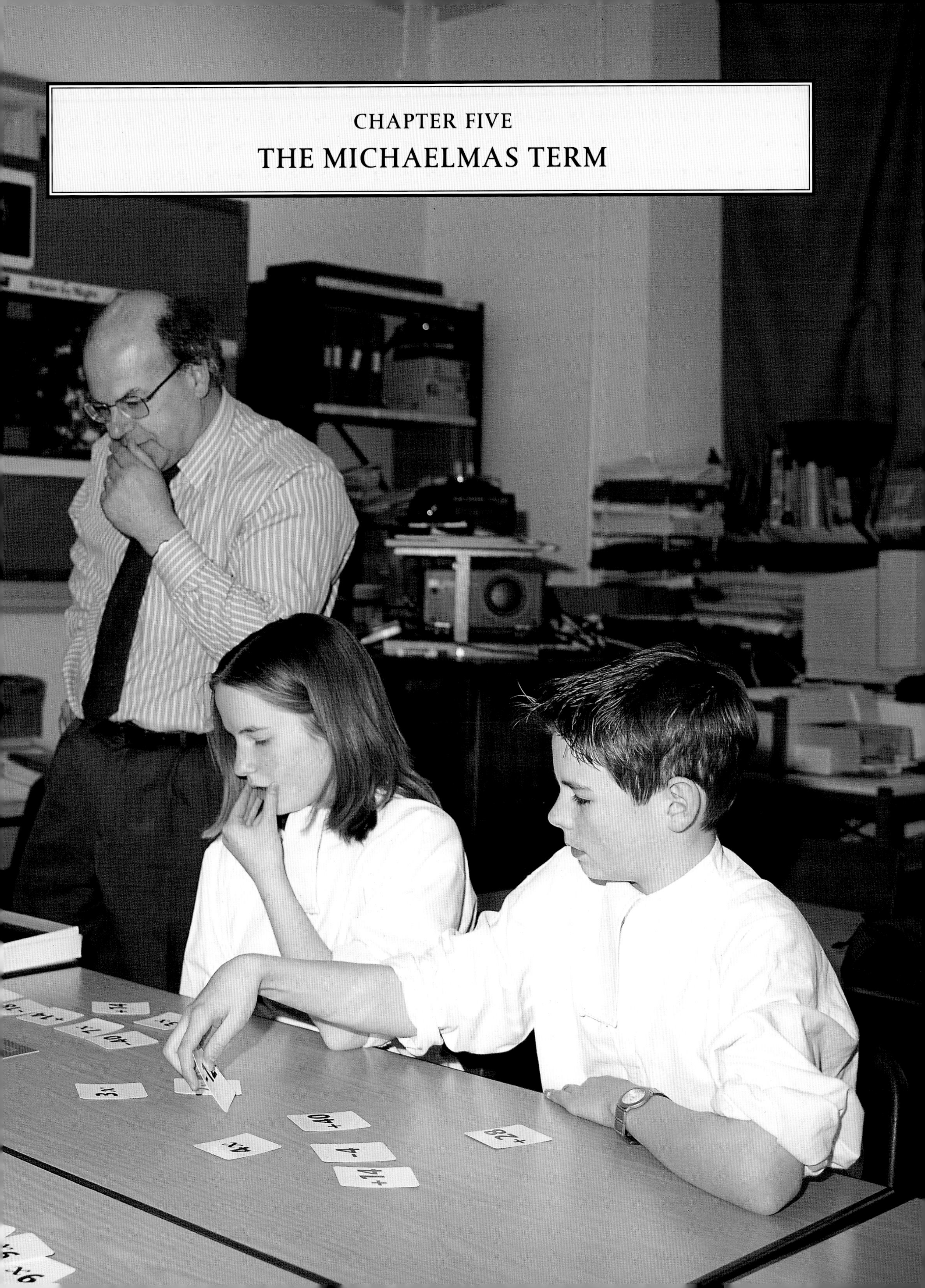

FIRST DAY OF TERM
WEDNESDAY 1 SEPTEMBER

IT'S THE FIRST DAY of the Michaelmas term and the academic year. The summer heatwave lingers into September, and the procession of cars increases as the 6.30pm roll call approaches. The asphalt behind the houses resembles a supermarket carpark as hatchbacks, saloons and people-carriers decant an assortment of children clad in colourful vest tops, soccer strips, shorts and trainers. Within the hour, summer clothing will give way to Housey coats and stockings.

Meanwhile, parents pile books and bags into their offsprings' arms, topped with duvets and sports kit, and heavy-laden family groups head purposefully through the back doors and up to the dormitories.

This year a surprise awaits the boys of Lamb B and Peele B: in their houses the open dormitories have been converted into study-bedrooms with three or four beds, workspaces and storage units.

The girls' houses were redesigned with cubicles in 1985, when the Girls' School in Hertford closed, and the School became co-educational. The boys are unused to semi-privacy. In Peele B, Alan from Clwyd, returning for his third year, takes the changes philosophically. 'The open dorm felt bigger, but I prefer this,' he says. 'It won't change the lifestyle of the house, though. It's only a bedroom.' Alan, who arrived in England the previous day from his father's army quarters in Germany, has arrived early.

Previous pages: Master of the Royal Mathematical School Alan Smith ponders a logical conundrum with Second Formers Georgia Bell, Edward Mathews, Rachel Chevill and Joshua Leakey.

The back asphalts.

Moving in. James Mitchell, Lamb B, with Dad in the foreground.

Along the corridor, his house matrons are still gearing up for the rush of boys. Yvonne Sheppard-Burgess and Hilary Breakwell, who both have children at the School, have spent the past three days preparing for this moment. They have attended an Induction Day for academic and house staff, and the Head Master's garden party. They have spent Monday stock-taking to be sure that uniforms are in good repair and that no stockings have gone missing. They have 'snagged' the house to check that repairs after the departure of summer course students have been completed.

The 'middle ladies' – named because the laundry rooms are in the middle of the houses – have been making up beds and putting out clean uniforms. And in Peele B, the new houseparents, Ian and Rosie Howard, are moving into their spacious, freshly-decorated accommodation.

Cricket pads, golf clubs and tennis rackets are piled in corners of the corridors linking Peele B and Peele A. Boys flood in and matrons' attention is required to reassure an anxious mother who has left some vital item of kit at home, and to sort out the boys' first problems of term.

Matrons are responsible for the children's physical well-being; the house parents and their deputies for their charges' social welfare, for running the house and for discipline. As 'neutral parties', the matrons provide pastoral care and are often the first port of call for advice and sympathy – and for first aid.

All matrons are qualified in first aid, and they now have computer skills. Medical records are held on the School's networked computer

system so that, when a child is referred to the Infirmary, their record is immediately available to the medical staff.

In Coleridge B, a group of fashionably-clad girls are chatting with housemistress Alison Röhrs. Col B has the distinction of providing this year's Senior Grecian, Kate Atkinson, who has returned early for pre-season training with the hockey team.

Pre-season training rugby players are trudging house-ward for a shower and change and a welcome cup of tea. In Lamb B, tea has already brewed and the lively Assistant housemistress Judy Simmonds, head of economics and business studies, is dispensing strong cups to parents, children and stray visitors, as small boys heave large suitcases through the melée.

The School shop has opened, and a patient queue of parents and children wait to collect shoes, house shirts and sportswear for their children. Kitting out is the priority, and few people have time today for the tables offering branded mugs, ties, CDs, sweaters and other gifts and memorabilia, including the invaluable Book of Housey Slang: a useful extra for the new entrants beginning the first of their seven years' education.

Equally valuable for the new intake – and the rest of the community – is the 56-page pocket size *Christ's Hospital Calendar*. In addition to the all-important dates for holidays and leave weekends, the booklet contains the daily timetable from rising bell at 7.15am to tea at 5.30pm, and details of chapel services, counsellors, surgeries, academic staff and their subjects, house staff, Button Grecians, and a day-by-day calendar of the term's events with blank pages for notes. Spelled out in detail at the end of the book is the School's policy on alcohol and drug abuse and the anti-bullying code, printed on pages 197–8. The final page, with new entrants in mind, is devoted to a layout of the classrooms.

At the end of a tiring day – of separation from home, friends and family, of travelling, catching up with schoolfriends' summer news, and of readjusting to the Housey lifestyle – the first chapel service of term is scheduled for 7.30pm: a welcome opportunity to relax and recharge spiritual batteries in an oasis of calm.

ST MATTHEW'S DAY

The St Matthew's Day service on 17 September at St Paul's, with the march through London from railway station to Cathedral to Guildhall, is the first opportunity for the new intake of eleven-year-olds to experience a ceremony whose origins lie in the ancient practice of City merchants to observe the feast day of St Matthew.

The occasion also provides a challenge for the whole School. Just two weeks into the academic year, the newly-formed Choir must rise to the occasion of singing in St Paul's Cathedral, the Band must demonstrate the skills needed to play in time and in tune while marching in formation. The new drum majors must be mace-perfect, and the new second formers must show they can march in step.

It takes considerable confidence for a young child to march in Tudor dress through the City of London, under the gaze of City workers and surprised tourists wielding video cameras.

THE FOUNDATION HYMN

Praise the Lord for our Foundation,
     praise him for our holy name,
Christ our host and our salvation,
     yesterday, today, the same.
In his tender love he sought us
     when we needed most his aid,
by the hand of man he bought us
     to the home his love had made.

Praise him for religious guiding,
     for the royal founder king,
for the ancient House providing
     shelter 'neath her kindly wing.
Prosper, Lord, with heavenly blessing,
     lives of those who love her peace;
with thy love their hearts possessing,
     make their number to increase.

Praise him for th'unbroken story,
     linking present with the past,
old world habit, civic glory,
     time-worn customs newly cast.
Praise him for our spacious dwelling,
     ringed with downs and woodlands fair,
wind and storm and sun forthtelling
     all his word in earth and air.

Brothers, best with righteous living
     shall our grateful thanks be paid,
lifting up with hearts forgiving
     holy prayer in duty made.
Praise we thus the God of heaven,
     Christ our saviour and our host,
With the Lord of spirits seven,
     Father, Son, and Holy Ghost.

R W Wilkinson MUSB, FRCO
Director of Music, Christ's Hospital 1902–1929.
The Ven A W Upcott DD
Head Master of Christ's Hospital, 1902–1919.

St Paul's Cathedral, 17 September 1999.
The choir and the brass ensemble.

In Horsham, the day begins at 6am, with the 130 members of the Choir and the fanfare musicians leaving at 7.20am for the train to London Bridge, a coach transfer to St Paul's and a 9.30am rehearsal.

'Singing in the Cathedral gives you a great sense of pride; you feel part of something important. And St Paul's has great acoustics,' agree Isabel Rankine and Rowena Thornton, Deputy Grecian choir members.

By 10.45am anticipation is mounting on the steps of St Paul's as the congregation awaits the arrival of the School. Choristers' parents chat with their children, Old Blues make contact with their contemporaries, Governors gather in a side-chapel to collect their wands, and early arrivals start taking their seats in the nave.

As the sun shines from a blue sky, traffic comes to a halt behind police cordons, and shortly after 11am, the distant sound of the Band announces the imminent arrival of the School.

The body of children had marched to Christ's Hospital railway station at 8.50am, taking the special train to Cannon Street station, then marching with the Band down Cannon Street and round the Cathedral forecourt to enter by the North Transept. The congregation are in place, leaving the Treasurer to welcome the Lord Mayor and Sheriffs on the Cathedral steps, and make their ceremonial entry through the West Doors.

'It's absolutely marvellous,' say Michael and Gillian Clenshaw who have travelled up from Sussex to share the experience with their daughters Jessica and Kate (Coleridge B). 'Watching the School march through the City is very rousing and very moving.'

Coleridge A lead the School's march from St Paul's Cathedral to the Guildhall after the service.

At exactly 11.25am the Governors, bearing their wands of office, form up along the aisle, facing inwards for the procession of clergy, Sheriffs and Aldermen of the City of London, the Lord Mayor and the Treasurer of Christ's Hospital. Everyone escorted by the Lord Mayor walks on his left except for the Worshipful the Treasurer, who walks on his right, the only person to be so privileged apart from the Monarch.

The Lord Mayor, Lord Levene of Portsoken, presenting 'largesse' to James Busby.

The Order of Service includes lessons from the first letter to Corinthians and St Matthew's Gospel read by Senior Grecian Kate Atkinson and the Canon in Residence, who also leads prayers with a School Chaplain. The sermon is given by the Rt Revd Dr Tom Butler, Bishop of Southwark. The music includes Mozart's 'Laudate Dominum', with a solo by Sarah Fairfax (Col A), and the anthem 'My Beloved Spake', from the 'Song of Solomon'.

The congregation join in a setting of 'The Beatitudes' arranged by Peter Allwood, the hymn 'How Shall I sing that Majesty', to the tune 'Coe Fen' by Ken Naylor (Old Blue and member of staff 1980–86) and the Foundation Hymn by the Ven A W Upcott (Head Master 1902–19), with music by R Wilkinson (Director of Music 1902–29).

After the Blessing, clergy and City dignitaries, the Lord Mayor and Lady Mayoress, and the Treasurer and Head Master process to the West Door, and the Clerk presents the Lord Mayor with the List of Governors of Christ's and Bridewell Hospitals as Joanna Marsh, organist at Christ's Hospital, plays the final voluntary.

Parents and Old Blues crowd the Cathedral steps as the entire School

Middleton A marching past the Lord Mayor in Guildhall Yard to the strains of the Band.

and Band march past, escorted by their house parents and staff in academic gowns. Mounted police lead them back along Cannon Street, with Coleridge A heading the procession behind their composed standard-bearer, Deputy Grecian Amy Greenhalgh.

City traffic comes to a standstill for the School to cross busy

The Band plays in Guildhall Yard as the Lord Mayor takes the salute.

Cheapside, from Queen Street into King Street, and the bells of St Mary-le-Bow ring out as the entire School approaches Guildhall, to be received by the Lord Mayor and presented with the annual Largesse – 20 pence each, rising according to seniority to £5 for the Senior Grecian.

Jennifer Vickery, who has travelled from Somerset for the service, can't resist a proud wave as her twelve-year-old son Ben comes into view, marching with Lamb B. She is rewarded with a discreet grin.

'Ben's very aware of the sense of tradition,' she remarks. 'The School gives the children a good grounding and structure for their future life, and celebrations like this provide an opportunity to motivate them.'

The history of the St Matthew's Day is given on page 209.

FOUNDER'S DAY DINNER

Founder's Day Dinner is held each year on, or close to, the birthday of Edward VI. It is organised by the Stewards, a group of, mainly, Old Blues who underwrite the Dinner financially. Their Chairman, this year John Gillham, Donation Governor and former Almoner, also chairs the Dinner.

It is traditionally held in London, and this year at the Drapers' Hall in the City on Tuesday 12 October. The Stewards invite the main speaker, usually, but not invariably, an Old Blue who has had a distinguished career or given exceptional service to Christ's Hospital, often both.

This year the honour was given to General Sir Garry Johnson, KCB, OBE, MC (Middleton A 1948–54) who, before proposing the Housey toast, spoke forcibly about the new challenges of the 'information revolution' and how the new digital age will set unprecedented demands for schools to meet. His belief was that Christ's Hospital is well placed to meet these challenges and is working well to provide the right educational environment for the new millennium.

In conclusion he quoted a contemporary politician: 'Education is the most powerful force in our society because it can lift people from the dis-

THE HOUSEY TOAST
The religious, royal and ancient Foundation of Christ's Hospital: may those prosper who love it and may God increase their number.

Founder's Day Dinner at the Drapers' Hall, 12 October 1999.

advantages of their background and carry them any distance, to the very limits of their potential, far beyond the expectations and horizons of their parents. It is the single most powerful tool in the fight against poverty.' This, he suggested, neatly summed up the ethos that has sustained Housie in the past and will continue to do so in the future.

Breaking with tradition – or perhaps starting a new one – this year the Stewards invited a more recent Old Blue to respond to the Housey toast.

Kate Atkinson, Senior Grecian, engages the attention of Old Blues, left to right, Bill Stevens, Colin Bell and David Garlick.

97

Ben Monaghan (Maine A and Lamb A 1982–89) made an outstanding response and spoke with great warmth and enthusiasm about how the School had prepared him and his generation for careers in the modern world, a very different one from that which older Old Blues had encountered on leaving the School. It was now a world where the majority of colleagues were from other countries and had multi-lingual skills, where age was no longer relevant to respect or success and where the buzzword was 'diversity': diversity in the wider range of opportunities open to young people.

Paying tribute to the teaching staff for achieving ever improving academic results, he concluded 'what still counts most is not the knowledge you start with but your ability to learn. Not the ability to fit in with a small like-minded group, but the ability to motivate those with very different backgrounds to your own. Not a tendency to accept immediately what you are told, but instead to apply a healthy scepticism, even some cynicism, before committing your energies to the task. To be at ease whether wearing a Blue Coat, blue jeans, or a blue suit.'

THE LORD MAYOR'S SHOW

Participation in London's civic pageantry means an early start on Saturday 13 November for the Christ's Hospital Band. The coach leaves Horsham at 7.15am and by 10am the musicians are moving into their places in Gresham Street, just west of Guildhall, ready to march off through the City streets.

At the head of the long and colourful procession are gold-clad musicians of the Mounted Band of the Household Cavalry, followed by the Mounted Escort of the Life Guards, the new Lord Mayor Clive Martin in his gold coach, and a detachment of pikemen, musketmen and bargemen in their historic uniforms.

The lengthy wait for the 10.50am scheduled departure means that almost everyone at the head of the procession is taken unawares as the

Members of the Busby family enjoy a day out at the Lord Mayor's Show, 13 November 1999. James, senior Drum Major, and his twin George, Second Monitor and a trumpet player, are about to take their places in the Band, which will head the Procession. Their mother, Mary Busby, left, and sister Charlie, with her son, Jack, will be among the admiring spectators lining the route.

mounted musicians strike up and move off five minutes earlier than expected. But the School Band falls swiftly into step behind the pikemen, skilfully avoiding equine deposits as they march towards the Mansion House under sunny blue skies.

By the time the parade reaches St Paul's Cathedral, the streets are thronged with cheering, flag-waving crowds, and the order of the procession has changed. Now it is Drum Major James Busby, followed by the Housey Band, who proudly leads the procession to the Law Courts at the end of the City route.

Meanwhile, Santa Claus – bringing up the rear – is just moving off along Gresham Street.

FIELD OF POPPIES

Ben Hayfron plants his poppy in the Quad on Remembrance Sunday.

Remembrance Sunday, 14 November, at Christ's Hospital achieves an extra dimension with the ceremony of poppy planting.

After morning service, the School emerges from Chapel to form a horseshoe across the centre of the Quad, with the Founder's statue at midpoint. Shortly before Big School clock strikes eleven a small procession emerges from the Chapel cloisters, moving slowly along The Avenue to the War Memorial.

Senior Grecian Kate Atkinson and Second Monitors Sophie Naish and George Busby, each carrying a wreath of poppies, are followed by the Treasurer and the Clerk, the Head Master and Chaplain.

The Grecians hang their wreaths, then take up position with the rest of the party facing the School. Prayers, and the Last Post played by a trumpeter on Big School bridge, are followed by the traditional two-minute silence, Reveille, and final prayers.

Following the blessing at 11.15, the School, the staff and visitors solemnly remove their buttonhole poppies, plant them in the Quad, then disperse silently under sombre grey skies, leaving a green field with a thousand drops of scarlet.

MONITORS DINE WITH THE TREASURER

Early in the term the Senior Grecian, Kate Atkinson, and the Second Monitors, Sophie Naish and George Busby are invited by the Treasurer, Susan Mitchell, and her husband John, to an informal dinner at their home a few miles from the School. George's twin, the senior Drum Major James Busby, is invited too, and the Clerk, Michael Simpkin, and his wife Joy complete the party.

'The Treasurer and the Clerk usually meet the senior pupils only on formal occasions,' explains Susan Mitchell, a Hertford Old Blue. 'It helps them and us if we can get to know each other at the beginning of the year. The Grecians come in mufti, and they tell us about themselves and their aspirations. We tell them a little about our rôles and answer their questions, and we are interested to hear what they have to say about the School. This year we have a lively and spirited group and a very engaging Senior Grecian.'

The Grecians are happy to find that the menu offers an agreeable change from their regular diet, and they enjoy the accompanying wines too. The Treasurer abstains from the wine so that she can drive them back to their houses by 10.30pm, the time agreed with the Deputy Head for their return.

SPORT IN MICHAELMAS

The 1st XV in action against Dulwich College.

A description of the considerable sporting facilities at Christ's Hospital is given in Chapter Three, but it is proper here to record the rugby and hockey results in the Michaelmas term.

Rugby
Not the best results in Christ's Hospital rugby, but there were many problems to encounter in a difficult season. An unprecedented number of injuries in all age groups, contributed to poor results in most teams. The total return from inter-school matches across the whole range of sides from Under Thirteen B to 1st XV was: Won – 31, Drew – 2, Lost – 72.

The 1st XV suffered thirteen losses against two wins but encouragingly some of the lower teams, such as the 3rd XV, the Under Fifteen B, the Under Fourteen A and the Under Twelve's achieved much better results, giving more hope for future years.

Girls' Hockey
An excellent season for the 1st XI and the Under Fourteen's led the girls' hockey results, with an overall return from all inter-school matches from Under Thirteen to 1st XI of: Won – 28, Drew – 14, Lost – 30. The first XI

1st XV Rugby team: Will Avenell* (Captain), George Busby*, Tom Hurdman*, John Noble*, Laurie Cook, Daniel Pearce, Moses Annoh, Liam O'Reilly, James Busby, Lewis Hughes-Evans, Barney Davies, David Kirkpatrick, Sam Masters, Nick Hoath, Paul Lacey.
* Denotes colours.

1st XI Hockey squad: Jo Tansley-Thomas (Captain), Kate Atkinson (Vice Captain), Gabriella Maselino, Kate Walton, Kim Miller, Rose Greenhalgh, Vicki Bell, Amy Greenhalgh, Sarah Moon, Natalie Williams, Emma White, Lizzy Avenell, Nikki Whitely.

won nine of their sixteen games drawing three and losing four, while the Under Fourteen played fifteen games, winning eight, drawing three and losing four.

CHRISTMAS AT CHRIST'S HOSPITAL

As Christmas trees and boarding houses are decorated, and seasonal celebrations are packed into the first ten days of December, the Chapel becomes the focus of attention in the last week of term.

The annual public Carol Concert, with mince pies and glasses of wine in the Dining Hall, is followed two days later by the Visitors' Carol Service; on a chill December evening parents, families, Old Blues and other invited guests pack Chapel pews for a service of eight lessons and carols.

As the procession of chaplains and servers approaches the altar, the Choir sings Ralph Vaughan Williams' setting of 'This is the Truth sent from Above', the first of several Choir carols, including a lively 16th-century carol in Spanish requiring considerable linguistic dexterity.

The congregation joins in familiar carols including 'Once in Royal David's City' and 'In the Bleak Midwinter'; and the traditional lessons are read by three pupils: Tom Swanborough-Nilson, Vicky Bell and John Noble; and by matron Yvonne Siddle, master and house tutor Nick Bailey, the Bursar Rachel Adams, house master Andrew Phillips, and the Treasurer, Susan Mitchell.

The service concludes with a rousing 'Hark! the Herald Angels Sing' and organist Joanna Marsh plays Bach's 'In Dulci Jubilo' and Messiaen's 'Dieu Parmi Nous' as the congregation departs, many of them heading for the theatre for the Big Band Millennium Concert.

The retiring collection raises funds for the School's millennium year charity, the Imlil Community Project in the Atlas Mountains of Morocco.

On the following day, the Head Master's assembly in Big School is followed by the School's own Carol Service, attended, this year, by the School President, the Duke of Gloucester. On Saturday – after the end of

After the Carol Service the President meets a number of pupils in the Head Master's house, from Second Formers to Grecians, and including his own presentees, Guy Nicholson and Ariadne Mitchell-Kotsakis.

Here His Royal Highness is meeting Lucy Morgan and admiring the extra buttons on her sleeve which signify that she is the Band Captain. George Busby and Kate Atkinson are in the background.

Left to right: Stuart Basset, Mark Davey, Catherine Williams and Ellie Mitra, Directors of the community nativity play 'Sherlock Holmes, the Christmas Mystery', performed on 24 December 1999 in Peele B dayroom.
Below: Catherine and Ellie prompt some of the more apprehensive members of the cast.

term service and senior school prizegiving – the children depart for home at the conclusion of a busy Michaelmas term.

Looking back on the term, Kate Atkinson, Senior Grecian, lists four highlights: 'Reading in St Paul's and having lunch with the Lord Mayor on St Matthew's Day; talking to General Sir Garry Johnson and other Old Blues at Founder's Day Dinner in London; laying wreaths with the Second Monitors on Remembrance Sunday; and meeting HRH The Duke of Gloucester at the Carol Service.'

Kate is also discovering the weight of responsibility carried by the School's senior pupil: 'There are not enough hours in the day, mainly due to sports commitments and public exams. I soon discovered it was impossible to go from A to B without getting diverted to C: you are never off duty, and people are under the illusion that I know the answers to random questions or have the ability to do everything. They are sadly mistaken! It has certainly been a steep learning curve.'

The pupils have gone home to enjoy their Christmas, but the School is far from deserted. Footsteps make a satisfyingly crunchy sound as they tread up the Avenue. Snow fell all yesterday evening and now, on a bright Sunday morning, the whole site lies under a white blanket. The sky is a clear blue, the sun shines low in the sky, and a bitingly cold wind sends the temperature well below zero. The snow had, apparently, melted slightly on impact with the still-warm earth but, as the temperature dropped overnight it has refrozen, and now the pathways are covered in sheets of rucked ice. Ahead, also making for the Quad, is one of our Security Guards, Richard Beale, who with his wife and two small daughters, has been lured from the warmth of his home to explore this arctic landscape.

The Quad is predictably beautiful but why are there so many signs to the ladies, gents, and car parks? Even more strangely, why are there two plastic buckets, filled with chunks of bright yellow sponges, immersed in now-frozen water? Outside Dining Hall, crushed in the frozen slush, lie streamers wishing someone a Happy New Millennium and, just feet away, are the stocks. Not just one set, but two, and a whipping post. Have we, one wonders, in the face of parental opposition and flouting legislation, decided to resort to well-tried and time-honoured methods of correction for wayward pupils? No, indeed. It is just that a private group had hired the Dining Hall for a Medieval Banquet last night, when a whole ox was roasted on the hallowed grass of the Quad, while hundreds of costumed revellers braved the snow and threw wet sponges at each other.

And this is what Christ's Hospital is like, out-of-term. The Freemasons have already had their Carol Service; others will surely follow. Christ's Hospital is a beautiful place, and beauty has a value. Its premises and facilities are hired out by Quadrant Events, part of the trading arm of Christ's Hospital Enterprises Limited, at a commercial rate and in return the customers enjoy an idyllic setting for their functions. And a warm one, too, since radiators have been installed in Dining Hall.

The permanent residents of Christ's Hospital look a little askance at these visitors. Surely it is our territory, they think. But no. They are sojourners too, and must accept the presence of strangers as legitimate though impermanent members of this community. The site is big enough for all of us. A breathtaking walk around The Mile sees only the Director of Music and his wife, also venturing out to enjoy the scenery. Their four children have stayed at home, watching television, too old now to be excited by snow. Of such is life: we are all consumers, in our different ways, of Christ's Hospital out-of-term.

A very important building for many of Housie's young residents – the Tuck Shop.

CHAPTER SIX
THE LENT TERM

CANDLEMAS
WEDNESDAY 2 FEBRUARY 2000

IT IS THE FLUTTERING SURPLICES that cause concern as the sacristans bend low beside the vestry to fan the flames in the thurible. Enthusiasm may be overriding prudence in the desire to burn incense on the glowing charcoals; but the concern is unfounded. All is well. Soon the chaplains with the sacristans process slowly into Chapel. The congregation remains in semi-darkness. Incense wafts around. Gradually eyes pick out the tea-lights that sparkle and twinkle on the altar steps. Some are even placed on the altar itself, or nestle in the niches of the reredos. It is beautiful, peaceful, and rich with significance.

For tonight Candlemas is being celebrated, the winter festival that recalls the presentation of Jesus at the Temple, and candles are much in evidence. After the processional hymn, 'Ye who own the faith of Jesus', there is the Collect for Purity, the Confession and Absolution, and the special Collect for Candlemas, 'Let us pray that we may know and share the light of Christ. Almighty Father, whose Son Jesus Christ was presented in the Temple, and acclaimed the glory of Israel and the light of the nations: grant that in him we may be presented to you and in the world may reflect his glory; who is alive and reigns with you and the Holy spirit, one God, now and for ever. Amen.'

This particular act of worship, with its emphasis on ritual, is in marked contrast to the normal Chapel services. Old Blues of an earlier generation will remember very different forms of worship, when even the lighting of a votive candle would have caused a stir. Today, the boundaries are less clearly defined.

MUSIC IN LENT

THE PURCELL ROOM CONCERT THURSDAY 3 FEBRUARY 2000

All day they have travelled, from points north, south, east and west, to watch Christ's Hospital play at the Purcell Room. The musicians left in the morning, by coach from the 'Back Ash' behind Lamb, loading harps and harpsichords, xylophones and double basses into the luggage compartment, along with the tuck and 'civvies' that experienced participants know to bring. By 6pm familiar faces are seen among the crowds at the Thames-side cafeteria and Christ's Hospital pupils, in their distinctive uniforms, are being pointed out to wondering strangers.

The programme is breathtaking in its breadth and complexity. It contains a Concerto in C for Two Trumpets and Strings (Vivaldi), played skilfully on D trumpets by Guy Vesey and Ben Allwood; a remarkable solo performance by sixteen-year-old Liz Pannell singing 'Piangero' from Handel's *Julius Caesar*; Alex Shuckburgh displaying vibrant skill in Fransisco Tarrega's guitar solo 'Recuerdos de l'Alhambra', and the Piano Quintet in F minor Op. 34 by Brahms. Ben Chewter accompanies thirteen-year-old Sarah Brooks (flute) in Arrieu's 'Sonatina' and Andrew Saunders accompanies Brigita Ziferman (violin) in Ernst Bloch's haunting work 'Simchas Torah' from *Baal Shem*. The Choir's diction is superb in

Previous pages: In the Art School Smith O'Connor instructs Natalie Smith on making a plastercast of Charlotte Keenan. Jason Marsham and Tom Seligmann are in the background.

At the Purcell Room, clockwise: Victoria O'Gorman and Robert Lomax (oboes), Una Kosanovic and Jemma Batte (bassoons), Amelia Bloore and Sam Neild (horns) and Daniel Cizek and Nicola Smith (clarinets).

John Thwaites rehearsing Zheni Kanani, violin, and Andrew Saunders at the piano before the concert.

Schubert's 'Christ ist Erstanden!' and they are joined by piano duetists Rejoice Amadi and Mary Ampah in Brahms' *Liebeslieder* Op. 52, 'Wie des Abends Schöne Röte', and 'Wenn so lind dein Auge mir'. Pianist Andrew Saunders brings the first half to a magnificent conclusion with Beethoven's Piano Sonata in F minor Op. 2 no. 1, and Prelude in B flat, Op. 23 No. 2 by Rachmaninov.

The second half begins in total darkness as Katherine Crosse weaves a beautifully mysterious web with her flute solo – 'Syrinx' – by Debussy. The stage suddenly bursts into life and light with the Allegro from Vivaldi's Concerto in A minor Op. 3 No. 6, with Pippa Reveley displaying remarkable skill and dexterity on the xylophone. This is followed by the Allegro from Beethoven's Wind Octet in E flat and then, setting a much gentler tone, Sarah Fairfax sings 'A Hymn to the Virgin' Op. 13 No. 2 by Edmund Rubbra, accompanied by Helen Mayhew on harp. Ciprian Ilie, a new Deputy Grecian from Romania, plays Malcolm Arnold's 'Fantasy for Unaccompanied Trumpet' with great skill and composure, and Andrew Saunders accompanies Zheni Kanani, another new Dep, in a captivating performance of Brahms' Sonata for Piano and Violin in G major Op. 78 No. 1. Jessica Greenfield's rich and smoky voice is sensitively and ably supported by Alex Shuckburgh, Ciprian Ilie and James Maddren in her interpretation of Antonio Carlos Jobim's 'Desifinado'; and the jazz sextet brings the concert to its conclusion with a skilful yet light-hearted display in Alex L'Estrange's arrangement of 'Funky Chicken'.

It was remarkable to note how well, in this concert, our new Deputy Grecians acquitted themselves. Coming from Rome, Romania and Lithuania, as well as the UK, they have shown great depth of character as they adjust, not only to a new School, but also to a new culture and even language. These performances in the Purcell Room are of the highest quality, both in range and depth, and great credit and appreciation must go to Peter Allwood and his team for their vision and perseverance in staging such an enjoyable event.

PIANO DAY SUNDAY 6 MARCH 2000

Today is Piano Day, when 129 budding pianists from the School perform their best pieces before Julian Jacobson, Professor at The Royal College of Music, on the new Steinway Model B grand piano in the Court Room. Arranged in their year groups, the participants are supported by their peers as they battle with sheet music, pedals, and performance nerves, to produce their best. At the end of each section of pupils Professor Jacobson points out weaknesses and commends strengths, before finally making special commendations in each year.

Those so commended receive a chocolate egg and formal recognition that will be reflected in their end-of-term reports. Standards, skills and performances vary enormously, but that is not the issue. The issue is that, under the direction of John Thwaites as Head of Piano – himself a performer of the highest standard – and Peter Allwood, pupils who otherwise would not have the chance to learn piano, let alone perform on such a noble instrument, are given the opportunity to develop their musical potential.

A few parents are here – those who live locally and can make the journey, for such a short time, worthwhile; otherwise most children perform alone, looking only for the watchful nod or the affirming smile from supporting staff to sustain them. It is character-forming, growing up at Christ's Hospital, and becoming independent so young. The absence of familial support at public performances is accepted and understood as an unavoidable corollary to boarding school life. Only occasionally it would be a little luxury if a parent could be there, just to give a hug in response to so much effort and hard work.

THE ANGUS ROSS MEMORIAL CONCERT SUNDAY 2 APRIL 2000

The programme mentions that 'The Carpenters' deserve credit and one wonders, therefore, if the former pop group have had any part in the preparations for this year's Angus Ross Memorial Concert. But no, the allusion is to the School's own carpenters who have worked so hard to provide banking on the Big School stage so that over 180 singers can be accommodated, standing and sitting, comfortably and safely, for tonight's concert. For it is on a massive scale. Not only have three choirs joined – the Christ's Hospital Chapel Choir, Christ's Hospital Choral Society and Invocation, the choir of professional singers who come together under the directorship of Joanna Marsh, Organist at the School: they have been joined by Christ's Hospital's Sinfonia, to perform three well-known and much loved musical works.

Dr Peter Southern, the Head Master, quietly welcomes the event's patron, Marjorie Ross, widow of Angus. Peter Allwood – brilliant and hardworking producer of this event and conductor for the evening – raises his baton and, as late-comers settle in their seats, the Concert begins.

Edward Elgar's 'Pomp and Circumstance March No. 1' opens the first half and, recalling the tradition of the last night of the Proms, the audience joins the massed choirs in singing 'Land of Hope and Glory'. Some may feel concern at such an unashamed display of nationalism: others feel no such qualms, and sing with all the fervour and volume they can

Julian Jacobson, Professor of Piano at the Royal College of Music, giving advice on Piano Day.

Jonathan Howard, one of four commended in his year group.

Sir David Willcocks, the celebrated choral conductor, rehearsing the choir in a day-long workshop for Belshazzar's Feast for the Angus Ross Memorial Concert.

The Angus Ross Memorial Concert.

Belshazzar's Feast: *Peter Allwood, conductor, with David Wilson-Johnson, principal soloist.*

produce. This rousing start is followed by 'The Enigma Variations' by Edward Elgar, when the Sinfonia – consisting of professional and amateur musicians, including Christ's Hospital pupils, under the guest Leadership of John Ludlow – give an impressive display of their skill.

The concert resumes with William Walton's *Belshazzar's Feast*, which depicts the events of Daniel Chapter v in which Belshazzar, King of Babylon, gives a sumptuous feast. Suddenly, the hand of God appears and writes, in judgment, on the wall: MENE, MENE, TEKEL UPHARSIN – 'You have been weighed in the balance and found wanting', The guest baritone David Wilson-Johnson sings with chilling tone and clarity, and the choirs support him with breathtaking vibrancy. A complex and demanding work is executed with professional skill and exceptional virtuosity.

This is the thirteenth annual Angus Ross Memorial Concert, an event which has become one of the great musical traditions of Christ's Hospital. The concerts started in 1987 with a performance of Carl Orff's *Carmina Burana* and, in the intervening years, a wide range of musical treats have been offered. The occasion owes its existence to the generous support given by Marjorie Ross after the death of her husband, Alan Alistair Ross, in 1984. 'Angus' as he was always known, was an Old Blue (Barnes A, 1930–37) who went on, after serving in the second World War, to enjoy a brilliant career in advertising.

He always remembered the solemn Charge and committed himself to do all that he could, during a particularly difficult period of Christ's Hospital's history, to support the School. In 1967 he became a Donation Governor; in 1974 he joined The Council of Almoners, and in 1976 became Treasurer and Chairman of the Council. He was a devoted 'Son of this House', and the Memorial Concert held each year in his name – which brings together pupils and staff as well as participants from the wider community at Horsham and beyond – is a fitting tribute to his life.

Confirmands leaving their service with the Bishop of Chichester, the Right Reverend Eric Kemp and the School Chaplains.

BAPTISM AND CONFIRMATION

Confirmation lessons start immediately after the Michaelmas half-term. Each Monday, after an early and rushed tea, the young candidates assemble in the Court Room to receive instruction in the Christian faith from one of five members of staff, including the Senior Chaplain, the Revd Munna Mitra and his wife, the Revd Nicola Mitra. To begin, often amid giggling and a little nervous excitement, a candle is lit by a pupil. The Chaplains then explain some aspect of the faith, which will later be discussed in groups with the tutors.

Questions range from the predictable, (Why isn't God a woman?) to the fantastic. It becomes clear that, while some pupils come from 'churched' backgrounds, others know nothing at all of the culture of the Church, let alone its practices, traditions and doctrines. But this is a safe environment, in which difficult issues can be examined and, hopefully, clarified.

Gradually the day for Confirmation, Sunday 13 February, draws near. The tutors wonder if they have done enough to prepare the twenty-five pupils for the solemn step they are taking. Is this for them and their families simply a rite of passage – something to be done in preparation for adulthood – or have they grasped the much deeper significance of the step? That it entitles them not only to make their communion; it also signifies taking on adult responsibilities within the mystical Body of Christ, the Church.

A weekend retreat at Micklepage, a converted farmhouse in nearby Nuthurst, from 22 to 23 January, helps to clarify some of these issues. Under the guidance of the Chaplains and other leaders – a master and three senior pupils – the candidates are invited to meditate on the important step they are taking, and all feel that their faith and their commitment has been strengthened by this time together.

Five candidates have been baptised on the previous Friday, in an even older rite. Now the time has come for them all to declare their desire for full admission into the Church of Christ. At Confirmation the Right Reverend Eric Kemp, Bishop of Chichester, who is soon to retire, officiates. In his address he invites the pupils whom he had just confirmed to consider a sign he observed outside a garage, which read, 'Stop here for service and repairs', and to reflect upon what that might mean for the Church in the twenty-first century.

CONFIRMED ON
13 FEBRUARY 2000:

Oliver Adams
Christina Asafu-Adjaye
Mark Belassie
Siobhan Brade
Michael Brierley
Katherine Clenshaw
Katherine Crawley
Stephanie Crouch
Rachel Elliott
Karen Elphick
Robert Gauntlett
Isabella Gill
Nicholas Hageman
Benedict Harrison-Burns
Lucinda Hutchins
Charlotte Keenan
Eleanor Mitra
Jodie Murray
James Musson
Krishan Singh-Gill
Thomas Smart
Stephen Stagg
James Swatton
Constance Usherwood
Matthew Vyner

The Confirmation Service is both joyful and emotional, as parents realise just how much independent thought and action by their children has enabled them to persevere with the training. The tutors are also touched as they see their young charges take this momentous step.

Tea for candidates and their families is served afterwards in Dining Hall, when presents are given by parents and godparents, while Bishop Eric mingles among the guests. Confirmation is a significant occasion in the life of Christ's Hospital, indicating a desire by both parents and pupils to learn far more than the national curriculum requires.

LOVE-IN
MONDAY 14 FEBRUARY 2000

Sorting out who has which bloom is the task of the monitors, with Senior Grecian Kate Atkinson in charge.

St Valentine's Day provides an opportunity for all members of the School to have fun sending flowers to favoured friends, who seem to have little trouble identifying the source of each fragrant tribute.

The millennial St Valentine's Day brightens a grey and drizzly Monday, with pupils paying 50p each for the privilege of wearing their own clothes throughout the day. Well before lunch, a group of monitors clad in suits, dinner-jackets and smart frocks can be found in Dining Hall among bunches of decorative balloons, sorting through 800 roses and carnations delivered by a bemused wholesaler. Their task: to decipher the handwriting on hundreds of small red cards and attach them to the relevant flower for distribution during junior and senior lunch sittings.

The single blooms have been pre-ordered by pupils prepared to pay £1.60 for a rose, or 80p for a carnation, to convey their affection, with Barnes B house captain Vicky Bell smoothly co-ordinating the ordering, sorting and distribution.

The monitors also cope with gifts left alongside the buckets of flowers.

Some take their flower-giving very seriously . . .

. . . . and some tables do better than others.

Among them an outsize, brightly wrapped box for Middleton A Grecian Anton who tries to open it discreetly under the table. The box contains a helium balloon from an admirer in Barnes B which, a few minutes later, comes adrift from its tether on the handle of a water jug and soars gracefully into the distant rafters – a scarlet heart-shaped reminder of a colourful celebration.

Down below, the girls of Coleridge B and the boys of Peele B seem to be accumulating more than their fair share of flowers, with the girls of Barnes A cheering as Lil (Lower Erasmus) receives her thirteenth flower. The rose proves too much for the jug accommodating the other dozen, which overturns and drenches the table with water.

A team of Barnes A girls with housemistress Lois Helyar are as busy as the monitors: they are raising funds with small packets of pink-wrapped chocolates as a high-calorie alternative gift: 160 packets have been ordered at 80p each.

Younger girls too are collecting flowers and 'snuggles' from the monitors, with Barnes B third-formers Sadie, Ariadne and Natalie amassing more than a dozen roses and carnations between them; and the boys are doing remarkably well, with Stuart of Lamb A (Great Erasmus) accepting a wrapped bunch of carnations.

As a result of the lunchtime celebrations, around £600 is raised for this term's Chapel charity, Friends of the Young Deaf.

Barnes A make and sell bonbons in aid of The 100 Years On Appeal.

THE SPITAL SERMON AT ST LAWRENCE JEWRY NEXT GUILDHALL

THURSDAY 2 MARCH 2000

The antechapel is suddenly full of people – shaking hands, divesting themselves of wet coats, sorting out wands, greeting old friends. For this is the time of the annual Spital Sermon, when Aldermen of the Corporation of London, with their Lord Mayor, as well as representatives of Christ's Hospital and King Edward's School, Witley, congregate in the City to honour the ancient custom of hearing the Spital Sermon.

The venue is the beautiful, intimate church of St Lawrence Jewry Next Guildhall, the official chapel of the Guildhall, which was almost destroyed during the blitz of London in the second World War. Designed by Sir Christopher Wren in 1670, and now restored to its former glory, it offers a noble, classical interior for this ancient service.

Due protocol is observed as the Lord Mayor, Alderman Clive Martin, with his Marshal, Sword Bearer and Mace Bearer, escorted by the Treasurer, Mrs Susan Mitchell, and her opposite number Mr Richard Abbott, Treasurer of King Edward's School, Witley, process to their seats through a corridor of wand-bearing Governors. But the atmosphere is neither stiff nor cold. Indeed, the relationship between the City of London and its famous charity schools is very warm and supportive.

The Lord Mayor with his esquires, Aldermen and representatives of the Judiciary, as well as officials from the Corporation of the City of London, sit on the south aisle: the Head Masters, the Governors and representatives of the two schools sit on the north aisle. The choir assumes its customary place in the gallery. There is a great sense of antiquity and

St Lawrence Jewry next Guildhall.

tradition in the unfolding of the service; factors which are reinforced by ancient symbols of authority – the Lord Mayor's Sword and the Mace, and the Governors' green wands – and the natural and unassuming use of ceremonial gowns and Tudor Housey coats.

This year it is the Senior Pupil of King Edward's School, Witley, who reads the lesson from 1 Peter 2:11–17. It is an honour conferred on the two schools in turn. The Rt Rev Ian Harland, the Lord Bishop of Carlisle, preaches the Spital Sermon, which revolves around the theme of 'The Spread of Truth', in which he exhorts the congregation to, 'Honour all men. Love the brotherhood. Fear God. Honour the King.'

Twenty eight members of the Christ's Hospital Choir have travelled with Peter Allwood and Joanna Marsh to lead the singing and to sing the anthem, 'The heavens are telling the glory of God', by Haydn. They conclude the service with a beautiful rendition of Cesar Franck's 'Panis Angelicus'.

After the service the Choir and the governors make the short journey to Guildhall to catch up on Housey news and enjoy a finger buffet. The Choir members are polite and responsive as they engage in conversation, but it soon becomes apparent that a miniature quiche and two small sausages are not going to assuage the thirst or hunger which has been mounting since breakfast. It is only on the way home, when the coach is able to stop at a 'Drive-In' McDonalds in Battersea – enabling the pupils to enjoy a portion of chips and a milkshake – that the demands and tensions of the day can finally be addressed and satisfied.

For a privileged few one of the most enjoyable aspects of attending the Spital Sermon is taking lunch with the Lady Mayoress in the Lord Mayor's private apartments at the Mansion House. The preacher at the service was Lindy Martin's principal guest. Among the others were the Head Masters, Treasurers and Clerks of the two schools associated with the Spital Sermon. The Lady Mayoress this year insisted on informality and after an excellent meal her only concession to tradition was to propose the Loyal Toast, and the only speech was a brief word of thanks from Christ's Hospital Treasurer Susan Mitchell. The Lord Mayor looked in briefly at the end of lunch, but had no time to enjoy the food before his next appointment called him away.

The history of the Spital Sermon is recorded on pages 209–10.

Peter Kuo taking part in the all-day relay for Middleton B on 26 March. Peter hopes to join the Sappers.

DRAMA IN LENT

A MILLENNIUM PAGEANT AT THE IRONMONGERS' HALL
9–10 MARCH 2000

Christ's Hospital's ancient and dynamic link with the City of London is again given expression as pupils from the School join professional singers and actors, as well as opera star Marilyn Hill-Smith and students from The Guildford School of Acting, in staging a Millennium Pageant. Entitled, 'All At Sea with the Shipwrights', its aim is to celebrate the growth and development of shipbuilding in England.

Produced and directed by Margaret Hunter, who has many years' experience in radio and drama production, and staged in the noble Ironmongers' Hall, the pageant centres around the dispute between traditional English shipwrights and their 'foreign' rivals who were based along the Thames at Rotherhithe. Samuel Pepys, who became Secretary to the Admiralty in 1686, features as a pivotal figure in the conflict.

It was in the execution of his rôle at the Admiralty that Pepys championed the cause of Christ's Hospital as the most appropriate establishment in which the Royal Mathematical School, as a centre for teaching navigational skills, should be based. His close involvement with Christ's Hospital is graphically depicted in the vast historical painting by Antonio Verrio which now hangs in the Dining Hall.

The pageant, staged to packed audiences, has been attended by HRH The Duke of Edinburgh, as well as dignitaries and senior players in the vibrant and complex business community which makes up City life. Christ's Hospital pupils, though now quite at home in their rural Sussex setting, still belong to that metropolitan life, and it is both heart-warming and humbling that our trumpeters, drummers, singers and actors have been invited to take part in such a prestigious event.

The pageant is being presented by The Worshipful Company of Shipwrights, and the antiquity of the livery companies is reinforced by the presence of the Pikemen and Musketeers of the Honourable Artillery Company who impressively line the carved and pannelled staircase to the Great Hall. It is extraordinary that the traditions of the City have not, over the centuries, become fossilised simply because they are ancient. These richly attired and strangely armoured footmen have all been trained members of the Territorial Army, equipped to engage in any modern conflict. On this occasion they are simply wearing their Tudor costumes.

The Christ's Hospital pupils, for the most part, are wearing their Housey uniforms which speak more clearly of our historic links with the City of London than any hired costume could. Only some of the Second Form girls wear reproduction costumes from the 18th century, which have been taken from the store at Christ's Hospital's Museum. Guy Vesey, Ciprian Ilie, Ben Allwood and Sophie Channer give impressive performances on trumpet; Amy Redwood and Sara Fairfax sing like linnets; Pippa Reveley is calm and competent as ever on the snare drum. Louise Ayling and Astral Pembleton-Fraser, in rotation, play the part of young Miss Cloves. Other Second Form pupils enthusiastically depict crowd scenes. They are all warmly applauded.

An observant onlooker would have noticed that the pupils perform their parts most ably and professionally, being ready, and on cue, to carry out their rôles with clarity and great presence. They would not have noticed that these same pupils – who had travelled for two hours by coach – were hungry, very thirsty and rather tired, yet gave of their best without stint. That, perhaps, was the greatest reason to applaud.

GUNSLINGER 24–25 MARCH 2000

The perennial problem with house plays for Head of Drama Jeffrey Mayhew is that the general ambition is always to do something light or funny. 'And, of course,' says Jeffrey, 'the heart sinks in the directorial

The cast of Gunslinger, *a Wild West pastiche performed with great style and energy by Thornton A in a variety of disguises.*

bosom because you know, and only too well, that "light and funny" is extremely difficult to achieve.'

But *Gunslinger,* Thornton A's house play, proves to be a Wild West pastiche with endless scope for humour. Nevertheless, it enshrines a dark vein of satire that gives pause for more serious reflection when the singing and laughing is over.

The play is directed by Deps. Chris Thomas and James Kent-Winsley supported by Jeffrey Mayhew and all the characters, male and female, come from Thornton A. Thus emerges a glorious charivari – the hero, Gunslinger Speed (Damian Lebas); the tart with the heart, Belle Tenderloin (Chris Hunnisett); the cowgirl, Dungaree Lil (Charlie Beringer); the swaggering outlaw, Angel 'Kid' Mcgrew (Craig Paine); and many more, all playing and singing with great style and energy and supported by the tinkling piano of Wild Willy Fifty Fingers (Paul Ward).

Above all, the production enjoys the support of the whole house – pupils and staff, led by Sean O'Boyle – at its very best. 'I don't care to count the shows I've worked on in one capacity or another but this is one of the most endearing' concludes Jeffrey Mayhew.

The Almoners Termly Visit dinner on 16 February 2000 welcomed new Council committee members, from left to right: Bill Richards (Audit), Phyllis Hoffman (Chairman, Distinguished Service Selection), Richard Carden (Securities), Michael Pickard (Chairman, Audit) and Arnold Allen (Governor Auditor) . . .

. . . and thanked retiring members Brian Hogben (Governor Auditor), Roger Dixon (Chairman, Audit), Evelyn Cowie (Chairman, Distinguished Service Selection) and Neville Osmond (Chairman, CH Club).

HISTORY DAY
28 MARCH 2000

At mid-morning break Batman and Robin are here, with Robin Hood, grinning broadly. A splendid figure from the Civil War leans against a door frame. A sinister figure from the twentieth century in leather cap, moustache and jack boots identifies himself as 'Stalin, The Master of Terror'. They have all joined the throng in Common Room on this Tuesday morning, as is customary, to hear the Head Master's Notices. French *femmes fatales* are here too, daintily sipping their coffee, alongside Hollywood molls, and the actor, not the king, James Stewart. For this is the Third Form History Day when – through a variety of costumes and techniques – members of staff, drawn from all disciplines, talk to groups of pupils, in rotation, about their hero or heroine of history.

The day is being addressed with varying degrees of seriousness by both pupils and staff, the intention being to stir up a sense of excitement about historical figures and events, rather than simply teach them in a didactic sense. The fancy dress shop in Horsham has been able to supply a variety of costumes with great flair and ingenuity.

The pupils are slightly nervous at the beginning, not knowing if this is a formal class or whether other, more relaxed, ground rules can apply. But soon they enter into the spirit of the day, setting aside the more traditional patterns of classroom behaviour and entering into a corporate time machine, by which they can travel backward in time to the sixteenth century. The focus of one particular group is Edward VI, royal founder of the School, and they struggle with Jane Seymour through her painful and long labour; rejoice with the whole of Britain at the birth of a male heir for Henry VIII, and lament when this bright star begins its downward descent, at the age of fourteen, with the onset of measles and smallpox.

They become totally absorbed as the King grows weaker, succumbing to a chill which turns into pulmonary tuberculosis. They are totally silent

and absorbed as the awful details of his fatal illness emerge; thinking of him as a fifteen-year old friend and colleague, possibly by now on the UF, who has shown so much flair and promise, and who now is to be struck down before he reaches his prime. And they enter with real thought and intelligence into the conspiracy theories that inevitably surround the late and frankly suspicious burial rites.

Had he been poisoned, so a popular conspiracy ran, by supporters of Mary Tudor's Catholic cause? Their eyes open wide, their faces are intent, and their bodies remain quite still as these issues are addressed.

And so a double period, some seventy minutes, passes quickly and enjoyably. It is time to refasten our seat belts and head for the cyber age of the twenty-first century. In the next classroom Stalin is engaged in an ideological struggle with a thoughtful pupil and insists, without recanting on his theories, that he has only wished to stir up interest in the person of Stalin. That he didn't, of course, personally hold with his views. After break another group of pupils is addressed, and it is only before lunch that the costumes can be set aside for clothing more appropriate to this cold, early Spring, day.

Of such are the benefits of School life. Common Room was hilariously enriched by the presence of colleagues dressed in a motley array of costumes; the pupils were given a glimpse of the excitement of history – the opportunity to enter in a personal way into the life of another; and those staff who took part were enabled to give expression to unexpected and unusual characters from the past. These History Days happen twice a year; and each time a different Junior year group benefits from them. We would all be poorer without them.

OPEN DAY
SATURDAY 1 APRIL 2000

Open Day is a great success. Despite the overcast weather, around 700 people arrive in pairs, families and some three-generation groups – far more than expected, as the October event is usually more popular.

Tours of the 250-acre campus leave from the Octagon every twenty minutes from 12.15pm until 3.30pm, but most visitors are lining the paths across the Quad for Band Parade. There is enthusiastic applause for the Band and for the three drum majors' perfectly synchronised mace-tossing. Inspired by the audience, the School marches into Dining Hall with unusual panache: in step, in formation, heads held high. 'Fantastic, just fantastic,' breathes a visiting Australian.

By 1pm the Theatre is packed to hear Head Master Dr Peter Southern and Second Deputy Head Bob Sillett give a half-hour introduction to the School and the assessment and selection process – a talk which will be repeated at 3pm, after a musical performance to showcase the School's considerable talents.

Afternoon tours of classrooms and selected boarding houses are led by eighty pupil volunteer guides, each equipped with notes of which rooms and buildings are open.

Useful crib sheets list vital statistics such as current enrolment (472 boys, 328 girls in 16 houses, each accommodating around 50 pupils);

Big School is a centre of activity on Open Day. The academic curriculum can be discussed with teaching staff and there is ample opportunity to explore the School and investigate methods of entry.

number of places for Second Form entry (around 120), information technology details (240 networked computers, 3 servers, 1 main ICT room, 6 'nests' of computers in teaching blocks and libraries, with five PCs in most houses).

The crib sheet even lists distinguished Old Blues, from Lamb and Coleridge down the centuries to the four current heads of Oxford colleges: St Anne's, St Hilda's, New College and All Souls. Small wonder that the young guides seem so confident and well-informed as they introduce newcomers to the School.

During the day, the visitors spend time in Big School, looking at displays, talking to academic and admissions staff, and enjoying complimentary tea and squash.

Carol Moore has regularly brought her son Adam Manning, aged ten, to the Theatre workshops for young children. Adam loves acting and writing 'stories which seem to go on and on until they are novels', and regrets that he is getting too old for the workshops. He is particularly impressed with the Band, 'But I was worried that they had to wait so long for their lunch,' he adds. Adam hopes to enter the School in 2001.

Jill and Tim Spinnery's daughter Emily, a flautist, hopes to enter the School in 2002, following in the footsteps of sister Louise who left in 1991. If she is successful, she may well come across Sarah Rushton's daughter Flynne. She already plays violin, clarinet, piano and recorder and is attracted by the musical tradition.

By the end of the afternoon, more than 250 families have filled out forms requesting further information on entry procedures and Carol Blackwell, who co-ordinates the day, can relax for a while before planning the next one.

The Marching Band is appreciated, but not impeded, by the visitors on Open Day.

Jessica Pinder provides more than a guide service for a family on a tour of the School.

118

The juniors are off on the steeplechase.

SPORT IN LENT

This year, the Steeplechase was held in fine weather in early April. The Senior Boys category was won by Richard Smith and the House cup went to Middleton A. Intermediate Boys winner was Tom Passmore, with the cup awarded to Middleton B. The Junior Boys category was won by Ben Maddox, the cup going to Maine B.

The Senior Girls winner was Laura Nightingale, the Intermediate winner Eliza Wheeler and the Junior winner Lucinda Hutchins. All three cups went to Coleridge A.

Not only the pupils ran the Steeplechase – several members of the staff were also seen to be taking part, and reaching the finish as muddy and exhausted as their younger rivals.

Nicola McCabe, a Third Former, running for the juniors; some doughty also-rans; and consulting one of the time keepers.

RESULTS IN THE LENT TERM

The 1st VII netball team, including (left to right) Erin Lettis (WD), Flora Nabena (GD) and Gaby Maselino (GK) in action.

Netball
The first and second teams returned outstanding results, with the 1st winning the Sussex League Division 2.
Overall results: Played: 78; Won: 46, Drawn: 3, Lost: 29. 1st VII Played: 14; Won: 13, Lost: 1. 2nd VII: Played: 13, Won: 12, Lost: 1.

Association football
Soccer is the major team sport for boys in the Lent term and has the good fortune to have Steve Gatting, the former Arsenal and Brighton player, as School coach. The popularity of the game is shown by the School turning out five senior teams plus under 15's, under 14's and under 13's teams.

The season saw a slow start for the 1st XI but then gradual improvement as the term progressed. Losing their first four games the team could have become dispirited but, during the second half of the term, they played some attractive and stylish soccer to end up with a number of excellent wins and a final count of played 13, won 5, drawn 2, lost 6, with 23 goals for and 23 against.

Junior girls' netball: Polly Hughes, with Jean King, scores for the U14 team against Epsom College.

Rugby Fives
Rugby Fives enjoyed a particularly good season with an increasingly high standard of Fives being played. The results were the best for at least twenty-five years, with sixty per cent of all matches won and the B teams sometimes playing opposition A teams and still winning.
Overall results: Played: 52, Won: 31, Lost: 21. The 1st played: 12, Won: 8 and Lost: 4.

NETBALL SQUADS
1st's: Sophie Naish (Captain), Helena Barnet-Lonergan (Vice Captain), Nicola Batchelor, Erin Lettis, Natalie Williams, Flora Nabena, Gabriella Maselino, Jo Tansley-Thomas, Sarah Moon.
2nd's: Agnes Rothon (Captain), Sarah Moon, Erica White, Rehanne Isaac, Nicola Whitley, Jhanelle Osbourne-Burke, Tamara Tinawi, Alice Holdsworth.

ASSOCIATION FOOTBALL
1st squad: Anton Dankwah (Captain), Tom Trewick, Leon Langton, Dan Hedges, Dan Pearce, Dominic Roberts, Ben Allwood, Andrew Tang-Pullen, Keith Smart, Liam O'Reilly, Sandy Ryan, Homan Mahmoudi, Sam Neild, Gavin Salvage, Ben Walker, Adam Parmenter.

BOYS' HOCKEY SQUAD
Ed Marland (Captain), John Brown, Tim Evans, Laurie Cook, Ned Ashley, Ed Hayes, Tom Cairncross, Dan Ramsay-Smith, Toby Davies, Moses Annoh, James Busby, George Busby, Guy Vesey, Lowell Lewis, Nick Hoath, Mikael Glazier, Dan Cizek.

RUGBY FIVES TEAM
Huw Aveston* (Captain), Ben Smithson*, Neil Green*, Mark Hutton, Adrian Hill.
Also played: Nicholas Rumball, Ed Hawke.
    * Denotes colours

National Schools' Championships
Senior singles: Huw Aveston reached senior finals. Ben Smithson won the 'Second Plate'.
Senior Doubles: Huw Aveston & Ben Smithson reached the quarter finals.
Colts Singles: Neil Green reached semi-finals.
Ed Hawke won the 'Second Plate'.
Colts Doubles: Neil Green and Mark Hutton reached semi-finals.

West of England Open Schools' Championships
Senior Singles: Huw Aveston reached semi-finals
Colts Singles: Ben Ford losing finalist of the 'Plate'.

Boys' hockey

An optional team sport for boys during the Lent term is hockey, played on the superb all-weather pitch on Little Side. Matches against schools such as St John's, Lewes Grammar, Epsom, Hurtwood, Eastbourne and Ardingly look familiar to many Old Blues – but not at hockey, which has only been played by boys at Christ's Hospital in more recent years.

For comparative newcomers to the game the results of played 12, won 6, drawn 2, lost 4, with 28 goals for and 15 against show great promise for the future. However, perhaps the team's most cherished result was beating the Girls' First XI 4–0!

Rugby football sevens

The School enters four senior seven-a-side tournaments each year: the Sussex Tournament, Worth, the Surrey and the National School Sevens

Ed Marland, Captain of the 1st XI, on the attack.

at Rosslyn Park. Unfortunately the disappointing results of the fifteen-a-side season in the Michaelmas term were repeated during the sevens tournaments, with the School being eliminated at the early stages on each occasion. Once again injury and lack of fitness and practice seemed to be the main reasons but, as in the XV's season, the team's attitude and morale was impressive in the face of adversity and there were several good individual performances.

The under thirteen sevens team played in similar tournaments in the Lent term and, although giving some highly spirited performances, failed to progress into any of the latter stages. They were particularly unlucky not to progress further in the Surrey Tournament, failing to qualify only on points difference.

Squash rackets

The first ever Christ's Hospital European Squash Tour having taken place in Spain in October, the boys first and second teams were well prepared for the Lent term season of School matches. Although they did not win all of their matches, the teams went from strength to strength and produced some outstanding individual performances.

The Girls' squash team did even better, managing to win all of their matches.

Squash has very definitely made its mark at Christ's Hospital, developing from a minor hobby to a senior sport in the last five years. Much credit for this transformation has to go to coaches Andy Williams, Paul Edwards and Julie Knott.

RUGBY SEVENS
1st squad: Will Avenell, George Busby, James Busby, Toby Davies, Sam Masters, John Noble, Nick Hoath, Carl Blakey, Alex Woodbridge, Moses Annoh, Samir Burns, Nick Rumball.
Under thirteen squad
James Mitra, James Maxwell, Edward Avenell, Woon-Young Kim, Mark Belassie, Sam Morgan, Jason Marsham, Sam D'Arcy, Rupert Munro, David Hayden.

SQUASH RACKETS SQUADS
Girls Jessica Daniell, Anna Martinelli, Kate Walton, Claire Gladding, Gemma Quinn, Rose Greenhalgh, Rebecca Cook.
Boys' 1st: Tom Cairncross (Captain), James Clipsham, Leslie Lubwama, Andy Moore, Sam Kaikai, Guy Matthews.
Boys' 2nd: Ed Marland, Sam Curtin, Tom Curtin, Neil Green, Chris Ansell, Tom Webster.

SERVICE OF THANKSGIVING FOR THE LIFE OF 'BILL' KIRBY, 1903–2000
MONDAY 3 APRIL 2000

While the steeplechasers spatter through the mud in Shelley's Wood, a more solemn occasion is taking place in Chapel. In the presence of some two hundred Old Blues, aged between twenty and ninety, a Service of Thanksgiving is being held for Old Blue and former Master at the School, Cecil Francis Kirby, universally known as 'Bill'.

Born on 16 March 1903, Bill had been admitted to Christ's Hospital in 1914. He became House Captain of Peele A and gained a Musical Exhibition to Gonville and Caius College, Cambridge, where he read Biology. He had always hoped to become a doctor, but he was persuaded by his mentor and former Head Master, William Hamilton Fyfe, to return to the School as a master of Biology and Elementary Chemistry.

He is remembered as being gracious and courteous, but tough and determined in the teaching of his disciplines and in the care of the boys put under his charge as House Master successively of Lamb B and Maine B. His interests were wide and varied. He loved swimming and water polo; Gilbert and Sullivan operettas; dogs, and walking them in the countryside around the School; bee-keeping and honey production; and brewing his own special brand of mead. He served in the Royal Signals during the second World War and in the post-War Territorial Army, in which he developed signalling skills which he was keen to pass on to his

Among the many Old Blues to attend the memorial service for Bill Kirby were Eric Beauchamp (right) and Barclay Hankin, who is displaying a framed drawing of Kirby's Lab. which he produced for Bill's 80th birthday.

pupils as an enthusiastic and active leader of the Officer Training Corps (OTC).

Bill retired in 1963. He had great support from the School, being allowed to build a bungalow in the grounds overlooking the playing fields, and being granted a laboratory in his former classroom where he could pursue his experimental work. He continued to live and work at Christ's Hospital until old age and infirmity led to residential care in a nursing home in Slinfold. He died there on 20 February 2000 aged 97 years, and bequeathed his entire estate to Christ's Hospital.

Four generations of Old Blues have gathered to give thanks for his life at the Chapel service, many bearing first hand recollections of their tutelage under Bill. He was a complex character – full of kindness to the weaker pupils, but intolerant of the lazy or self-indulgent. He was indifferent about his personal appearance and mostly wore old army clothes, much-mended and worn. He was an eccentric, who used extraordinary means to communicate his subject, some of which would be considered inappropriate by today's standards. He never married, but could be charming to women, and was particularly close to his mother.

And so, for Christ's Hospital, another era passes with his death. Bill was able to live and work in a way which simply would not be possible today. His pupils won't forget the way that he befriended the vulnerable, supported the weak, and saw potential in the most unlikely places. It is appropriate that his life is remembered, with thanksgiving, during this special, millennial year.

EASTER HOLIDAY

Any chronicle of events during April in the year 2000 must include a weather report. For it has rained, and rained and rained. Not just the occasional, seasonal, shower, but such heavy continuous rain that even our hardy Head Master has been seen wearing a protective hat. And the rain has had a major effect on the events of the holiday which, from the School's point of view, centre on the progress or otherwise of the Grecians' residences. For at this point they are open to the skies, and therefore vulnerable to whatever the skies may deliver. The ground has become fluid and glutinous, forming into fantastic peaks and ridges as heavy wheels churn and mould it as they navigate the site.

The Steward's department undertakes key works during the holidays, which include renewing the electrics and erecting new ceilings in the East Block Classrooms; renewing the plumbing in the New Science School; converting dormitories into studies and 'cubies' in Thornton B and Maine B; strengthening the roof of the Tube between Lamb and Barnes; modifications in the Prep Block prior to decanting, and laying tarmac on the new East and West Car Parks and their adjoining road.

While estate and ground staff hammer and saw, wire and dig, Quadrant Events are busy co-ordinating the many events which they have booked. There is a staff member's wedding; the Provincial Grand Chapter of Sussex Masons meet in Big School; Horsham Primary Schools hold their Music Festival in the Theatre; and The West Sussex Road Safety Competition Final is held in Big School while the West Sussex Primary Care Managers are in the Theatre. The Royal Society for the Protection of

The cycle touring group in Chipping Camden during the Easter holiday. Left to right: Markus Ernst, Frank Pattison, Alex Wodzianski and Theodore Usherwood.

Birds volunteers also settle in the Theatre, as do the Rotary Club District Assembly.

TRIPS AND EXCURSIONS

Although not on site, many pupils are still involved during the holiday, with staff, in furthering their studies, pursuing their hobbies or participating in sporting activities. Members of the CCF attend an Adventure Training and Duke of Edinburgh Camp at Capel Curig, North Wales, from 5–12 April. The Scouts hone their sailing skills on the Norfolk Broads from 8–15 April.

Meanwhile students of Russian leave for a week-long visit to Kiev, from which they return on 16 April. During that time, from 14–21 April, the basketball team are on tour at Platja d'Oro, near Barcelona; the French Grecians are on a study visit to Toulouse; and a field teaching trip is being held on Dartmoor for Deputy Grecian geographers.

GERMAN DEPARTMENT EXCURSIONS

The German Department is another which is involved in overseas trips, organised by Frank Pattison, Head of German, who writes:

The Department organises four major activities in Germany every year: the exchange, the study visit, work experience, and the Rhine visit. During the Easter holiday our pupils entertain thirty boys and girls from our partner school in Ansbach, northern Bavaria. The Germans arrive here at School on 8 April and are taken to their hosts' homes on 11 April for ten days. The return visit will take place at the beginning of the summer holiday, when the School party will travel to Ansbach for a fortnight. They will stay at the homes of their German partners and be offered a varied programme of activities, visiting Rothenburg, Regensburg, Munich and Nuremburg, attending school, and taking part in a number of social events such as parties and barbecues.

The annual Grecians' study visit takes the fourteen German Grecians, accompanied by four of the German staff, to Munich and Nuremburg during the October half term. Here they explore the history, art, culture and cuisine of Bavaria, visiting King Ludwig's palaces at Linderhof and Neuschwanstein, medieval Nuremburg, the churches and galleries of Munich, Hitler's monumental stadium for his party rallies, the concentration camp at Dachau, the baroque churches at Ettal and Wies and, of course, the Hofbrauhaus.

For twelve UF pupils unable to take part in an exchange, the department organises a visit to the Rhine valley. They spend a week in youth hostels in Cologne and Bacharach, a castle with spectacular views of the Rhine, and visit the towns, villages and castles of the Rhine gorge.

Seven of the Deputy Grecians studying German will spend part of their summer holiday doing work experience in either Bamberg or Ansbach. They will undertake a variety of jobs: in a school library, a café, a travel agent, the offices of an engineering firm and even a sausage factory.

As the holiday draws to a close academic staff and matrons have a staff development day; cricketers selected for the forthcoming Barbados trip return early for pre-season training; and those who have a mind to can browse among the antique books, prints, and magazines at the Antique Book Fair, held in Dining Hall from 28–30 April.

It is strange being at Christ's Hospital during the holidays. Teaching colleagues are occasionally sighted in the Quad, or in Common Room, but their privacy is respected and they are not necessarily drawn into conversation. Most take the opportunity of going away – to bask in the sun or to read a long-awaited book. The children of staff are also seen; the older ones, as like as not, doing some work for Quadrant Events, for which they will be paid slightly more than pocket money; the younger ones careering around on bikes and kicking footballs, or swinging a cricket bat in areas which would certainly be out of bounds during the term.

And so the weeks pass and suddenly the last day of the holiday arrives. Returning parents need tea or coffee and a biscuit from the house parents as gentle enquiries are made about the holidays, work, and any social problems, hopes and concerns that may have arisen. This year many boys' parents choose that opportunity to ask about the implications of the new all-through houses, and to seek reassurance that the net effect will be to offer better facilities than the existing structures can provide.

While they talk the house becomes full of happy, boisterous children who, in a well-tried routine, fill tuck lockers, put up posters, play on computers and greet old friends. Soon Dining Hall will be filled with hungry Housey-clad pupils. The Head Master's Assembly will be held in Big School. Chapel will host an act of worship, and the Quad will be criss-crossed with groups of children. Christ's Hospital may, very successfully, offer hospitality to outsiders on a commercial basis during the holidays, but during the term it is definitely the domain of the pupils.

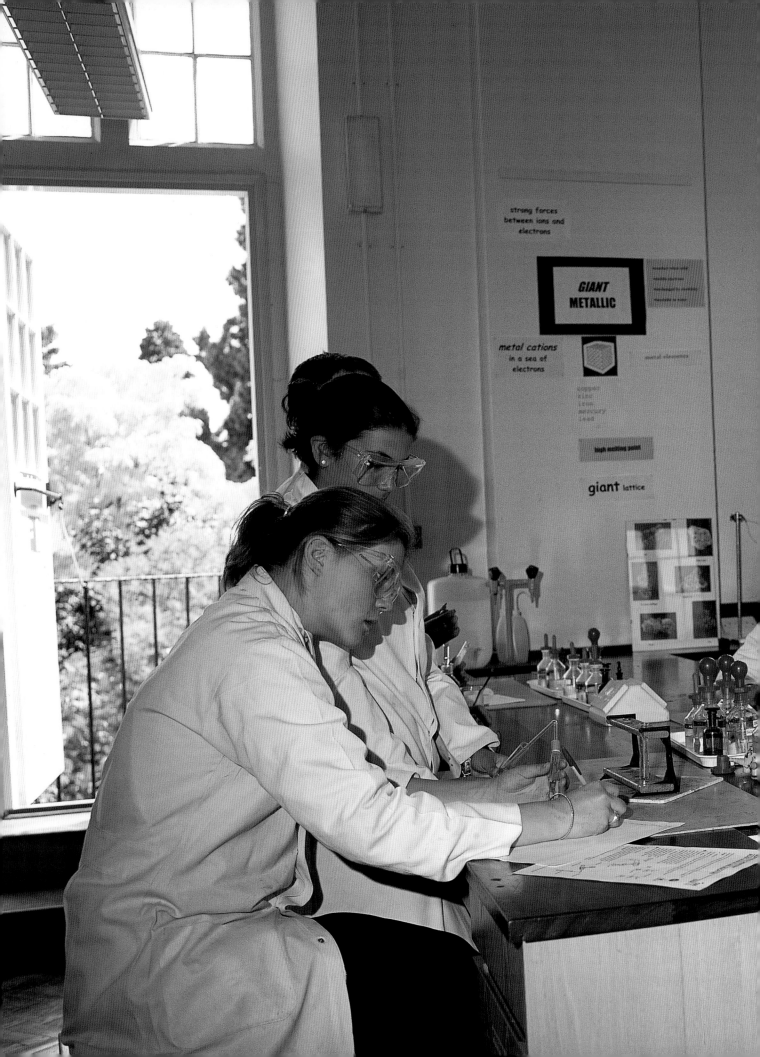

CHAPTER SEVEN
THE SUMMER TERM

PARENTS' FORUM
30 APRIL 2000

COMMUNICATING WITH PARENTS is a priority for the teaching and academic staff; and especially for Head Master Dr Peter Southern, who hosts open forums where parents can bring major problems and minor queries for discussion.

At the start of the Summer term, around three dozen parents of Little Erasmus pupils, having settled their children, congregate in the Riches Lecture Theatre for a fifty-five minute session with Dr Southern before he leaves to join in the first chapel service of term.

It's a relaxed, informal occasion, in which Dr Southern offers considered answers to a range of questions. Topics include history or geography choices for GCSE; the closure of the Arts Quad while it accommodates temporary classrooms; the range of activities available on Sundays; recommended amounts of pocket money; age restrictions on sail training and the provision of Livery Company funds to enable students to work in tall ships.

Considerable time is spent discussing the scheduling of leave weekends and the possible rescheduling of the School year to provide terms of equal length, before the group move on to the layout of School reports, the International Baccalaureat, SATs tests for eleven- and fourteen- year-olds, and the effects of the new Curriculum 2000 on A-level students.

Also discussed are the issues surrounding a child arriving a year later than his or her peer group, attitudes on the rugby pitch and the tidiness of house kitchens.

'This was our first parents' forum, and it was really good,' say Philip and Diana Hodson, parents of third-former Luke (Peele B). While Valerie Davies, mother of Charlotte (Barnes B) agrees. 'We all have concerns, but I feel you can talk to the Head Master at any time.'

NEW ENTRANTS' DAY
SUNDAY 7 MAY 2000

At the start of each Summer term, the children who will enter the School in September spend a Sunday afternoon at the School with their parents. After a brief address and prayer with the Head Master in Chapel, they meet their houseparents and explore the campus guided by their 'nurse-maid', the boy or girl now completing their first year who will act as mentor to the newcomer.

Among this year's new intake will be Mary Rendle, the first girl to be presented by Christ's Hospital Club Old Girls' Association under their Millennium Presentee scheme. With many CHCOGA members subscribing to the donation, fund organiser Mrs Valerie Hill was elected to serve as Donation Governor, taking an active part in selecting the presentee: the daughter or granddaughter of an Old Girl.

Mary will enter Leigh Hunt B. She lives in Jersey with her mother, an Old Hertford Blue of the '60s. Mary enjoys singing and dancing, plays the 'cello and is interested in drama. She is a good swimmer, enjoys netball and is learning badminton – a range of interests which will stand her in good stead in the Christ's Hospital community.

Previous pages: A UF class in the Salters' School of Chemistry. Left to right: Lucy Foster, Meera Singh, Eve Dawoud, Rachel Simm, Jenny Williams, Head of Chemistry, Stevie Parish, Gemma McMahon and Ryan Wickens.

Mary Rendle, the first CHCOGA presentee to the School, with her mother.

EXAMINATIONS

The Timetable for the Summer Term is dominated by the complex programme of GCSE and A-level exams organised by David O'Meara, Examinations Officer at the School.

External examinations in May and June 2000 are taken by 1 Third Former (1 GCSE), 1 UF (1 GCSE), 107 GE who take 9.3 GCSEs each on average, 93 Deputy Grecians who take a large number of modular papers, 3 A Levels, 4 GCSEs and 13 short courses in all. 113 Grecians take 2.95 A levels each on average, most of which involve many modules.

The results for the main exam years are:

	A*	A	B	C	D	E	N
A level (%)	n/a	34	29	17	13	5	2
GCSE (%)	14	24	33	24	4	1	

The venues used are: Big School, Court Room, Language laboratory, Music School, Dr Hackett's laboratory, John Denison's classroom and David O'Meara's classroom, on at least one occasion using three of these at once. The busiest day is Tuesday 13 June, when 407 papers are sat, 212 in the morning and 195 in the afternoon. Many pupils have an exam in both the morning and afternoon, and some take four modules on that day. The second busiest day is Tuesday 6 June with 364 papers.

The A level syllabus will change completely in September 2000 and become entirely modular. There are also changes to GCSEs due in 2001, but they will not be as fundamental.

'I don't like to think how long it takes to organise!' remarks David O'Meara. 'Hardly a day goes by without there being something to do on the exams front. The most obvious tasks are getting entries from Heads of Department, which takes two or three full days twice a year; printing individual statements of entry and timetables, and sorting them for delivery, which takes a full day for a large session (probably about six times a year); organising seating which takes a whole day for the summer session; checking deliveries of papers which takes about six half days; and sorting them for use in the exam sessions, which takes half a day at the height of the season. These are the "hidden" tasks, which people do not see. Then there is the higher profile of being present at the start and end of every paper, which makes for long days in the exam season. Results days take most of two days, when the results are received from the Examination Boards, twice in the summer holidays.

'The biggest bane of my life as Examinations Officer is changes to entries. These can take up to half a day each to implement, and I usually miss something. It also takes up a lot of time chasing pupils who are absent, only to be told, "I gave that up in January".'

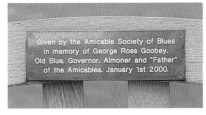

Plaques commemorating Old Blues and Amicables Michael Pearey, Clerk 1986–98, and George Ross Goobey, Almoner, Governor and a benefactor to the School, on benches in the Garden Quad, presented by the Amicables. The idea of creating a knot garden here was conceived by John Gale and it was laid out and planted in 1999 in preparation for the centenaries celebrations in 2002.

THE AMICABLE SOCIETY OF BLUES REMEMBER THEIR COLLEAGUES
THURSDAY 4 MAY 2000

It is cold with a raw dampness as some fifty Old Blues gather beside the War Memorial outside Dining Hall. They have come to honour four former students. Two – Leslie Foxton (Peele A 1938–45) and Geoffrey Urquhart-Pullen, known as Roy, (Peele B 1941–8) – died as young men, in the service of their country; the other two – George Ross Goobey and Michael Pearey – each died after a lifetime of service to their country and their School. Today, in two separate ceremonies, the latter organised by The Amicable Society of Blues, they are remembered and honoured by their families and friends.

The plaque on the south wall of Dining Hall is covered by a blue velvet curtain as colleagues recall the bravery of their friends under fire; and a portion of Scripture from Revelation (21:1–7) is read before the curtain is drawn aside. Trumpeter Cyprian Ilie plays the 'Last Post', before the Senior Chaplain offers a Prayer of Dedication, and the brief ceremony closes with 'Reveille'.

After a few moments to pause and reflect, the group moves across the Quad to the Garden Quad, where the groundsmen have put everything into immaculate order. Now, in the middle, on two gravel beds, facing each other across the knot garden, stand the new garden seats – deep-seated, high backed, broad-hipped, handsome, light wood seats, which lend real tone and elegance to an already beautiful spot.

The Senior Chaplain officiates as prayers are said. The Head Master reads from the First Letter of St John, Chapter 4, 7–12: 'Beloved, let us love one another: for love is of God; and everyone that loveth is born of God; for God is love.' We consider these sentiments during Psalm 96; the Christ's Hospital Collects and the Lord's Prayer follow before the seats are dedicated to the glory of God in the service of Christ's Hospital.

Such acts of remembrance are a further reminder of the ethos of Christ's Hospital, and one of the factors on which the corporate life of the School is built.

Mike Pearey was apparently small enough to sit comfortably inside his settle when he joined the School at the age of nine. After service in the Royal Navy he returned to the School to serve as its Clerk until his death in 1998. George Ross Goobey, Donation Governor, former Almoner, Father of the Amicables, and with a long and distinguished career as an actuary, had also maintained a close contact with the School. Neither would have expected to be so remembered. But this is typical of the way of Christ's Hospital: a small investment at a critical stage often reaps huge dividends for the School in later life.

Leslie Foxton fell in the Korean War, and Roy Pullen died on a reconnaissance flight in the Suez Crisis. Mike Pearey and George Ross Goobey served over a much longer span. The Marching Band honours them with a Salute and a March Past to the tune of 'Army of the Nile'. The Amicables continue to remember them over their lunch in the Court Room.

Michael Wates, Chairman of the Wates Group, with the Senior Grecian, Kate Atkinson, and the Head Master performing the topping out ceremony at Grecians' West.

THE TOPPING OUT CEREMONY AT GRECIANS' WEST

5 MAY 2000

It is unusually warm and sultry as a small group gathers at noon on the south side of the new Grecians' West residence. Michael Wates, CBE and Chairman of the Wates Group, which has the contract for the two buildings, greets the Head Master, the Clerk, the Senior Grecian Kate Atkinson, the Steward, Philip Obeney and other members of the School community who have come to watch.

The new house parents Neil and Marlene Fleming, for Grecians' West, and Stephen and Amanda Walsh, for Grecians' East, have now arrived with Peter Smith (Services Manager), John Morley (Buildings Manager), Richard Churchman (Grounds and Estate Manager) and Brian Wilson (Works Co-ordination Officer). At 12.30pm Michael Wates climbs the ladder to the temporary platform erected near the partly-constructed building and, accompanied by the Head Master and Senior Grecian, makes a short speech of welcome. He speaks with warmth, of both his pride in the teamwork that has developed between the different agencies, and of the excellent relations which have been maintained between Wates and the Clerk, Michael Simpkin, and Philip Obeney.

Dr Southern responds with typical warmth and sincerity and raises the Union Jack, alongside the green and white Wates flag. After applause

Michael Wates presents him with a handsome ceremonial trowel dating from 1884, as a reminder and a symbol of the excellent spirit of co-operation which has characterised the enterprise thus far.

Some wonder what exactly a 'topping out' ceremony signifies. It is, we are told in a thoughtfully provided leaflet, an ancient tradition which normally takes place when the roof or the highest point of the building is finished. It is a time for celebration, when workmen of different trades – as well as the architect and the future occupant – give thanks for works accomplished thus far and look forward to its completion.

As formalities at the site draw to a close the group moves to the Court Room where the drinks and refreshments are being provided by Wates. This gives an opportunity for further questions: is the work up to schedule? Have there been particular difficulties from working in the clay soil?

Clare Hebbes and Simon Johnson, of the Structures and Services Unit at Ove Arup & Partners, are very helpful. Yes, exceptionally deep foundations of two and a half metres have been dug, to avoid the zone of dessication that must be afforded to the large trees which surround the site. Yes, the site is being built to an exceptionally high specification, so that it not only looks good, but will, hopefully, withstand the wear and tear to which future generations of teenage children, and other residents, will subject it in the next hundred years and more. Yes, the mud has, on occasions, been troublesome, but it is very satisfying to work on a building which is aesthetically so pleasing, and which blends so well with the original Aston Webb and Ingress Bell style of architecture. They are particularly pleased that so much trouble has been taken in the choice of bricks – the colour blends very well with the rest of the site. Yes, it is unusual that so much care has been taken in the selection of building components, so that they are not only beautiful and durable, but they can also be easily maintained, or replaced if they were to be damaged.

And so it is a time for celebration, for discussion, and gentle enquiry as to whether the buildings will be ready in time for the Grecians to occupy on 4 September. We must hope so; much depends upon it.

This whole programme of renewal is like a complex game of chess, in which pieces must be moved in a prescribed order. The topping out ceremony on this hot, late spring, morning is an exciting opening move.

CCF INSPECTION
THURSDAY 18 MAY 2000

It is the weather, again, that gives cause for concern about the success of the day. There is no doubt that the pupils are drilled to perfection: indeed the parade-ground calls of Parade Commander Peter Gogalniceanu, Grecian, Mid B, and Sarah Freeman, Guard of Honour Commander, Grecian, LHA, have been heard for days before as they meticulously trained their troops. Nor is there any doubt that Rear Admiral Michael Haskins, Deputy Commander in Chief of US Forces in Europe, will execute with precision and dedication his rôle as Inspecting Officer. It is just the weather – will it rain and cause havoc with the Band?

In the event the day is overcast but dry as the troops march on to the Quad. They stand rigidly as Rear Admiral Haskins is led among them,

Waiting for the helicopter rides was well worth while.

Rear Admiral Haskins, USN, inspects the Guard of Honour with Squadron Leader Stannard and School SS1 WO1 Rick Smith on the right.

The Admiral has time for a word with several of the cadets. Here he is talking to Nicola Williams and Jessica Clenshaw.

asking questions, making comments, showing admiration for their high standards. Those in the ranks remain impassive unless spoken to, but the occasional and discreet wiggling of toes or twiddling of thumbs indicates a raw need to keep the circulation flowing. Three pupils do faint, but they are quickly attended to. The Guard of Honour stand to attention, then at ease, transferring their rifles from one shoulder to the other.

The Band, immaculate and professional as ever, are inspected too, and forge their own relationship with the Rear Admiral. Duty done, the Band leads the combined services, and the Guard of Honour, on the March Past and Salute. At the command of 'eyes right' they give the salute, and all those watching – pupils, staff and parents – are moved to applause.

Admiral Haskins is the highest-ranking officer from overseas yet to carry out the annual CCF Inspection at the School. He is warm and gracious, not only in the execution of his formal duties, but also, after they have concluded, in moving easily and informally among the crowd of onlookers. With obvious pleasure he invites questions, and is not apparently fazed by the renowned directness of the pupils. 'Have you ever killed anyone?', asks a Second Former. 'What does it feel like?' We don't hear his answer.

Slowly he returns to the official party and on to the Head Master's house. The Band and contingents march off to an early lunch after which a British Army Gazelle helicopter arrives, which is to spend the afternoon whirring and buzzing over the School, taking groups of pupils, and the Head Master, on a breathtaking aerial tour. Only then do the first, gentle, spots of rain appear.

SPEECH DAY
SATURDAY 20 MAY 2000

Under sunny skies, Speech Day passes smoothly through time-honoured traditions, undisturbed by demonstrators picketing at the gates to protest at the possible sale of part of the Foundation's land for housing.

During the Chapel Service the Lord Mayor of London, Alderman Clive Martin, and his civic party, the Sheriffs, the Head Master, Treasurer, Clerk, Almoners, Donation Governors, staff, parents and children, sing 'O Praise Ye The Lord', and echo the choir in Colin Mawby's 'Christus Vincit'. The lesson, read by Second Monitor George Busby is followed by 'How shall I sing that Majesty'. Prayers are followed by the Foundation Hymn and the Blessing.

School and Band readied for the March Past, diminutive Olivia Bartleet (Col A) appears composed as she takes the long walk along the Avenue from the west cloisters to the civic party gathered in front of Dining Hall. Having presented a posy to the Lady Mayoress, she achieves a graceful curtsey and proceeds gravely to the east cloisters to warm applause.

The Band strikes up, and the Lord Mayor acknowledges each house in turn as they march smartly past, then head off for a barbecue lunch while the visitors adjourn to Dining Hall. The Senior Grecian and Second Monitors join the top table, and other Grecians join the visitors' tables for lunch and coffee, followed by the Loyal Toast and the Housey Toast. Graces are said by Second Monitors George Busby and Sophie Naish.

During coffee the Treasurer, Susan Mitchell, makes a speech honour-

The Lord Mayor's procession from the Head Master's house is led by the City Marshal Brigadier Neill O'Connor, followed by the Sheriffs Alderman Robert Finch and Pauline Halliday and the Lord Mayor's Chaplain, the Revd. Canon Alan Coldwells. The Swordbearer Colonel Mark Carnegie-Brown and the Serjeant-at-Arms and Common Cryer Colonel 'Tommy' Tucker (bearing the mace) are followed by the Treasurer, the Lord Mayor Alderman Clive Martin and the Head Master.

ing the City's Common Cryer and Serjeant-at-Arms, Colonel 'Tommy' Tucker, and presents a gift to mark his retirement.

The formal events conclude with Speeches in Big School. Guests enter to Purcell's Symphony from *The Faerie Queen*, performed by the Symphony Orchestra led by Brigita Ziferman (Col B).

The eight verses of the 'Votum' are followed by a remarkable performance by Grecian Andrew Saunders (Lamb A) and the Symphony Orchestra of his 'Fantasy Overture' for piano and orchestra – a submission in his A-level GCE portfolio which is enthusiastically applauded by an appreciative audience.

Kate Atkinson's Oration, confidently and eloquently delivered, follows the tradition of providing an encapsulated history of the School year, with thanks to various people who have contributed to it. Much of what she says is included in these chapters. The following extracts demonstrate the eloquence of her style and items which are not otherwise dealt with.

THE ORATION

It is a great honour for me to welcome you here today.

In preparation for this oration, my Lord Mayor, my idea was to concentrate on life at Christ's Hospital at the turn of the last century during its last days in London. It would be fascinating to know what pupils of that era would think of Housey life at Horsham in the year 2000. I doubt that any

Bob Sillett gives a final word of reassurance to Olivia Bartleet before she presents the Lady Mayoress with a posy, which she does with great aplomb,

after which the Lord Mayor takes the salute from each house in turn – Middleton B currently marching.

The Senior Grecian, Kate Atkinson

of them could have imagined the ways of the School today, as the past hundred years have seen a 'Century of Progress'.

Now we complete our coursework on networked computers, are able to search for information on the world-wide web, maintain links with the outside world by mobile 'phone and submit articles to *The Blue* by e-mail. Many classrooms and all boarding houses are equipped with televisions and video players, and visual effects are added to lectures through computer-linked projection devices. We can pop down to the Sports Centre, play hockey on the astro-pitch, skate on the half-pipe or gain access to the Library and its resources with our personalised electronic swipe cards.

Old Blues of the 1900's might recognise certain traditions which still uphold and define our year, and the strong links we have maintained with our roots in London, as can be seen by the annual visit of the whole School to the City on St Matthew's Day to receive our largesse. Today's traditional march past would be familiar, but the fact that this is an English Oration might be slightly unexpected. The same distinctive Housey uniform is being worn, but they might be surprised to find the girls wearing it too!

Our close ties with the City are still displayed by the livery company presentees who continue to wear their unique badges on their Housey uniform. . . . My Lord Mayor, there are links between your livery company, the Stationers, and Christ's Hospital. Our Treasurer, Mrs Susan Mitchell [is] a fellow liveryman, [and] in 1652 money was left in the Will of Christopher Meredith (also a Stationer) to provide Bibles 'for the poore children of the said Hospital'. To this day the tradition of presenting Bibles to the Grecians at the leaving service endures, as does the Charge delivered by the Head Master in words that have been used since at least 1784. . .

Kate then describes the changes resulting from the Master Plan, and the structure of the houses. She remarks:

Apparently pupil suggestions for the new houses include ensuite showers, lifts, internal 'phones by each bed and vending machines to provide twenty-four hour chocolate supplies!

After describing the numerous musical events of the year, not least that the Marching Band again led the Lord Mayor's procession, and that:

The music school has released two CDs in the past year. 'Century of Progress' was released in the summer which mainly features the Marching Band, with supporting tracks from various ensemble groups and the Showband, and was Mick Davison's parting legacy. The choir, under the direction of Mr Allwood, produced a CD of Christmas carols, aptly named 'Silent Night'.

Senior among those leaving this term is Elizabeth Cairncross, Deputy Head, to take up the Headship at Wells Cathedral School. Here she is seen at a dinner party given by the Head Master in her honour, talking to Thelma Pearey, widow of the former Clerk.

After an account of the sporting activities in the School, and their varied results, Kate moves on to thank members of staff who are leaving:

> The modern languages department say farewell to Mr Nordgreen, who originally planned to stay for one term but, fortunately for us, stayed for two years, and Mrs Charbonnieras, who has taught in both the French and Russian departments for the past four years, and has assisted on Russian study visits. Dr Dillow has been appointed Head of the Sixth Form at the British School in the Netherlands. He is currently head of higher education, assistant house master of Maine A, coach of the 4th and 5th soccer XIs and of the 3rd XI cricket team. His knowledge of universities and their courses is unsurpassable, and his ability to find somewhere that offers the slightly more unusual courses will be sorely missed.
>
> Mr Phillips leaves to take up the post of house master at his old house at Mill Hill School. In his time he has been house master of Thornton B and more recently Maine B as well as teaching French, Latin and classical civili-

Two of the other teaching staff leaving this term: Dr Jonathan Wolstenholme in his IT classroom and Andrew Phillips, right, talking with the under-13's cricket coach, Alan Pilgrim.

sation. He has taken charge of the cross-country teams, the organisation of the steeplechase, and coached junior cricket teams.

Dr Wolstenholme will move to Radley to become head of ICT. His patience with those of us who are slightly less computer literate has been immense, and we are very grateful for all the time and energy which he has spent ensuring that the network of computers is fully functional. He has also been involved in setting up computer networks in schools in Romania, using not only old CH computers, but persuading other companies to donate machines which they no longer use.

Mr Endacott retires after twenty one years at Christ's Hospital. Currently the head of careers, he has previously been house master of Lamb A, Coleridge A (when it first became a girls' house) and Peele A. He was also part of the coaching team that produced the 1st XV rugby side which remained unbeaten.

Rachel Adams retires this year as Bursar. She has been with the Counting House since its days in London and has served the Hospital with a variety of high-powered ideas, introducing modern technology to a quill-driven accounts department as Finance Officer for twelve years and as Bursar for six.

Mrs Cairncross came to Christ's Hospital fifteen years ago as Senior Mistress, and was promoted to Deputy Head after the retirement of Mr Rae in 1990. Throughout this time she has taught in the English department and has been tutor to an endless list of tutees. Colleagues and pupils alike will remember her as being approachable at virtually any time, about virtually any subject and for her unmistakable sense of humour even in adverse situations. We wish her well in her new post as Head of Wells Cathedral School.

We would also like to congratulate Mr Shippen on completing one hundred terms here at Christ's Hospital.

Scouting is her next subject, about which an extract appears on page 69. She remembers the success of St Valentine's Day when:

> The efforts of the School Monitors raised more than £600 for the Friends of the Young Deaf, and I would like to thank them for all their hard work and support throughout the year, and give special thanks to the Second Monitors, Sophie Naish and George Busby.
>
> At the turn of this new millennium the opportunities offered here at Christ's Hospital both academically and outside the curriculum are unrivalled. I believe that pupils at the turn of the last century could not have envisaged the international dimension which life at Christ's Hospital has taken, as has been shown by the vast number of trips, expeditions and tours that have taken the 'good name of Christ's Hospital' to places far and wide. However, despite all the changes which we have seen over this 'Century of Progress' the Foundation is still committed to serving its original charitable ethos. While we stay firmly rooted in both our traditions and our base here at Horsham, there is a real sense that we are reaching out to embrace change. It is through that change that we will spread our message to more people than ever before.

Kate's oration is followed by the response from the Lord Mayor who expresses his enjoyment of the day's events, and warms to his theme of voluntary service, commending the lead shown by Christ's Hospital staff and pupils.

A spirited performance of Sibelius's 'Karelia Suite' and the National

VOTUM

Unum concentum tollite
Læto, sodales, sono;
Et vota Christo fundite
Nostræ domus Patrono.

Nostro favete carmini
Amici, quotquot estis,
Quos cura tangit Hospiti
Cæruleaque vestis.

Ut per priora saecula
Sic tempus in futurum
Det fausta Deus omnia
Et Ipsum adjuturum.

Ne noceat concordiæ
Contentio proterva,
Neu tabes obsit corpori
Neu febrium caterva.

Mores honesti suppetant
Et utilis doctrina
Et litterarum gloria
Et recta disciplina.

Ludi viriles floreant,
Qui præbeant salutem
Fraterna per certamina
Et nutriant virtutem.

*Artes palaestra floreant,
Per gratum quae laborem
Et robor addunt corpori
Et robori decorem

Artes colantur gymnicae
Per gratum quae laborem
Et robor addunt corpori
Et robori decorem.

Sit in dies felicior
Vigore domus verno
Et floreat, ut floruit,
Honore sempiterno.

*Verse specially composed by Dr Haig Brown for the Girls' School, where the piece was known as 'The Carmen'.

Words by Revd W Haig Brown LLD (CH 1833–1842).
Music by H Collingwood Banks (CH 1869–1877).

The Lord Mayor, Alderman Clive Martin, on a walk about with Robbie Kirkland, left, and Richard Poole.

The Treasurer, the Lord Mayor, William Fraser, Jemma Batte, Charlotte Gray and the Lady Mayoress after the unveiling of the memorial plaque to William Hornby Steer.

Anthem brings events to a close and the civic party, Almoners and Donation Governors depart to the Grand March from *Aida*.

Most visitors take the opportunity to visit classrooms and the Art School, and a small crowd gathers in the east cloisters for the unveiling by the Lord Mayor of a plaque to one of this century's most prominent Almoners and benefactors, William Hornby Steer (1899–1993). The ceremony, which includes an introduction by the Clerk, recollections by William Fraser and a prayer of dedication by the Revd Gary Dobbie, is attended by the two Hornby Steer Scholars, Jemma Batte (1998 entry) and Charlotte Gray (1999), both of Leigh Hunt B.

Tea is served in the Theatre marquee and visitors and children relax on the playing field in the last of the day's sunshine.

PEELE B HOUSE REUNION
FRIDAY 26 MAY 2000

The day has been meticulously planned, but no amount of forethought can influence the weather. The skies are overcast, but there is the promise of better things to come. So as the thirty six Old Blues assemble in the day room of Peele B at 10.45am, there is every expectation that they will soon be practising their line-up and drill in preparation for Band Parade at lunch time. Refreshments follow and, as they greet each other and study the notice board for news of absent friends, the Head Master welcomes them. Maurice Hall, Chairman of the Peele B Association and joint organiser with Old Blue and Almoner Peter Bloomfield, then calls the Roll. A tour of the house follows, led by three current house members on the LE, until it is time for marching practice to begin.

Then comes the rain, at first a drizzle, but by lunch time a persistent downpour; and Band Parade is cancelled. Sad but undaunted the Old Blues lunch in Dining Hall before a group photograph is taken on the dais. Afterwards the Head Master, the Clerk and Nick Thompson, the architect of the Master Plan and himself an Old Blue of Peele B, outline

Some of the Peele B Old Blues at their reunion in the Court Room.

Below: Ian Howard, house master of Peele B, addresses the meeting, with Mark Curtis, the Partnership Director, in the foreground.

Peter Bloomfield, one of the organisers of the event.

the scope and progress of the building and refurbishment programme. Nick, in pouring rain, escorts a group to the new Grecians' West residence, before they return to house for tea – and for wet jackets to dry out.

After a short break guests and staff make their way to Chapel for perhaps the most profound part of the day. Here Gary Dobbie presides over a simple yet moving service which opens with the Foundation Hymn and closes with The Charge, read from the steps of the altar by Alderman Sir Richard Nichols, OB. All then remove to the Court Room for pre-dinner drinks before enjoying an excellent meal in the company of former and present Peele B house staff. For some this is the end of the occasion, but others return on Saturday when, in drier conditions, they are able to see around the Design and Technology School before repairing to the Bax Castle for final reminiscences.

For some this is the first time they have returned to Christ's Hospital in fifty years or more. For everyone it is a moving and memorable occasion – indeed, it is described by one participant as 'magical'. And so it should be. Barnes A had a reunion on 12 May; Coleridge A has one on 17 June. These occasions are intended to be entirely pleasurable, catching up on lost years and renewing old acquaintances. Christ's Hospital is a living body, not a dead institution, and its corporate life is unique. It is not simply a school which takes its personality from its present incumbents: it is the sum of all the lives – good and bad, private and public – that have ever touched on Housie, that makes it so special.

Flora 2000 transform the chapel and the displays are greatly admired by many visitors.

Below: Barbara Harris, Chairman of the Festival, left, talks to Rosie Howard.

FESTIVAL OF FLOWERS
2–3 JUNE 2000

This is the special millennial Sussex Area Festival of Flowers, organised by NAFAS (National Association of Flower Arrangement Societies), by arrangement with Quadrant Events. Women, predominantly, who can distinguish and appreciate countless flowers, plants and shrubs have come in hundreds, possibly thousands, by car and coach, to see the floral exhibits.

Barbara Harris, Chairman of the Festival, explains that the event has been planned for over two and a half years, and it is obvious that a great deal of research and preparation has gone into the displays. Dining Hall and Chapel are full of formal arrangements, while Big School and the Court Room offer refreshments on a sultry and overcast day. The Chapel cloister provides shelter for all kinds of stalls, selling driftwood to dried flowers, and two classrooms in the New South Block serve as makeshift shops for plant sellers.

Against a background of chamber music played by a string quartet of pupils, visitors circulate among the displays in Dining Hall, which focus on the history of Christ's Hospital and centre, appropriately, on the

founding of the School by the boy King Edward VI. Surrounding displays depict key events in the life of the School, including the Great Fire of London and the granting of the Royal Charter in 1673 for the Royal Mathematical School, commemorated in the Antonio Verrio painting which hangs above it.

Old Blues from Charles Lamb and Samuel Taylor Coleridge to David Bawtree, Dennis Silk and Michael Wilding are depicted in appropriate displays; while in the Chapel Sir Frank Brangwyn's murals which adorn the walls are represented by floral creations which give fresh and vivid expression to their subjects. There are large and small displays, traditional and *avant-garde*, blending together to bring a new dimension of colour and beauty to their magnificent surroundings.

The pulpit in Dining Hall looks so noble with its hanging foliage, its hop boughs and dried flowers. So does the fireplace in the Court Room. But flowers fade and the splendour cannot realistically last beyond its two allocated days. The pupils return from half-term on Sunday and by then all trace of this breathtaking festival will have gone. Physically, at least, but not in the memory. For the vision of colour and rich greenery against the red-brick and timber backdrop has been received and – in the process of redevelopment and refurbishment which is being worked out at the School – it will surely find fresh expression.

A string quartet plays in the decorated Dining Hall and, below, the pulpit is bedecked with its own display.

THE MATHIESON MUSIC SCHOOL
SATURDAY 10 JUNE 2000

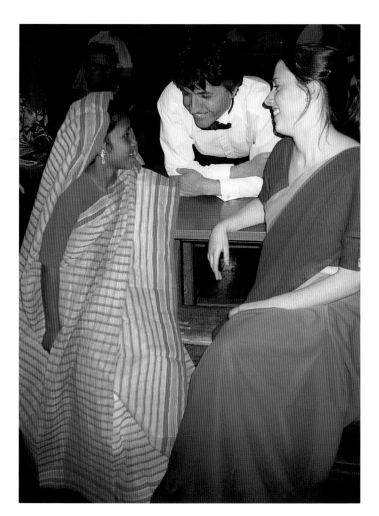

One of the dancers from the Mathieson Music School with John Hancorn, voice teacher at Christ's Hospital, and Old Blue Felicity Hill who is having a gap year at the Mathieson School.

It is an unusual sight, in the middle of term on a balmy Saturday evening in June, to see strangers picnicking in the Quad. They are local visitors and members of the School who have come to watch, even take part in, a concert by the Mathieson Music School from Calcutta.

Suddenly in their midst appear six small Indian girls dressed in saris of the most delicate shades of orange and red. They are tiny, almost doll-like and, at a word from their Head Mistress, Agnes Sarkar, begin a series of traditional dances among the guests. As they perform with confidence and grace older Indian boys appear, laden with traditional refreshments. Their cook, who lives and works with them in Calcutta, has been working in Peter Allwood's kitchen all day to produce over 1,000 onion bhajees.

The concert takes place in Dining Hall. It isn't just a concert, it is a real celebration of music, song and dance, mediums which can traverse and transform barriers of culture, language and race. The pupils from the Mathieson School – dancers as well as musicians – are joined by the Christ's Hospital Choral Society, the Horsham Children's Choir and Youth Choir as well as the School Concerto Ensemble.

Peter Allwood has arranged a full and varied programme with Anup Biswas, the visionary founder of the Mathieson Music School, and an internationally renowned solo 'cellist. They have included 'bhagras' – dances from the Punjab – demonstrated with skill and stamina by the dancing group of nine teenage boys; 'ragas', melodic phrases which are re-interpreted on different instruments in different ways; and a variety of items sung by the School Choral Society and played by The Concerto Ensemble with the Mathieson pupils.

Peter Allwood, who is now a Trustee of the Mathieson Music School, visited it when he was on a tour of India some years ago and was at once attracted by both its musicality and its ethos which so closely accords with that of Christ's Hospital. The school's vision and purpose is to remove children from the poverty of Calcutta and enable them to develop musical and academic skills to equip them for employment in the wider world. The school now has forty pupils, all boarders in a house named after Thomas Fanshawe Middleton, an Old Blue who became Anglican Bishop of Calcutta in 1813.

Christ's Hospital has supported the school through Gap Year students, who have given freely of their time in assisting teaching music theory and in practical care of the children.

CH COMMUNITY PLAY
14 & 16 JUNE 2000

Part of the cast of Murder at the Vicarage.

The Friends of Christ's Hospital Arts annual buffet, organised by Barbara Wolstenholme, precedes the first of the two sold-out performances of Agatha Christie's *Murder at the Vicarage* performed by the School community. 'The children await these staff and community productions with unholy glee,' notes Jeffrey Mayhew, Head of Drama. '"Did you see Mr Brown in those tights! . . . and Mr White snogging Miss Grey . . ." and so on. But when the house lights go down and the giggling is stifled, what magnificent support they do give us.'

Those confidently treading the boards include box office manager Jackie Davies as the intrepid Miss Marple; Bill Avenell as the befuddled Inspector; David Williams and Leanda Thornton presiding over the Vicarage; Bob Sillett, seen but not heard on this occasion, as the corpse; Almoner Moyna Gilbertson looking and sounding as though she's just returned from Poona and Jenny Barwise missing no opportunities for comedy in the maid's rôle.

This is a production being played for all it is worth by a cast enjoying itself hugely, deftly directed by Paul Ward and with a fine realistic set by Roberto de Pino. And it *is* worth it – the full house is delighted and is already looking forward eagerly to the next community play.

Three former Head Mistresses of the Hertford School, left to right: Elizabeth Tucker, Ruth West and Jean Morrison . . . and the three Reverend Old Blues who conducted the service, Bridget Woollard, Judith Thompson and Dorothy Green.

HERTFORD OLD GIRLS' REUNION
SATURDAY 17 JUNE 2000

Across the country, 218 Hertford Old Girls and three Hertford Head-mistresses awake to one of the warmest days in an otherwise indifferent summer, select something smart from their wardrobes and set off in happy and expectant mood for their old School site. The occasion is a millennium celebration and recollection, organised by the Christ's Hospital Club Old Girls' Association, of the School's historic time in Hertford, and of the girls' sole occupancy of the Hertford school for about eighty years before being re-united with the boys at Horsham in 1985.

The eldest of those present is Hilda Morgan (Gibbs, Ward 6, 1920–6), and the youngest, Jacqueline Savill and Caitriana Steele (Wards 5 and 8, Coleridge B), who finished their education at Horsham in 1987, were admitted to Hertford in 1981 and 1980 respectively and moved, with 280 fellow pupils, to Sussex in 1985 when Hertford finally closed its gates.

They are joined by Elizabeth Cairncross, Deputy Head, Leanda Thornton (house parent of Hertford Girls' House) and five current Blues, (Kate Barwise, Rachel Harris, Alison Harrison, Ellen Mayhew and Lucy Morgan, Band Captain) each immaculate in her Housey uniform.

Many have travelled with friends from School days, and all congregate in All Saints' churchyard where they are welcomed by the three 'Holy Old Girls' who have planned the service – The Revds Bridget Woollard (Ward 3, 1966–73), Judith Thompson (née Lillie, Wards 1 and 7, 1953–63) and Dorothy Green (née Steel, Wards 1 and 2, 1946–55), The crowd swells and excitement mounts as greetings and news are exchanged, while inside the church the choir of Old Girls, brought together for the occasion by Susan Walsh (Evans, Wards 1 and 3, 1959–68), are being put through their paces by the Director of Music for the day, Jean Taverner (Staff, 1963–85), supported by Catherine Ennis, organist (Ward 6, 1965–71).

The Service of Recollection and Thanksgiving, held at the parish church by kind permission of the Vicar, the Revd William Kemm, starts at 11am with the choir's confidently joyful rendering of C Villiers Stanford's familiar setting of the 'Jubilate' in B flat. This is followed by the

Organist Catherine Ennis, left, and Director of Music Jean Taverner.

Elizabeth Cairncross introducing Leanda Thornton, house parent of the Hertford house at Horsham, with the five Blues who also attended.

hymn 'Lord, for the years your love has kept and guided, urged and inspired us', and then comes Bridget's warm welcome and introduction. She speaks of the School's history at Hertford, and recognises, on behalf of all those present, how deeply important the School has been to the girls educated there. In introducing a short period of silent reflection and individual prayer for sick and absent colleagues, she reminds us that about 460 members of Christ's Hospital's past communities have their graves here.

The Service moves on through Psalm 63, to H. Lawes' traditional chant, and the first reading, from Colossians 3, vv.12–17 by the Treasurer, Susan Mitchell (née Hamilton, Wards 1 and 7, 1947–56) to the Anthem, Schubert's four part setting of 'The Lord is My Shepherd'. For those who had sung, years ago, under the direction of Mr Comley, and all his successors, this choir's delicate, controlled and sensitive rendering brings memories of long and painstaking choir practices; could we ever have sounded as good as this?

Kerren Simmonds, who chairs CHCOGA, is the main organiser of a very successful day.

The Foundation hymn is followed by 'Looking Back', a presentation of voices and memories from a variety of sources about the girls' experiences of School life, devised and led by Judith Thompson and read by Old Girls representing each generation. They include some humorous as well as some gaunt reminders of life at the School from the 1780's through to the 1970's. All are evocative of their time. In the 1930's, for example, the explanation given to a girl enquiring what was adultery? 'It's a form of self-indulgence, dear – like talking in the dormitory.'

The familiar prayer, '...the Maker and Builder of every house not made with hands...', used at the dedication of Hertford's new buildings in 1906, is followed by Stanford's triumphant settting, and Jean Taverner's masterful conducting of the 'Te Deum', sung at full throttle. Miriam McKay (née Radley, Ward 7, 1976–83) gives the second reading from Philippians 4, vv.4–9, and after prayers for the School from Dorothy Steel, Miss West (Headmistress 1942–72) reads The Charge with little diminution of her well-remembered powerful delivery. The service ends with the Hertford Grace.

Joan Newall, Secretary of CHOGA from 1958–68, being presented with a bouquet. Joan's support for the membership and her practical help has been continuous for over forty years.

Kathleen Duncan and Dr Janet Porter.

Nearly 180 of us make our way to the Richard Hale School for a reception and an excellent lunch organised by Kerren Simmonds, who chairs CHCOGA (Ward 2, 1957–66). It is another opportunity for Old Girls to enjoy their reminiscences which, judging from the noise level, are extensive and enlivening.

All of the three former Headmistresses, Miss Jean Morrison (senior mistress 1965–82 and Headmistress 1982–86), Miss Elizabeth Tucker (Headmistress 1972–82) and Miss Ruth West (Headmistress 1942–72) are guests of CHCOGA for the occasion, as is Elizabeth Cairncross (Deputy Head at Horsham). Tradition is observed with the Graces and the 'Carmen', followed by the Housey toast, proposed by Kerren Simmonds.

Elizabeth Cairncross prefaces her address by introducing the Grecians who each tell the appreciative audience of their aspirations for the future. Ellen Mayhew, for example, plans to spend eight months in China before reading Chinese at University.

Elizabeth speaks movingly about how difficult it is to leave CH – a diverse community of people who would never have met in any other way than at the School. She speaks of the support and involvement of Old Blues and Governors and of the great strength of the School, continuously evolving to meet the ever-changing needs of education and society. Elizabeth thanks Jean Hayes (Ward 6, 1944–51) and all previous editors for inviting her to contribute to the Old Girls' Newsletter each year. To great applause she is presented with a flute as her leaving present from CHCOGA. It has been her choice, she tells us, as she is studying to play the instrument.

The day is a very happy celebration of the past, and among the most successful of all the Old Girls' reunions in recent years. But as the company moves from the church to the reception and lunch, the focus of the day gradually swings from recollection of times past towards optimistic anticipation of the School's future. The Grecians' descriptions of their exciting plans inspire the older generations by the wide range of opportunities being seized by girls at Christ's Hospital in the year 2000, matched by Elizabeth Cairncross's vision and strong messages of evolution in the School's approach to education and of its capacity to respond to change in society in the 21st century.

PARENTS' DAY
SUNDAY 25 JUNE 2000

The Band rehearses Beating Retreat.

The decision has been made that this year Parents' Day and Old Blues' Day will be held as separate events and so, in comparison with other years, it appears that there are fewer parents than usual. Whether that is true or not is impossible to know. Those who do join the pupils on an overcast but mild Sunday seem relaxed and assured as they experience a slice of Housey life. Some are already waiting outside Chapel, where Full School Chapel has been held half-an-hour earlier than usual, for more time to be free to enjoy the company of family and friends.

Most people assemble in the Quad to watch the Marching Band practise their complicated routine for this year's Beating Retreat. They seem to have already reached a high degree of proficiency, but Band Master Terry Whittingham watches them closely, giving instruction or correction here, and encouragement there.

As the Band marches out through the eastern cloister thoughts turn to lunch. Some parents collect their pre-booked packed lunches from the Scout Hut, while others return to house to picnic on the lawns, perhaps to enjoy a barbecue, which has been laid on by at least one house. Some houses provide music to accompany the lunch break – most typically with the use of keyboards – but it has been known, in previous years, for harps or even full-sized pianos to be dragged out on to the front lawns.

Replete, if by now a little sticky-fingered, some parents make their way to the Octagon where an outdoor concert involving the junior pupils is staged. The Training Wind Band entertains us with marches, and the junior girls sing a medley of songs.

. . . and there are mini bus tours around the campus.

While the concert is under way Senior Prize Giving begins in the Theatre, and it is Elizabeth Cairncross, the First Deputy Head, at this her last Senior Prize Giving, who presents the prizes. Decorum is as ever preserved as pupils receive their awards, until Andrew Saunders responds to her congratulatory handshake with a peck on the cheek. Not to be outdone, Grecian and School Monitor Tom Cairncross gives his mother a generous hug as he receives his prizes. And before formalities draw to a close Mrs Dimopoulos, mother of Alex (Grecian) and Dinos (LE) presents Elizabeth with a number of gifts which have been bought with donations from parents, in due recognition for all that she has done to support the School and its pupils during her fifteen years here.

During Prize Giving, some parents have been looking at pupils' work, on display in the Design and Technology School, and in the Art School. All demonstrate work of an extraordinarily high standard of skill and flair. Others have wandered into Big School to purchase a cake from Coleridge A's cake stall, or to buy some item of Housey memorabilia,

For many parents, tea time (here, on the lawn at Lamb) provides an opportunity to enjoy a relaxing day with their children and to become better acquainted with house staff.

offered by Quadrant Events, and a few have strolled from the Quad to Peele B's produce stall in aid of The 100 Years On Appeal.

By this time the clouds have lowered and the temperature has dropped, and many houses decide to break with tradition and hold their teas inside the day rooms instead of on the lawns. Fairfields, the School's caterers, not only provide the food and drink for this, they also provide someone to dispense them, so house staff are again free to wander, mingle and chat. It may be that nothing of any particular weight is discussed, but the simple fact of staff and families being together and having time to talk is of great value at this busy, and often stressful, time of year. House parents are in a unique relationship with their charges. The pupils will probably spend longer with them than their natural parents while at School, and they may exert a greater formative influence upon them. But they are only substitutes, and the few opportunities in the year when house staff can share with parents the hopes and concerns of the pupils in their care are very important.

Most parents have left by six o'clock, but others choose to stay and accompany their children to a choral service of Family Communion in the Chapel at 6.30pm.

SPORT IN SUMMER

Cricket: House Cup Tie finals, 5 July: Lamb v Peele, with Mike Gladding umpiring. Peele are the winners.

Cricket

The general view of cricket this term was that teams under-performed and should have done a lot better. Matches that were lost might have been won if teams had taken their chances and not given so much away.

All teams turned in poor results with the exception of the Under Twelve's, so there is hope for the future. That hope was re-inforced by the success of the touring team in Barbados during the summer holiday. A full report of the cricket and netball matches there starts on page 165.

1st XI Results: Played: 13, Won 3, Drawn 1, Lost 9.

Girls' Tennis

Girls' tennis reached new heights this year, the players having spent a week in Spain for pre-season training. Unfortunately the term was excep-

Close of play on Big Side.

IST XI CRICKET TEAM
Toby Fraser-Gausden* (Captain), Martin Jackson*, Neil Green*, James Busby*, Ben Walker*, Moses Annoh, Hugo Holland, Sam Curtin, Leon Langton, Alex Woodbridge, Johnny Sheppard-Burgess.
Also played: Andrew Sheppard-Burgess, Adam Smith, Ben Smithson, Anton Dankwah.
    * Denotes Colours.

tionally short this year which meant few matches could be played and players were lost to examinations near the end of term. Nevertheless, wins were achieved against King Edward's Witley and Ardingly, before a defeat by City of London Freemen's School and the match against Bedales being rained off. The team was consistent when winning and the players developed their skills throughout the year. Even when losing they never lost their spirit.

A visiting team from Toowomba Grammar School, Queensland, on 25 June.

Under 15's
The under fifteen tennis team had a very successful start to the season, winning all four of their early matches. A convincing 6–0 defeat of Seaford was followed by wins over Ardingly and the City of London Freemen's School. Matches lost towards the end of the season all went down to the last round. For every match that the team played they always managed to get at least four victories out of a possible nine.

Under 14's
The under fourteen team only lost three matches in the whole season which was a very good start to competitive match tennis. A good sign for the future!

Ben and Daniel Allwood (left) playing James Maddren and James Maxwell in a doubles final.

Boys' tennis
The senior boys had a good season with a number of significant victories, including St John's, King Edward's Witley and an 8–1 thrashing of Seaford. The first team also performed extremely well in the Sussex League. At the conclusion of the first round they were desperately unlucky not to qualify into the winners pool, relegated to third on a count back. In the second round the team performed very creditably, Liam O'Reilly winning most of his matches. The second team didn't perform so well, only winning one of their matches.

U 13 Sussex Schools Tournament
Christ's Hospital was represented in this highly competitive inter-school event by James Maxwell and James Maddren who, after excellent performances in the early rounds, reached the semi-finals. Here they lost to a strong team from St Andrew's who went on to win the competition.

Christ's Hospital Junior Tournaments

Over 65 boys took part in singles and doubles tournaments to decide the House Champions within each year group.

The winners were:

U 15 Singles: Daniel Allwood, Mid A; U 14 Singles: Daniel Foster, La B; U 14 Doubles: Mark Davey & George Chamberlain Pe B;

U 13 Singles: Tom New, Ma B; U 13 Doubles: Tom New and Jason Marsham, Ma B

U 12 Singles: Paul Fosker, La B; U 12 Doubles: Paul Fosker and Harry Doyne-Ditmas, La B

The two best players on the Third Form and LE together with the UF semi-finalists then entered a second competition for the Hamburger Cup, donated by a former School tennis coach. In the semi-final Daniel Allwood lost by a narrow margin to James Maxwell, a Third Former, who went on to play James Maddren, another Third Former, in the final which was won by Maddren 7–5, 6–2.

Swimming

Having once been a major competitive School sport at Horsham, swimming has lapsed in more recent years, which is surprising in view of the excellent pool in the School's own Sports and Social Centre. Happily, the summer of 2000 saw a resurgence of competitive swimming and the emergence of a large squad of very keen swimmers that enabled the School to compete seriously again, with the girls performing particularly strongly to maintain their unbeaten record throughout the season.

The results were: Senior Girls won 5; lost 0. The Senior Boys won 1, lost 2.

Girls' athletics

The School participated in five inter-school meetings, involving girls from the 2nd Form through to the LE, with some excellent results.

There were many excellent individual performances throughout the term which contributed to team results; particular mention should go to Ilona Motyer, Nikki Jay and Jean King who were selected to go to the Sussex trials to compete in the discus, high jump, 100 metres and shot putt. All performed well and Ilona Motyer was chosen to represent Sussex in the discus.

GIRLS' TENNIS

1st Team: Helena Barnett-Lonergan (Captain), Sophie Naish, Anna Martinelli, Jessica Daniell, Sarah Jones, Jo Tansley-Thomas, Kate Atkinson.

Under 15 Squad: Felicity Sweatman, Jemma Charman, Annie Charman, Rosalind Hodgson, Lara Hutchings, Bill Passmore, Bella Busby.

Under 14 Squad: Thea Vernon-Jones, Georgina Culverhouse, Ilona Motyer, Polly Hughes, Jean King, Laura Freeman, Mary Clare.

BOYS' TENNIS

1st VI: Ben Allwood (Captain), Andrew Moore, Alex Dimopoulos, Liam O'Reilly, Tom Hurdman, Keith Smart.

2nd squad: Guy Matthews, Homan Mahmoudi, Ben Edwards, Nick Hoath, Josh Hollis, Walter Gilbert, James Clipsham, Tom Williams, Sam Romp.

An informal game of water polo in the Sports and Social Centre.

SENIOR GIRLS' SWIMMING SQUAD
Sarah Freeman (Captain), Rehanne Isaac (Vice Captain), Joelle Crawshaw, Elisabeth Aston, Zoe Smithers, Nikki Whitley, Elisabeth Avenell, Michelle Leong, Rowena Thornton, Jennifer Hawke, Emma Dods, Stephanie Coaten, Jessica Fleming, Emma White, Natalie Elliott, Nikki Williams, Alex Choa.

SENIOR BOYS' SWIMMING SQUAD
Toby Davies (Captain), Sacha Wolstenholme (Vice Captain), Adam Scott, Alex Wodzianski, Sam Neild, Andrew Quine, Guy Vesey, William Owen, Peter Kuo, Chris Ansell, Samir Burns, Josiah Rose, Ben Sweatman, Harry Tewkesbury.

The Band marching in the grounds of the US Ambassador's residence at Regent's Park in London, 4 July.

BEATING RETREAT
AT THE US AMBASSADOR'S RESIDENCE
4 JULY 2000

Throughout the day Americans around the world have been celebrating this 224th anniversary of the Declaration of Independence, and the American community in London is no exception. Under lowering skies caterers, floral arrangers and red-coated Masters of Ceremonies are busy on the lawns of Winfield House, the US Ambassador's official residence in Regent's Park, London, equipping a huge white marquee for the imminent arrival of 2,000 invited guests.

While the catering arrangements are being seen to, another agenda is being worked out, womb-like, in the basement, where musicians of the Marching Band are establishing themselves, deliberately out-of-sight of any guests. For they are to make a surprise appearance, as part of the formal ceremonies of the evening. The Band Captain and drum majors make a brief sortie to the open-air, shortly after their arrival at three o'clock, to view the slightly undulating, grassy terrain on which the Band is to march. They return to lead the Band out at four o'clock for a rehearsal. In half-Housey they march the course, concentrating more on their manoeuvres rather than the music, and acquainting themselves with this unusual environment.

As the familiar strains of the marches fill the air, waiters, organisers, workmen and security officers, too – apart from the marksmen on the roofs – temporarily forsake their tasks to watch this unfamiliar activity. The Band, unperturbed, marches, plays and wheels. After an hour of painstaking preparation under the vigilant eye of Band Master Terry Whittingham they are invited to enter the marquee and enjoy a Ben-and-Jerry's ice-cream, or a piece of cake; an offer which is accepted with enthusiasm.

But at six o'clock they, Cinderella-like, return to their basement and

Part of the wind section in the grounds of Winfield House, the US Ambassador's residence at Regent's Park, London, 4 July.

remain hidden while, overhead, the guests arrive. Royalty, certainly, are expected and heads of governments, as well as members of the diplomatic corps, captains of industry, leaders in *academia*, and icons of the entertainment world. As the guests assemble the musicians eat sandwiches, drink Coke and munch through crisps and cookies, before the command comes to don full-Housey and appear in the courtyard, ready, with instruments and music. Within minutes playing cards are put away, hair smoothed, stockings pulled up and Housey coats donned, before instruments of varying size and weight are manhandled through a narrow corridor, and an even narrower stairway, to the open air.

Suddenly it is serious and real as the Band march in formation, silent apart from a single drumbeat, through puzzled crowds across the lawns to their rendezvous point under the trees. Poised, they wait while the US Marine Corps present Colours to the Ambassador, Philip Lader, and then their cue comes. With typical, but extraordinary, calmness and authority James Busby, Senior Drum Major, gives the command, 'Band, by the left, quick march', the drums produce their familiar heart-stirring beats, and the air is suddenly filled with the strains of 'Washington Post'.

It is fascinating to watch the amazement of the guests as the pupils, in their ceremonial Housey uniforms, some resplendent in tiger-skins, march and play with such precision and elegance. The Ambassador gives his address and a vocalist sings the 'Star Spangled Banner' which the Band accompanies. Many continue to stand to attention, or even salute, as the National Anthem – uncertainly by some – is sung. A complex sequence of marching and countermarching follows, which is accompanied by tunes with a distinctly American theme – 'King Cotton', 'The Thunderer', 'Stars and Stripes' and 'St Louis Blues'. The display is brought to its close by the march, 'Semper Fidelis'.

The Band returns in silent and admired formation to their basement, while Louise Bigott of the Embassy staff arranges for more Ben-and-

Jerry's to be delivered. A small group of Grecians, with the Band Master, return to the lawns to be introduced to the urbane and gregarious Ambassador in his Stars-and-Stripes-festooned gazebo. One breathless Grecian thinks she had seen Ralph Fiennes; certainly Roger Moore and Sean Connery have been spotted, as well as the Duke of York and Prince Michael of Kent.

Throughout their routine the musicians perform to the highest standard, and the professionalism runs deeper. Unbidden they pack away their instruments and tidy up the basement, so that a last search only reveals the Band Captain's saxophone, still waiting to be packed into its case, and a few half-empty Coke cans.

FINALE

As operas draw to a grand finale, so the Summer term reaches a climax, as pupils and staff – already tired and strained from the exigencies of the School year – find extra strength and tolerance to cope with the most demanding time of all, the Last Week of the Year. Experienced hands know that they need to put more wine on ice, and grab sleep as and when they can, because the normal routine will be turned on its head. House parents brace themselves for a possible onslaught of pranks and other misdemeanours as pupils revel in the pre-holiday, post-exam atmosphere. For others, too, there is apprehension about leaving; especially those for whom the School has become home, father, mother and family.

The official countdown starts this year on Sunday 2 July with Full School Chapel, at which the Head Master preaches. This year he has thoughtfully moved the service from the evening to the morning, so that football fans can watch the final of Euro 2000 between France and Italy.

In the evening there is a concert in Big School entitled 'Concertos Galore', in which the School's distinguished musicians play virtuoso solo pieces to the accompaniment of an orchestra composed of pupils, staff and professional musicians. Bob Sillett, the School's Second Deputy Head reports:

Ciprian Ilie, trumpet, and Katherine Crosse, flute, two of the soloists at the 'Concertos Galore' concert, 2 July.

'This evening I had the privilege of enjoying one of those very special moments at Christ's Hospital. The Concertos Evening in Big School featured five outstanding musicians accompanied by a semi-professional orchestra: Katherine Crosse on flute; Brigita Ziferman on violin; Ciprian Ilie, trumpet; Zheni Kanani, violin; and Andrew Saunders, piano. They all produced performances of the highest quality. The audience was stunned by the sheer talent on display, which was reflected in the level of continued applause which they all received. Altogether an evening of stunning and spectacular musicianship by five very talented musicians.'

On Monday 3 July there is the Leavers' Party – staff leavers, that is, – which, in the fine weather, is held in the Head Master's enviable garden. Some staff have only been here briefly as GAP students; others have devoted almost a lifetime to the care and nurture of children at the School. Kate Atkinson pays tribute to them in her Oration, pages 137–8.

BIG BAND SUMMER CONCERT

On Wednesday 5 July, fresh from their triumphs in Regents Park, many members of the Marching Band don waistcoats and bow-ties and delight a packed Theatre audience with the Big Band Summer Concert. The evening is hot and sultry, an ideal environment in which to hear Vicky Bell's clear voice singing a Dusty Springfield medley; or Jessica Greenfield's warm rendition of 'Desifinado' and 'Nobody Does it Better'. Other vocalists, Harriett Chubb, Ciprian Ilie, Candy Rider and Guy Vesey sing Glen Miller's classic, 'Don't Sit Under the Apple Tree' with controlled swing and style. Instrumental soloists include Tom Cairncross (trombone) playing 'The Way We Were'; Guy Vesey and Ciprian Ilie joining on trumpets to play 'Spanish Flea'; and percussionists Tom Lodwick and James Maddren drumming up 'Dance with the Devil'. The Band who, by now, are in 'swing' mode, play other popular pieces with flair and confidence, and the Concert draws to a glorious, rumbustious conclusion with Blackwell & Hammer's 'Great Balls of Fire'.

LEAVERS' CONCERT

We just have time to draw breath from the Big Band concert before, on Thursday 6 July, another musical event is underway, this time the Leavers' Concert which is, in accordance with recent tradition, held in the Court Room.

One of the basic skills that all pupils learn – with more or less facility – during their time at Christ's Hospital, is that they must always be ready for a public appearance or performance; and this week is no exception. For, with instruments tuned, clothes changed and music found, the leaving musicians and singers have to appear, calm and composed, to play or sing in more classical rôles.

There are solos, duets and trios, even a quintet to play the 1st and 3rd movements of Mozart's 'Eine kleine Nachtmusik'. All give of their best. Some, like Andrew Saunders, will go on to pursue a professional musical career: he has already secured a place at The Royal College of Music on a Scholarship. Others will be content to remain very good amateurs. What is obvious and indisputable is that at this place they have not only been the recipients of the very best musical tuition; they have also had the opportunity of performing to a wide variety of people in a great range of venues. This evening's concert has an added edge; it is the beginning of the pupils' goodbyes, a way of saying 'thank you' and of giving something back in their performance to those who have given them so much.

After the break the Concert continues with more attractions, which include a violin solo by Brigita Ziferman; and contributions by singers Sarah Fairfax, Helena Barnett-Lonergan and Rejoice Amadi, with Sarah Fairfax and Lucy Gwynn singing a duet. Pippa Reveley rounds off the evening in The Quad with a candlelit performance on the marimba of Peters' 'Yellow after the rain'. It is a feast of good things, offered in gratitude by those who are leaving, and joyfully received by those who will remember them as round-eyed Second Formers, possibly difficult teenagers, and suddenly, now, mature, confident and graceful young adults.

GRECIANS' BALL

For the Grecians, Friday 7 July is dominated by preparations for the Grecians' Ball. For days, plants have been lugged and hauled from boarding houses to Big School, while coloured lights and spotlights have been rigged up and circular tables set in place for the diners. On the day itself Fairfields Catering install heated buffets and a bar, while Harry's Band sort out the balance of their instruments as multi-coloured spotlights are rigged up on the east and west block arches, and gigantic candles are set in the ground on the approach to Big School.

Some of the girls booked their hair appointments months in advance, and for them the afternoon is spent being curled and coiffured. Others employ less expensive methods of performing their toilette; but for all it is an essential part of the Grecians' Ball, this meticulous preparation – matching jewellery to shoes and nail varnish – and the actual wearing of the first and very special ball gown. The boys are hardly less particular in

Everyone looks their best for the Grecians' Ball, including invited members of staff. Neil Fleming, above, at the reception in the Head Master's garden, does it in style, and still makes time to take photographs.

their preparations in dinner-jackets or lounge-suits – or even more spectacular outfits, such as Kaeran MacDonald's magnificent ceremonial tartan.

By seven o'clock groups of Grecians have assembled outside their houses where, to the admiring glances and remarks of their house-mates, Neil Fleming photographs them in their finery. Gradually they process – some as couples, most in groups – towards the Head Master's garden, where they are offered Bucks Fizz before processing to Big School. It is an amazing sight to see pupils who, normally dressed in their traditional dark blue and white, blossom like spring flowers in dresses of the most gorgeous colours and fabrics. Tickets for the Ball have been in high demand, and only a select number of staff – with the Head Master and the Treasurer – are present. The Thai meal, miraculously provided by Fairfields on their limited catering facilities, is ably dispensed by Deputy Grecians, acting as waitresses and waiters. It is surprising that the music chosen to accompany the meal is a compilation of '50s and '60s songs, including romantic ballads and slow rock numbers by such artists as Perry Como, Andy Williams and Frank Sinatra. Today's Grecians – even the toughest rugby players among them – are romantics at heart.

By ten o'clock the meal is over and Harry's Band take the stage for the dancing. At this point it is best to draw a veil over proceedings and allow the Grecians their evening, untrammelled by prying eyes. Certainly dancing continues until the small hours and breakfast is served in the Grecians' Club from 6am. Some stay up all night, others return to house quite early to sleep, and only wake to attend Holy Communion in the Quad at 7am.

This is an odd time for all – this waiting. All week there has been the bustle of end-of-year activities, in between clothes being sorted and packed, lockers and pigeonholes cleared; long-overdue books returned to the Library. For most it is a time of great excitement; for others a time to dread. For them Christ's Hospital is a sanctuary and will be sorely missed.

Finally, early on Saturday 8 July, house teams go into overdrive to supervise the final packing and tidying-up of 'cubies' (sleeping cubicles), studies, changing rooms and dayrooms, so that all are ready for the Head Master's Assembly at 11.30am It is at this time that Dr Southern announces the appointment of next year's Senior Grecian and Second Monitors. Guy Vesey (Peele A), Chris Thomas (Thornton A) and Amy Greenhalgh (Col. A) are those chosen. Guy Vesey has also just been appointed Band Captain, and as he already has his academic buttons he has achieved the unique Grand Slam of honours. We wish him every success in his multifaceted rôle.

After a final march-in at Lunch Parade the pupils drift around until four o'clock when the Leaving Service is held. We wish them Godspeed, and fill with cups of tea, or even something stronger, the three-quarters of an hour that remains before Beating Retreat begins at six o'clock.

A breath of fresh air at the statue in the Quad.

The leavers' Bibles arrayed in Chapel under the careful eye of Jessica Pinder, Sacristan.

Nicola and Munna Mitra light the candles before the Leaving Service.

THE LEAVING SERVICE

Those who have been privileged to attend the Leaving Service at Christ's Hospital will know that it is one of the most moving and solemn events in the life of the School. And yet the highly-charged atmosphere of the Chapel at that tea-time, on the last Saturday of the School year, is not fed by sentimentality. It has much more to do with impending loss, and the recollection of shared experiences; and most face it with fortitude, bowing to the inevitable with calm acceptance. However, if there is sadness, it is alleviated considerably by the traditions which have become part of the service and therefore help to ritualise the separation.

These include the singing of the Foundation Hymn and the Hertford Grace and the silent procession of leavers in the nave and the moving hymn, 'Lord, thou hast brought us to our journey's end'. The Second Monitors and then the Senior Grecian bring up the rear of those to be called forward, and only then does the Head Master read The Charge, from the steps of the altar.

'I charge you never to forget the great benefits you have received in this place, and, in time to come, according to your means, to do all that you can to enable others to enjoy the same advantage; and remember that you carry with you, wherever you go, the good name of Christ's Hospital. May God Almighty bless you in your ways and keep you in the knowledge of His love, now and for ever.'

As ever, the occasion contains its extraordinary blend of stillness and formality shot through with constrained emotion, for the moment of departure from beloved friends has become imminent. But there is no turning back. New horizons beckon and new friendships will be forged.

159

For the moment though, as The Charge still rings in the ears, and perhaps settles in the heart, there are goodbyes to be said as autographs are written in newly-received Bibles. At this point it is best to maintain a discreet distance.

BEATING RETREAT

The evening has become cool for mid-summer as the Band, in full cry, makes its heartwarming, spine-chilling entrance under the Big School bridge to the strains of Strauss's famous 'Radetzky' march. The Quad by now has filled with parents and siblings, as well as Old Blues of all ages, intermixed with pupils and staff. Some occupy formal seating set in rows in front of Dining Hall. Others perch on ledges or lean against archways. Still others have brought picnic tables and chairs and, with an air of dogged determination, defend their pitches around the Quad. No-one is really supervising at this stage.

Daniel Sandham practising at the Chapel organ before the Leaving Service.

All eyes are fixed on the Band as they march and counter-march with practised skill and precision, moving with apparent ease from quick march to slow, through ellipses, circles and star formations, to the well-loved marches, by composers as diverse as Strauss and Sousa. We listen to 'New Colonial', 'El Abanico', 'Stars and Stripes', 'Star Trek', 'Royal Standard', 'Imperial Echoes', 'On the Square', and 'Semper Fidelis', before coming to Beating Retreat itself as we hear and watch the expertise of the drummers under the leadership of Pippa Reveley. The 'Raiders March',

Pippa Reveley, nearest to the camera, will lead the side drummers in their exhibition.

The Marching Band impresses, as always, by its performance.

Kaeran MacDonald plays the pipes from the roof of the west archway.

'Circle of Life' (from *The Lion King*), and 'St Louis Blues' continue the marches before Ben Allwood plays a most moving arrangement of the Last Post, which is this time incorporated into an arrangement of the hymn, 'The day thou gavest, Lord, is ended', followed by 'Dark Island' played on the bagpipes from above the west archway by Kaeran MacDonald, wearing the full dress of a Scottish piper, before the National Anthem. All too quickly the hour passes and the Band disappears beneath the eastern cloister arch to the sound of 'Sussex by the Sea' and 'Auld Lang Syne', played as a tribute to Band leavers. Suddenly it is all over. One feels shocked and numb.

Time to go.

CHAPTER EIGHT
THE END OF THE SCHOOL YEAR

ERM IS OVER, but School activity does not cease. Some of the staff are involved in holiday activities with pupils; Quadrant Events are busy with many and various bookings for the facilities in the School over the holiday period.

The advance party for the Scout Camp at Barnswood in Staffordshire leave the day after the end of term; there is Old Blues' Cricket Week starting on Sunday, and on the same day the CCF Army camp begins at Longmoor and the Duke of Edinburgh Gold Award adventurers leave for the Lake District.

In School many of the staff are completing end-of-term reports in time for tutors, house parents and the Head Master to add their comments.

PGL Travel arrive to set up their programme for the holiday. They bring 3,471 children and staff to the School for a variety of recreational projects in the holiday. Quadrant Events have arranged another seventeen events by various groups, and there will be several weddings in Chapel.

THE GRECIANS' RESIDENCES

It had been hoped – indeed many other factors depended on it – that the Grecians' residences would be ready for occupation by both pupils and house staff by the beginning of the Michaelmas term, 2000. But it becomes apparent by the middle of the Summer term that this target is not going to be met: at best, just the attached staff houses will be ready. This is a devastating blow. So much had depended on the availability of these buildings and now Sean O'Boyle, House Master of Thornton A, a member of the Maths Department, who also serves as chief statistician, goes into overdrive to see just how the Grecians can be accommodated throughout the School until the new residences are complete.

An ingenious solution is quickly found. Although Lamb (A & B) has been emptied to begin the process of refurbishment, it has not yet been gutted, and so it will, temporarily, accommodate a majority of the boy Grecians. The rest can be accommodated – in twos and threes – in their former houses, which will also provide much-valued support as they adjust to their new-found situation of being 'all-through'. The girl Grecians can stay in their present houses.

In the course of the year the decision was made that, from September 2000, the boys' houses would contain all the year groups, apart from the Grecians. The separation of 'junior' and 'senior' boys' houses, which has obtained since 1966, has come to seem impractical and undesirable.

The Marching Band at its final ceremony of the School year, Beating Retreat, 8 July.

163

The Steward, Philip Obeney, centre, explains some of the challenges encountered in the construction of Grecians' West as HRH the Duke of Gloucester turns to face the camera. Houseparents Marlene and Neil Fleming are on the left. On the right are the Head Master and Charles Forrester of the professional project management team, Gardiner and Theobald.

Considerable upheaval is needed to distribute suitable numbers of juniors among the former senior houses and to re-introduce seniors to former junior houses.

Some, both staff and pupils, initially expressed concern at this move, especially those senior boys' houses which have developed a clubby cosiness, but the decision is accepted with grace. The plans are carried out by the house masters with even-handed fairness and real altruism. Adjustments in attitude and practice are required by everyone, but there is a consensus of belief that this is in the best interests of the pupils and staff and reverts to a pattern which was successfully followed for many

The Duke also meets Ken Leadbeater, Head of Design and Technology, below. Crossing the back asphalt, below left, on the way to visit the D & T School, accompanied by the Treasurer, the Head Master, the Lord Lieutenant Mr Hugh Wyatt, and Supt. James Dale.

years in the School, and which matches the successful pattern within the girls' houses.

Work still progresses on the Grecians' residences and in October our President, HRH The Duke of Gloucester, will visit the School, ostensibly to open them officially, but in fact more simply to go on a tour of inspection. The buildings are to be finally completed during the Christmas holiday, 2000. The delays have, of course, been difficult for both staff and pupils, but the aim from the beginning of the project has been to build and finish to a high standard so that the Grecians' residences will last as long and look as good as the original Aston Webb design.

BARBADOS SPORTS TOUR – JULY 2000

For many of the staff the summer holiday is only part vacation, especially this year for Howard and Marjorie Holdsworth. They have spent the past two years organising and raising funds for a cricket and netball tour in Barbados. Howard reports:

After months of preparation fifteen girls and fourteen boys embarked on an ambitious, two-week combined sports tour to Barbados to challenge the best teenage netballers and cricketers on the island. The coaches were more than a little anxious as the cricketers had not enjoyed a successful home season and the netballers were going to have to pit their skills out of season, after just ten weeks of training once a week.

Everyone returned elated following a highly successful tour. The girls won 7 out of 10 matches and the boys won 4 games out of 6. These statistics are all the more remarkable when put into context: there were nine other schools from England on sporting tours in Barbados at the same time as us. Some were participating in the Sir Garfield Sobers cricket festival; others were playing against local schools and clubs as we were. No other cricket side won more than two matches out of nine, and none won a match against a Bajan school, only defeating other English schools. The three other schools playing netball, along with the Cambridge University side, recorded only a single victory each.

All the girls and coaches soon came to terms with the fact that the set-up in Barbados is much less organised than in the UK; some matches were cancelled or delayed at very little notice, but the games that did take place were evenly contested and the delays only served to spur our girls on to greater things. They all benefited from the coaching of Mrs Rowland-Jones and from the ever-encouraging Peter Carter who, with his wife Caroline, were invaluable assets on the tour.

Often the girls were pitted against highly skilful and athletic individuals who ranged in age from 13 to 30. The best performance actually came in a game in which we were defeated by 27–23. We led the adult side 7–4 after the first quarter. Just two days earlier they had defeated the Cambridge University 1st team with ease. The girls could not quite compete with the fierce intensity to overhaul one of the strongest club sides in Barbados, where netball dominates all other sports in the women's arena. The most exciting win was when the girls defeated another adult side under floodlights at the National Stadium by 31 goals to 29 in a nail-biting affair.

Although it is invidious to pick out individuals in a team game, special

Another goal! Natalie Williams, Sophie Naish, Sandra Bamfo and Agnes Rothon practising while waiting for the opposition to arrive.

Neil Green batting, on the way to victory against Coleridge and Parry School, Barbados.

mention must be given to Sophie Naish, the captain of the squad, for the exemplary way in which she carried out her duties both on and off the court. The most vociferous and extreme of motivators would have to be Jo Tansley-Thomas, for whom, along with all the other leavers, this tour was a fitting climax to their School sporting careers.

Tour Party: Sophie Naish (captain), Helena Barnett-Lonergan, Nicky Batchelor, Rehanne Isaac, Agnes Rothon, Jo Tansley-Thomas, Gabby Maselino, Alice Holdsworth, Anna Lewis, Sarah Moon, Nicky Whitley, Sandra Bamfo, Flora Nabena, Emma White, Natalie Williams.

Results:

	Played 10	Lost 3	Won 7
1st VII beat	Emmerton	29–11	
2nd VII beat	Emmerton	29–11	
1st VII lost to	BA Insurance Ballers	23–27	
2nd VII lost to	Pinelands	14–25	
1st VII beat	M and M Ballers	27–12	
2nd VII beat	Combined Primary	29–12	
1st VII lost to	Eden Stars	20–29	
2nd VII beat	Mpact Haggatt Hall	31–29	
1st VII beat	Banks Spurs I	32–9	
2nd VII beat	Banks Spurs II	31–10	

The cricketers were off to a good start with a fine win over North Star CC in a 35-over game, the regular length of matches in Barbados, thanks to some sparkling bowling and catching. The very next day we suffered a heavy defeat against a select Barbados Under-19 side. We lost Ben Walker and Alex Woodbridge through injury, but went on to win a thrilling game against the highly-rated Lodge School at the end of the first week.

In our next game we defeated the spirited Coleridge and Parry XI in front of the Treasurer, Susan Mitchell and her husband, John, in an excellent match. Unfortunately we were unable to reproduce our form the next day when we lost to Alleyne School by a narrow margin. Only Andrew Sheppard-Burgess, with his highest 1st XI score of 41, looked at ease.

We won the final game of the tour comfortably with a most satisfying team performance. Ben Walker bowled quite beautifully early on to take four wickets and Toby handled the bowlers well so that five others achieved success. Martin Jackson, who had become fond of Bajan wickets, and Hugo Holland made excellent use of a good batting track by adding 101 for the first wicket. Sam Curtin finished the tour with one of the biggest sixes you could imagine.

The team: Toby Fraser-Gausden (capt.), James Busby, Martin Jackson, Adam Smith, Hugo Holland, Moses Annoh, Andrew Sheppard-Burgess, Johnny Sheppard-Burgess, Ben Walker, Sam Curtin, Neil Green, Leon Langton, Alex Woodbridge, Richard Hawke.

Results:

		Played 6	Won 4	Lost 2
C.H		132 all out	North Star C.C.	95 all out
		(Johnny S-Burgess 3–19, Alex Woodbridge 3–26)		
Combined Island Under 19 XI				
		186–6 i.c.	C.H	96 all out
C.H		217–7 i.c.	Lodge School	190 all out
		(Neil Green 68, Martin Jackson 63)	(Alex Woodbridge 4–42)	
Coleridge and Parry School				
		175–7 i.c.	C.H	176–7
		(Martin Jackson 3–40)	(Martin Jackson 73)	
Alleyne School				
		148 all out	C.H	116 all out
		(Martin Jackson 4–21)	(Andrew Sheppard-Burgess 41)	
Garrison Secondary School				
		114 all out	C.H.	120–2
		(Ben Walker 4–16)	(Martin Jackson 67)	

Howard and Marjorie Holdsworth with Old Blue Jo Broomes, right, at a barbecue party for the whole tour party hosted by the three Old Blues resident on Barbados and held at the home of Michael and Ann Seakins.

As well as providing an excellent opportunity to play sport for a concentrated period, the tourists were also able to enjoy many other memorable activities and excursions. The highlights have to be the coach tour of the island with the very warm and generous Sheldon Branch, a native of Barbados who lit up the life of everyone; the day trip on the catamaran, when we had the opportunity to chill out, swim with turtles and an amazing variety of fish over coral reefs and wrecks; and the excursion to the Malibu rum factory followed by sumptuous food and water sports.

There was opportunity, too, to immerse oneself in the culture of another country, whether dancing to the rhythm of the local steel bands or at the extraordinary fish fry at Oistins Bay or worshipping at the open-air People's Church. We also met two Old Blues on the island: Michael Seakins and his wife Ann, along with Jo Broomes, at a barbecue which Michael and Ann kindly hosted. It was an evening that was greatly enjoyed and hugely appreciated by all. We also met the third Old Blue resident, Bob Showan, at the airport shortly before our departure . . . the drinks for all were most welcome.

The German Grecians' party relaxing during their study visit to Munich in October.

The pupils are indeed very fortunate to have such expert coaches as Peter Carter and Les Lenham, whose early morning shadow batting sessions caused many an eye to flutter. Caroline Carter was a very valuable and unflustered netball umpire. Sean Davey made a tremendous contribution with the boys' fitness and motivation, and shared the umpiring with the ever-bubbly Ken Suttle. His wife, Val, was invaluable as she massaged and mended broken bodies and spirits in her rôle as the tour nurse. Peter Sands came as the tour photographer, as well as helping Marjorie Holdsworth with ferrying people to and from the various venues.

OTHER END-OF-YEAR EVENTS

In August the Venture Scouts, with Deputy Grecians and Grecians, are on a tour to Poland; UF in the German Department visit Bacharach. The Chaplaincy take ten pupils from the GE, Deputy Grecians and Grecians to visit Taizé in Burgundy, France, and there is another journey for members of the CCF and Duke of Edinburgh's Gold Award to the Lake District. There is more: the Geography Department have organised a field trip for Deputy Grecians to the Cévennes, in France, and the Biology

The cast of As You Like It *and supporters in Bamberg during their German tour in December.*

Adrian Hill at the peak of his 4,274 metres climb in the Bernese Oberland in July.

Department run a field trip in Bideford, North Devon. Even though the Barbados tour might have been the highlight of the end-of-year activities there were others equally as important to those who took part. To identify a few of them: in July Adrian Hill scaled a 4,274-metre mountain in the Bernese Oberland which involved six hours of ice and rock climbing. Early in August the cycle touring club toured in the Carpathian Mountains, and in October the German Grecians went on a study tour to Munich. Both these events were under the leadership of Frank Pattison. In December, after highly successful performances in the theatre at the School, the cast of *As You Like It* toured in Germany.

PUBLIC EXAMINATION RESULTS

The Summer 2000 A-level results (page 129), announced in August, showed a 98 per cent pass rate and, perhaps even more significantly, the largest proportion – 63 per cent – ever of passes at grade A or B. Twelve candidates achieved three A grades or better; seven of those offered places at Oxbridge gained their grades, and everyone hoping for a university place was successful, mainly at that of their first-choice.

At GCSE the 95 per cent pass rate – grades A to C – was a record. Eight candidates had the distinction of nine passes at Grade A or A*.

The Head Master remarked that overall the results seemed to have matched the capabilities of the candidates pretty accurately, which (even in the era of league tables) is the only measure of a school which really matters.

LEAVING BLUES, JULY 2000

Some of the summer's leavers will take a gap year and a few will go straight into employment. The majority have decided on higher education at these universities or colleges. This list includes a small number of 1999 leavers who have taken a gap year before going up to university.

Bath	Clare Gladding	Biochemistry
Belfast, Queen's	Ian Baxter	English/Philosophy
Birmingham	Vinay Patel	Accounting / Finance
Bradford	Jonathan Moore	Peace Studies
Bristol	Edward Ashley	Economics / Accounting
	Angel Crocker	Theology /Religious Studies
	Kimberley Miller	Geography
	Lucy Morgan	Medicine
Brunel	Paul Carter	Music/Drama
	Leslie Copland	Product Design
	Isobel Fraser-Underhill	Communication/Media Studies
	Kaeran MacDonald	Industrial Design/Technology
Cambridge		
Girton	Katherine Crosse	Veterinary Medicine
Magdalene	Christian Ashby	Natural Sciences
St Catherine's	Daniel Chandler	Archaeology/Anthropology

CITY	Thomas Trewick	Sociology
COVENTRY	Martin Jackson	Industrial Product Design
DE MONTFORT	Nicola Smith	Management of Design & Innovation
DURHAM	Mary Ampah	Chemistry
	Katherine Atkinson	Economics with French
	James Busby	Geology
	Rebecca Cook	Archaeology
	Kate Cordery	English Literature
	Victoria O'Gorman	Chemistry
	Gemma Quinn	Arabic with Mid-East & Islamic Studies
EAST ANGLIA	Sophie Adams	English Literature with Creative Writing

EDGE HILL COLLEGE OF HIGHER EDUCATION

	David Hobbs	Field Biology & Habitat Management
EDINBURGH	Isabel Chandler	Chinese
	Adrian Hill	Chemistry with Industrial Experience
	Stephen Robson	Psychology
	Nicholas Rumball	Mathematics/Statistics
EXETER	Philip Firmin	Economics/Finance with European Study
	Toby Fraser-Gausden	Mathematics with Accounting
	Leslie Lubwama	French
HERTFORDSHIRE	Hayley Lashbrook	Sociology
KENT	Una Kosanovic	Social Anthropology with French
KINGSTON	Thomas Jeremy	Business Studies
LEEDS	Edward Hayes	Chemistry
LIVERPOOL	Shaun Rosier	Marine Biology
LONDON		

Imperial College

	Sarah Freeman	Materials Science & Engineering

King's College

	Elizabeth Aston	Nursing Studies
	Alice Chubb	Latin with English

London School of Economics

	Huw Aveston	Geography
	Kasparas Jurgelionis	Economics
	In Tae Lee	Economics

Queen Mary and Westfield

	Nicola Batchelor	Medicine

School of African and Oriental Studies

	Claire Goodridge	Politics
	Rehanne Isaac	History of Art
	Ellen Mayhew	Social Anthropology/Chinese

University College

	Jimena Bargados	Spanish/History of Art
	Petrut Gogalniceanu	Medicine
	Joanna Tansley-Thomas	Anthropology/Geography
	Brigita Ziferman	Economics

London Institute		
	Alex Dimopoulos	Product Design
LOUGHBOROUGH	Andrew Moore	Economics
MANCHESTER	Joseph Dormer	Pharmacology with Industrial Experience
	Hannah Shaw	Biochemistry
MIDDLESEX	Daniel Pearce	Business Studies & Management
NEWCASTLE	Peter Marquis	Electronic Engineering
	Bryony Passmore	Zoology
OXFORD		
Corpus Christi	Tom Cairncross	Modern History
St Edmund Hall	Sophie Naish	Classics/Modern Languages
St John's	Lucy Gwynn	Modern History
OXFORD BROOKES	Sarah Jones	Environmental Policy/Sciences
PLYMOUTH	John Noble	Surf Science/Technology
READING	Joelle Crawshaw	English Language / Literature
SHEFFIELD	Tracey Allen	Hispanic/Business Studies
	Benjamin Edwards	Mathematics
	Natalie Thomas	Philosophy
SOUTHAMPTON	Sophie Channer	Aerospace Engineering
	Mikael Glazier	Chemistry
	Sabrina Hawkins	English with Psychological Studies
	Erin Lettis	Environmental Sciences
ST ANDREWS	Jessica Daniell	Mathematics with French
	Thomas Hurdman	Environmental Sciences/ Marine Biology
STIRLING	Victoria Bell	Human Resource Management
	Peter Newman	Politics/Philosophy/ Economics
	Richard Smith	Human Resource Management
SURREY ROEHAMPTON	Charlotte Bull	Primary Education with Sciences
SUSSEX	Douglas Edwards	Environmental Science with European Studies
UNIVERSITY OF WALES INSTITUTE		
	Hayley Bridgman	International Hospitality Management
UNIVERSITY OF WEST OF ENGLAND		
	Timothy Gilroy	Valuation/Estate Management
	Matthew Smith	Business Information Systems
WARWICK	Adam Parmenter	History
	Ryan Pickett	Mathematics
YORK	Joel Jardine	English/Writing for Perfomance

171

CHAPTER NINE
THE CHARITABLE FOUNDATION

T HIS BOOK HAS TRIED TO CAPTURE the work and atmosphere of the School in 2000, as well as describing the opportunities afforded to its pupils. But Christ's Hospital is more than a leading independent school – it is also one of the UK's foremost educational charitable foundations. The book would therefore be incomplete without reference to the work of the team which has a dual rôle, first, in managing the charitable aspects of Christ's Hospital and, secondly, in providing some of the services which enable the School to meet the charitable objectives, summarised in the Mission Statement (page 17) and the Council of Almoners' strategic aims (page 216).

The indivisibility of the School and the charitable Foundation – indeed, their close inter-dependence – is recognised by all who serve Christ's Hospital. Nevertheless, in practical terms the Clerk of Christ's Hospital, Michael Simpkin, is the Chief Executive Officer of the Charitable Foundation and he works in close liaison with the Head Master as well as with the Treasurer, Deputy Chairman and Chairmen of Council committees.

THE RÔLE OF THE CLERK AND HIS STAFF

The main mission of the Clerk and his staff is to advise and support the Council of Almoners, as Trustees of the charity, and, by so doing, to facilitate the achievement of Christ's Hospital's primary charitable objective of providing a boarding education, in a Christian institution, to children in need. The work of the charitable Foundation focuses not only on the present but also notably extends into planning for the future. This work is carried out with due regard to UK charity, fiscal, educational and other statutory requirements. Frequent changes and fresh legislation ensure that the fulfilment of this clear objective is more of a moving target than it might at first seem; it is in fact a complex task requiring a skilled and professional team.

A large range of tasks – some of them shared with the School – is entailed. Alongside the contribution to policy making and strategic planning sit the application of parameters of need set by Council to the admission of pupils to the School, as well as the prime functions described below. For many years the Clerk and his team were located at 26 Great Tower Street in the City of London. A Christ's Hospital badge on the wall still commemorates the site but in 1987 the London Counting House team moved to a modern redbrick building at the School, behind the Court Room and to the side of Dining Hall.

Historically, the Clerk has, more often than not, been an Old Blue. Michael Simpkin is an exception, and in appointing him in 1998 the

Michael Simpkin, OBE, the Clerk of Christ's Hospital.

Tony Hogarth-Smith, Administration Officer, left, with Finance Officer Geoffrey Wheeler in the Treasurer's office.

Council secured a man with wisdom and commitment to the causes held dear by Old Blues, and with a wealth of relevant experience from an administrative background. Of course it is a team effort and there is a full supporting cast of some sixty-five, of whom nearly half maintain the estate buildings. A key member of this team is Vicky Haigh, the Clerk's secretary, who co-ordinates the protocol and organisation of all the major civic and ceremonial events in which the School is involved throughout the year.

FINANCE

Under the leadership of the Finance Officer, Geoff Wheeler, the Finance Department typifies the inter-relationship between the charitable Foundation and the School. The Department has responsibility for the control and monitoring of the Foundation's income-generating assets that subsidise the School on a scale which makes it unique. Christ's Hospital's substantial investment property and land assets are not typical of the charity sector and provide diverse challenges. The Department provides the usual range of day-to-day accounting services, such as payroll, for all parts of Christ's Hospital; parental contributions are collected; specific charitable trusts are controlled; and separate Trustees for the Christ's Hospital Pension Scheme are supported and advised.

ADMINISTRATION

Initial legal advice, health and safety, personnel and training, insurance and the management of the Christ's Hospital Museum, treasures and archives help to explain why Tony-Hogarth-Smith enjoys the ubiquitous title of Administration Officer. He, too, has a wide-ranging job portfolio which exemplifies the mix of day-to-day service with the longer-term aspects of charity management. The Scheme of Administration approved by the Charity Commissioners in 1990 is the instrument of governance which requires regular interpretation and updating and the Administration Officer is the immediate link to the Commissioners. Tony also provides secretarial services and support to the Court, the Council of Almoners, the Education Committee and various Committees and sub-Committees.

As part of his responsibilities for the Christ's Hospital Museum, Tony works closely with the Curator, Nick Plumley, and the Archivist, Rhona Mitchell, in the organisation and development of the Museum and its archives.

Carol Blackwell, Marketing Officer, in the Court Room with Mr S Swaine of Lockyear Motors, Horsham, a guest at a community visit.

MARKETING

The all-important task of raising awareness of Christ's Hospital is shared by several people and includes nurturing the reputation of the charity, the promotion of widespread interest amongst potential pupils, families and donors, fostering the historic links with the City of London, and maintaining communications with Governors, Old Blues and the local and wider Christ's Hospital community.

Carol Blackwell, the Marketing Officer, takes much of this responsibility and with her colleague, Celia Bryant, develops and implements initiatives to spread awareness about the unique ethos of Christ's Hospital across the country. These include open days for parents of prospective pupils; primary school induction days for head teachers, so that they can observe classes and talk with staff; community visits for representatives of local businesses, parish councils, clubs and associations; and the development of links with Directors of Education, journalists and the City of London.

Those taking part in a community visit cover a broad spectrum of local government, the professions, trades and other interests. Here the group, accompanied by the Head Master, Ian Humble, Operations Director of Christ's Hospital Enterprises Ltd and Carol Blackwell, walk in front of the Library to the Riches Lecture Theatre for a presentation on the ethos and rôle of the School in the year 2000.

In another example of shared tasks, the Head Master and the Admissions Officer, Patricia Gilbert, take a leading part in regional educational exhibitions and present 'roadshows' in a variety of the least affluent regions of the country to spread awareness of the School. The effects of such campaigns may be hard to measure, but perhaps the fact that the number of candidates sitting the entrance examination has risen from 165 in 1995 to 310 in 2000 gives a clue to the usefulness of this work.

The admissions process and the rôle of the Admissions Officer are described on pages 81–5.

MAINTAINING THE FABRIC

The grandeur of Aston Webb and Ingress Bell's 1900 layout and architecture of the Horsham School site, now Grade II Listed, rarely fails to impress visitors and parents, or to seem overwhelming to new second formers, before they have had time to develop and appreciate the feelings of historic place and welcome space which they will share with generations of Blues. Thirty-one major buildings, some physically linked, date back to the early 1900's; the New Science School opened in 1930; extensions were added to the backs of the sixteen Avenue boarding houses in the 1960s; the Arts Centre was built in the 1970s; the Sports and Social Centre opened in 1987, and several smaller buildings appeared in between times. Additionally, residential accommodation on site is provided for some 159 teaching and support staff. Now, in 2000, come the two new Grecians' residences and the start of the Masterplan, described on pages 78–81.

The challenge of maintaining the fabric of this large stock of buildings falls to the Steward, Philip Obeney. It has been a formidable task for generations and especially in times of financial difficulties. Inevitably, and rightly, meeting the expanding educational and social requirements of the School population has received financial priority. However, in proceeding with the 21st century Masterplan, equal consideration is given to the preservation of the stock of 100 year old buildings. Year 2000 is thus

Part of the Master Plan for the modernisation of the School results in the erection of temporary classrooms in the Arts Quad. These came as pre-fabricated units on low-loaders and were lifted into position by crane.

Mark Curtis, Partnership Director, with the Steward, Philp Obeney in the Court Room.

significant for the establishment of a detailed rolling programme for the refurbishment of the basic fabric and services of all the old buildings – ranging from roofs and rainwater goods to pointing, power supply and plumbing. Long-term budgets have been established and ring-fenced to enable this work to be carried forward, and for future maintenance requirements for new and modernised buildings to be added to the programme as they are completed. 'The balancing act of repairing and maintaining the fabric without interfering with the efficient running of the School is certainly a challenge,' says Philip. 'The new projects that form the Masterplan add another layer of complexity that has to be handled carefully and sensitively. This is a challenge that I relish and enjoy.'

THE CHRIST'S HOSPITAL PARTNERSHIP

The Partnership, headed by Mark Curtis, fosters and develops relationships with Old Blues world wide and with other supporters of the School, such as City Livery Companies and grant-making trusts, to keep them aware of current and future plans. The underlying objective is, of course, to secure continuing financial support through Donation Governorships, legacies, appeals, and for specific projects of particular interest to major donors.

The most immediate project in 2000 is The 100 Years On Appeal, described on pages 192–3, for which the Partnership provides extensive support to the Treasurer and the Old Blue Appeal Team, and advises donors on the most tax-efficient methods of making gifts. At School, Mark collaborates with physics teacher Andy Williams, who is co-ordinating Housie's own activities for the Appeal. During Lent term, each house is creating its own fundraising opportunities, which range from a five-a-side pay and play soccer match to the kidnapping of a (willing) Almoner, who is held to ransom. Pupils' efforts continue in the Easter

Ian Humble, Operations Director of Christ's Hospital Enterprises Ltd, includes the running of the School shop amongst his responsibilities. The shop sells sports clothing and equipment at competitive prices, as well as a range of Housey memorabilia.

holiday with their individual sponsored ideas, and activities wind up with major fundraising events in the Summer term.

Mark is supported by four executives: Anne Sartain organises house reunions for Old Blues and is production editor for the twice-yearly newsletter *Housey!*; Wendy Dicker works with trusts and Livery Companies and assists groups of Old Blues in forming collective Donation Governorships; Judith Law develops the database of supporters; and Janet Peckham keeps the office wheels turning. Together with Marketing Manager Carol Blackwell, the Partnership is also responsible for the Christ's Hospital website.

'We are always looking at how we can appeal to Old Blues across the age ranges,' says Mark. 'One recent innovation is the Young Old Blues scheme. Recent leavers are unable to afford the £13,065 currently required to become a Donation Governor, but they can build up a fund over the years and when they reach the midway point, we fix a future rate of contributions, regardless of the increase in education costs.'

CHRIST'S HOSPITAL ENTERPRISES LTD

The *Mail on Sunday*, on 27 April 1997, featured a report quite accurately headed 'The Richest School in Britain'. *The Sunday Times* in July 1999 and the *Financial Times* supplement in March 2000 ran similar pieces, albeit projecting the balance between wealth and benevolence more appropriately. The richest school it is, but, of greater if less sensationally newsworthy relevance, it is also the most philanthropic. Statistics which demonstrate the unique benevolence of Christ's Hospital are given on pages 219–20.

Nevertheless, the income from these riches can support only a fraction of those who need help; Christ's Hospital would like to do more. And so, as in most other independent schools, the facilities are exploited commercially through a trading company which covenants all its profits to the charity. Ian Humble, Operations Director, points out, 'Christ's Hospital is an academic institution, so not all commercial ideas are appropriate, but we aim to take Christ's Hospital into the local business communities.'

Although CHE Ltd is not part of the Foundation, the Clerk serves as its Chairman. The company has four operating divisions, employing some seventy staff who report to the Operations Director. Bluecoats Sports and Social Centre offers an extensive range of indoor sports and swimming activities through a members club. The Centre has a registered crèche and its café caters snacks and light meals for up to eighty people. During School holidays Bluecoats is booked by such organisations as the All England netball team, Sussex County Cricket Club and the British Pentathlon Association.

Quadrant Events, run by Mandy Russell-Price, co-ordinates the hire of School buildings for conferences, exhibitions, sporting events, weddings and for residential courses during the holidays, and Sporting Blues, led by Commercial Manager Annie Daniell, runs the School shop and mail-order business, both selling sports kit and a wide range of Housey memorabilia. Annie is engaged in developing new projects for CHE Ltd and she also arranges the Verrio tours for up to 20 groups of 50 visitors during the year. They come to inspect the famous painting in Dining Hall, visit the Museum, watch Band Parade and talk to the pupils who conduct their tour of the School.

Bp Media Design Group's manager, Jonathan McCulloch, and his team offer a graphic design and typesetting service for the School and outside commercial customers, and a website design service. The portfolio of customers is growing and includes some household name clients.

CHE Limited has expanded to become a recognised leader in the field of commercial development within the independent school sector and assists other schools with commercial ventures. Its profits benefit Christ's Hospital and, in addition, it saves the charity some £350,000 a year by carrying the overhead costs of the Sports and Social Centre and Bp Media Design.

One of many reminders of Royal patronage.

CHAPTER TEN
THE OLD BLUE COMMUNITY

Three distinguished Old Blues and former soldiers enjoy Founder's Day Dinner at Drapers' Hall, 12 October 1999. Left to right: General Sir Garry Johnson, KCB, OBE, MC, John M. Gillham, MC, KCSG, FCIOB and Lt General Sir Michael Gray, KCB, OBE, DL.

THE GREAT SPIRIT OF COMMUNITY which is engendered in most of the pupils during their time at Housie expresses itself in a number of ways after they leave the School. Some retain the close friendships they formed at School; others make their way in the world in the spirit of independence which characterises Old Blues and only return later in life to renew friendships and support the School. Indisputably, Christ's Hospital enjoys exceptional support from its Old Blues and this is greatly valued and fostered. Old Blues and Donation-Governors are welcomed to the School at many events during the year but it is mainly through the numerous Old Blue organisations that shared interests are pursued and lifelong friendships sustained.

CLUBS AND SOCIETIES

There are some seventy two associations, clubs and societies in existence in the year 2000 for Old Blues and other members of the Christ's Hospital community. Historical notes on the major Old Blue Clubs and Societies are on pages 212–3.

THE AMICABLE SOCIETY OF BLUES

On election to the Society of Amicables, each of the brethren receives a medal engraved with his name and date of enrolment.

The records and Minutes of the Amicable Society support its claim to have met continuously since 1629. From the beginning of the twentieth century these convivial meetings have been held three times a year, usually at the Innholders' Hall in the City of London, on Audit Night in February, in November to mark the accession of Queen Elizabeth I and on St George's Day to commemorate the Founder.

The present Society is limited to forty male full members, with a number of additional honorary members. Most 'brethren' are Blues of distinction; a few are non-Blues who have demonstrated a particular devotion to Christ's Hospital. Brethren proceed each year to the Presidency by seniority of election. Other officers include a Treasurer, currently Arnold Allen, and a Secretary, Richard Pearey, who in February succeeded Ian Allan, Father of the Society and Secretary since 1972. Geoffrey Shelley is the Secretary of the Amicable Foundation.

In November 1999 the President, Brother John Gale, chairs the last dinner of his memorable year of office, handing over the presidency to his successor, Brother Norman Jacobs, for the ensuing twelve months. During this period guests include the Treasurer, the Head Master and the Clerk, who address the Society about current aspects of the School and Foundation. Brethren are expected to bring guests to all dinners, which are noted for their robust, but not ribald, behaviour. Brethren 'brawl' with

Brethren and guests at the most recent of the Amicables' rare Ladies Nights, on 23 April 1999, included (left to right) James Forbes, immediate Past Treasurer of Christ's Hospital, John Gillham, Lady Shelagh Nichols, Sir Richard Nichols and Joel Jardine, Senior Grecian 1998–99. Brethren wear their Amicables' medals on pale blue ribbons until they have passed the Chair, when their medals are gilded and dark blue ribbons are substituted.

each other and the President throughout the dinner and are frequently, even usually, fined for so doing in 'bottles' – now, alas, devalued to a nominal £3. All fines accrue to the Amicable Foundation for the benefit of the School. At their best – worst – dinners are as good-naturedly boisterous as that of 1629 undoubtedly was.

John Gale, right, Amicables' President for 1999, instals his successor Norman Jacobs on Audit Night, 7 February 2000.

THE BENEVOLENT SOCIETY OF BLUES

The BSB, founded in 1824 at the instigation of the Amicables, and now a registered charity, is directed by a volunteer Board. The Society exists to help those educated or employed at Christ's Hospital and their dependents throughout their life, in times of need, hardship or distress, and to present children of Old Blues to the School.

BSB membership is open to Old Blues (and to others as non-voting 'Friends of the BSB') with a minimum annual subscription of £15. The Society has over 1,000 members and many remain in membership all their lives, seeing this as a meaningful way to respond to The Charge (p. 159).

The BSB's President is the Treasurer of Christ's Hospital, Mrs Susan Mitchell. Steve Webb is Chairman, and Treasurer David Marriott was succeeded by Richard McGregor on 25 January 2000. A full-time Secretary, Mrs Jane Hitchcock, working from an office adjacent to the Counting House, administers the charity, and is always keen to know of any Old Blue or former member of staff in need of assistance. Apart from maintaining membership records and handling applications for assistance, Jane's duties include organising committee meetings and the Annual General Meeting, held in London in January 2000. A meeting which, in earlier years, was strictly routine has now evolved into another of those delightful social evenings beloved of the Old Blue community, when the formal meeting is followed by a well-attended dinner, where friendships can be renewed, experiences shared and networking undertaken in a convivial atmosphere.

The BSB has assets of some £2.4 million at 30 June 2000, of which almost £2 million is represented by income-producing investments and £300,000 by outstanding loans to beneficiaries.

Details of the Society's grants and loans are on page 220.

The Board of the BSB meets in the Court Room.

THE CHRIST'S HOSPITAL CLUB

The objectives of the Club are twofold: 'the preservation and promotion of friendship and fellowship among Old Blues' and secondly 'the furtherance of the interests and prosperity of the Foundation and of the various School and Old Blue societies and organisations in any manner that may be thought expedient and in particular by rendering where practicable financial assistance and support by way of loans (with or without security), donations, subscriptions or otherwise to any such societies and organisations.'

Full membership is open to all Old Blues, staff, former staff, Almoners and Governors. Associate membership is available to widows or widowers of Old Blues, parents and step-parents of Old Blues and of current pupils, and any individual approved by the Management Committee. The subscription in 2000 is £15 for both categories of membership. Mrs Wendy Killner, the Club's full-time administrator, welcomes contact and enquiries from Old Blues and is usually the first point of contact with the Club for pupils at the School.

The Presidency of the Club is normally held for five years and Geoffrey Shelley was elected in March 2000, succeeding Richard Poulton, former Head Master. In 1999 the Club elected its first lady Chairman, Mrs Diana Gould, in succession to Neville Osmond. These posts are honorary appointments, as are the posts of Secretary, currently held by Peter Hill, and Treasurer, held by Keith Minter.

With some 3,500 members, the Club provides liaison between its constituency and the School through events such as Old Blues Day and

Leavers' suppers, as well as presenting children to the School occasion-ally. It runs a Careers Network, providing advice by volunteer Old Blues to those leaving School or considering a career change. The Club's Annual General Meeting, which fills the Court Room in March, is fol-lowed by a generous buffet which provides members with opportunities for reminiscing and socialising.

The Club finances the publication of the termly School and Old Blue magazine *The Blue*, and supported the directory of Old Blues, *Who's Blue*, which was published by Christ's Hospital Enterprises Ltd in 1997.

The Club incorporates the de-constituted Old Girls' Association which catered for Old Girls who left Hertford before 1984. The Association retains its autonomy, is self-financing, publishes an annual newsletter and arranges reunions in different parts of the country. Many of its 1,500 members have joined the Club independently, enjoying full benefits, but the Association – now the Christ's Hospital Club Old Girls' Association (CHCOGA) – ensures that all members belong to the Christ's Hospital 'family' through invitations to regional Club activities, Old Blues' Day, and other functions. CHCOGA is chaired by Kerren Simmonds, an ex-officio member of the Christ's Hospital Club Management Committee, who liaises closely with Wendy Killner.

Christ's Hospital Club Management Committee at the AGM, 7 March 2000. Left to right: Neville Osmond, immediate past Chairman, Susan Walsh, John Kennedy, Kerren Simmonds, Chair of CHCOGA, Chris Bruce-Jones, Diana Gould, Chairman, Peter Hill, Hon. Secretary, Keith Minter, Hon. Treasurer, Maurice Hall, Louise Pickett, Geoffrey Shelley, incoming President, Richard Poulton, retiring President, Helen Bradley and Bob Sillett. Colin Eley and Paddie Drake were absent.

The Club's twenty eight regional sections in the UK and a further seventeen overseas sections form *Le Cordon Bleu*, which promotes fellowship of all Old Blues world wide. The various Ward and House Associations are also affiliated to the Christ's Hospital Club. Many of these organise local Founder's Day celebrations and social events, and some support the School by presenting a child.

Richard Poulton, retiring President of the Christ's Hospital Club, chairs the AGM in the Court Room on 7 March 2000, supported by Diana Gould, Chairman, Keith Minter, Hon. Treasurer and Peter Hill, Hon. Secretary. Sir Richard Nichols, Lord Mayor of London 1997–8, keeps a watchful eye on the proceedings from his portrait, behind.

FREEMASONRY

Robert Betson (Lamb A, 1946–53) writes: At the end of February 2000 David Spackman (Lamb B 1938–44) succeeded Colin Eley (Lamb B, 1971–78) as Master of Christ's Hospital Lodge No. 2650 and so became the 103rd holder of that office; no significance should be attached to the Lamb B connection, which was just a coincidence! The Lodge is the lynchpin of Housey Freemasonry but there are two other Masonic bodies open to Old Blues, Governors, officers and masters: the Christ's Hospital Royal Arch Chapter and the Christ's Hospital Rose Croix Chapter. The current membership of the Lodge is about sixty, of whom six are not Old Blues.

Since its consecration in 1897, the Christ's Hospital Lodge has attracted those who feel the added affinity with the Housey ethos which Freemasonry provides, based as it is on the moral precepts of Brotherly Love, Relief and Truth. Charity and caring for others less fortunate play important parts in the rôles and objectives of both Christ's Hospital and Freemasonry.

Throughout its existence the Lodge has staunchly supported the various appeals for the School and regularly contributes to the Benevolent Society of Blues. When the Lodge celebrated its centenary in 1997 it marked the occasion by creating an Educational Bursary at Christ's Hospital, having raised over £12,000. The interest from this capital (about £800) is distributed each year to pupils with extramural educational needs not covered by the School. Similarly, £470 from table collections in the last two years has been passed to the BSB.

Housey Freemasonry is both worthwhile and enjoyable.

THE STEWARDS OF FOUNDER'S DAY

The Stewards of Founder's Day run themselves on a voluntary basis, so the post of Secretary requires an Old Blue with not only diplomatic and organisational skills, but also with time and energy to undertake substantial routine clerical work at critical times of the year, and doubling as Treasurer. Christopher Pearson had held the post very successfully for two years, introducing modern IT techniques, before handing over to Richard March in November 1999.

The Stewards organise and underwrite the costs of Founder's Day Dinner, held annually in October in the City in the magnificent Drapers' Hall, select and invite the principal speakers, and cover the costs of tickets for invited guests from the School staff and Grecians. Stewardship is open to any Old Blue, Donation Governor or former member of staff, subject to election and payment of the annual 'quota'; in 2000 there were 144 subscribing Stewards.

The Chairman of Stewards is elected annually for one year, and has an important rôle to play at the Dinner in welcoming and introducing the speakers. The Stewards hold two meetings a year in London to resolve everything from the venue and menu for the Dinner to the selection of speakers. These opportunities for social gatherings are not overlooked, and a variety of London restaurants of the livelier sort have seen parties of Stewards enjoying their post-meetings suppers.

An account of Founder's Day Dinner 1999 appears on pages 96–8.

THE NEWGATE CLUB

The Newgate Club was formed, very informally, in December 1997. Three

Newgate Club members on their Headlings Cup golfing day, summer 2000.

Old Blues RFC (founded 1873) in a lineout vs. Old Guildfordians. The Old Blue players are Simon Macpherson and Paul 'Chico' Konig.

1970's Housey contemporaries working in the City of London met and soon discovered many more Old Blues in the Square Mile. The Club's aim was to bring them together over occasional, and increasingly extended, lunch breaks. Since then, attendance has expanded to include Old Blues from much further afield and officers and staff of the School.

Meetings are fluid in terms of both timing and consumption! St Matthew's Day in September is a regular date, with two or three further gatherings during the year and a small but very popular golf tournament for The Headlings Cup in the summer. These are all informal occasions and the focus is on the School and Old Blue communities' activities. Each lunch provides Christ's Hospital societies and those involved in formal appeals with an opportunity to address those present.

The Club's surplus funds support a specific Christ's Hospital project of the membership's choice. In 2000 the Club is sponsoring the website 'oldblues.com' which has rapidly achieved great popularity for its postings of up-to-the-minute news and details of forthcoming events.

The founding members and co-Chairmen are Paul Chambers (Peele B, 1971–78), Michael Hiard (Coleridge B, 1970–77) and John Cullen (Peele A, 1971–78).

OLD BLUES SPORTS CLUBS

OLD BLUES RUGBY FOOTBALL CLUB

Present membership of the OBRFC is around 350 Old Blues and non-Old Blues, of whom 150 are playing members – a very healthy position for an old boys' club with its own ground and clubhouse at Motspur Park in Surrey. Current President is Andrew Cosedge (Old Blue), Chairman Ian Hoskins (non-Old Blue) and Club Captain Old Blue John Gower.

The 1999–2000 season was played in London League 2 South where the Club finished in ninth position out of seventeen. Overall results of the 1st XV were: played 25, won 11, lost 13, drew 1. Points for: 607, points against: 641.

Apart from the 1st XV, the Club fields Nomads (2nd XV), Bedouins (3rd XV), Chindits (4th XV) and a Veterans XV, although these teams do not play every week.

It is worthy of note that so many members of the Club over many years have returned to serve the Foundation in multifarious capacities, their comradeship and interest in Christ's Hospital having been kept active and nurtured during their younger years by the fellowship of rugby. It is to be hoped that present and future generations of Blues continue this tradition and that the Club broadens its scope and facilities to include girls' hockey at some time in the future.

OLD BLUES CRICKET CLUB

Old Blues cricket has been played on and off, certainly over the years since the School moved to Horsham. Under the leadership of Captain and Honorary Secretary, James Maxwell, it has become revitalised over the past few years, currently boasting in the region of sixty members and with a full fixture list during the season.

In 1999 the Club progressed for the first time beyond the first round of the Cricket World Trophy (for old boys' sides not involved in the Cricketer Cup) through a masterly call by the Captain after the match against Milton Abbey was finally abandoned to the rain. Until then Old Blues had had very much the worst of the contest. The next round, against St George's Weybridge, produced an outstanding Old Blues performance (302 for 2 in 50 overs), before beating Old Askeans in the semi-final. But luck was then to desert the team as appalling weather caused the final against Old Ellesmerians to be postponed until summer 2000, by which time the momentum of 1999 has gone and less than half of the first choice team were available despite a year's notice.

A number of fixtures in summer 2000 were affected by rain but losing in the first round of the Cricket World Trophy (prior to the previous year's final!) was followed by good wins against Letchworth and Butterflies. The Club considers Christ's Hospital its home ground and is always grateful for the support and assistance given by the School. There is a regular annual match against the School 1st XI (lost by Old Blues in 1999 but won in 2000) and a cricket week in July 2000, just after the School broke up, was resurrected after a gap of eighteen years, albeit with half the fixtures washed out by the incessant rain.

OLD BLUES GOLFING SOCIETY

Founded before the second World War, the Old Blues Golfing Society was run after the War by George Ross Goobey and given a new boost in 1984 by David Gibbs and Mervyn Dyer when the Society was re-constituted. There are now around sixty members of whom twenty to thirty turn out for meetings.

Old Blues about to enjoy a fine day's golf. Left to right: Mark Hammond, Mike Wilson, Chris Ward and Donald Payne.

Traditionally there are two meetings a year – spring and autumn - and various other matches on an occasional basis. The autumn meeting was held at Liphook on 10 September with twenty-seven entries for the Ross Goobey trophy, and included one lady, Rosemary Adkins, who went on to win. Mike Wilson was second, David Gibbs third and Robin Crane fourth. The Society hopes that Rosemary's success will encourage other ladies to join, and they were delighted to welcome Susan Mitchell, the Treasurer, as their dinner guest.

An innovation this year was the Masters' Challenge on 26 September, with Jim Endacott organising a team from the teaching staff to play OBGS at Mannings Heath, Old Blues winning 3 to 1. A second encounter at Wildwood on 27 April resulted in the teams drawing at two matches each.

At the spring meeting at West Surrey on 12 May the Atkinson Trophy was contested by twenty-two players. Chris Ward, playing off 10, was the winner with 41 points. Mark Hammond was only one point behind and Charles McKay, captain, third with 38 points playing off 4, having been round in only two over par.

The Society entered for the Grafton Morrish Trophy, an annual scratch competition for Old Boy teams from prestigious UK schools. Old Blues qualified for the regional finals at Knole Park in May, progressed to the final stages at Hunstanton and Brancaster before losing to St Edwards, Oxford. However, they were runners-up in the Committee Bowl, the subsidiary competition. This was the first time that Old Blues have won a trophy in the Grafton Morrish competition and their success was capped by a hole in one from Mike Harvey, a member of the team.

The year started with David Spackman as Captain, prior to handing over to Charles McKay at the spring meeting, with Dennis Quinn continuing as Honorary Secretary, a post he has held since 1993. New, particularly young, members are welcome and although handicap is not important they should be past the novice stage. Under 28 year olds pay only half charges.

OLD BLUES RIFLE CLUB

Thanks largely to the Platfoot family, Clive and his son Kim, the Rifle Club has been going for many years and meets annually at Bisley to compete in the Old Boys' Shooting Competition which follows the Schools' Ashburton Shield. Clive was in the Army VIII for both rifle and pistol shooting during the 1950's and 1960 and was also the Inter-Services Rifle Champion and winner of the Queen Mary Medal in 1958.

There are probably more Old Blues who have represented Great Britain and England in shooting than in any other sport. They are Stewart Armour, who left the School in 1932, and two younger Old Blues, Andrew Harrison and Simon Smallwood, who acquired their shooting skills at Christ's Hospital.

The Old Blues Rugby Fives squad. Back row: Bernard Atkinson, David Bawtree, Noel Osborne, Tim Bryant and Ian Torkington, master in charge of Fives; front row: Ben Smithson, Adrian Hill, Neil Green.

RUGBY FIVES

Rugby Fives has a long tradition at Christ's Hospital and the School is currently producing some excellent players – and results. Once again there is a small but active Old Blues Association, led by stalwarts Bernard Atkinson (Hon Sec) and David Bawtree, who play against pupils and Common Room on Wednesday evenings each week and have an annual match against the School every February.

Also every year in the Autumn, Old Blue Fives players going back to the 1950's meet at the School for some games and some serious socialising, usually ending up at the Boar's Head or some such local hostelry.

OLD BLUES REAL TENNIS

Although no facilities exist at the School for the game of Real Tennis, (but there seems a possibility that they might have done in its London days), there were sufficient Old Blue players for a Club to be formed by Neil Simms, a former master and Petworth Club player, in 1993.

Members gather for a full day's tennis, usually on a Sunday, about three times a year. This year matches were played at Merton College,

Oxford on 7 May, Holyport near Maidenhead on 2 July and Prested Hall near Colchester on 22 October, where fellow Old Blue Michael Carter has recently developed a new Club. Other matches have been held at Lords, Cambridge, the Harbour Club and Bridport. Christ's Hospital has been represented in the public schools Henry Leaf Cup over the years by Old Blues John Ward and Michael Carter. John recently won both singles and doubles in the over-60's World Championships in Bordeaux and was runner up in the over-50's doubles.

This is the game from which all racket sports were developed so tennis, squash and fives players are all in with a chance. The new Secretary, Richard McGregor who has succeeded Neil Simms, would welcome new players to the Club.

Representing Old Blues on 7 May in a real tennis match at Merton College, Oxford, are (left to right) Andrew Reid-Thomas, Chris Harding-Smith and Richard McGregor.

Memorabilia of CH: this set of mug, kiff bowl and salt cellar is in the proud possession of Paul Parker in Portland, Oregon, USA.

Guy Nevell, who was our guest of honour at lunch in Portland, Oregon, 22 September 2000, for his liaison rôle, on behalf of Christ's Hospital, with the British Schools and Universities Fund in the USA for thirteen years.

THE HUNDRED YEARS ON APPEAL

This Appeal, run by a Steering Group comprising the Treasurer Susan Mitchell as Chairman, Christopher Pearson as Vice-Chairman, Partnership Director Mark Curtis and the Clerk, Michael Simpkin, was launched, with a special edition of *Housey!*, in January 2000 in celebration of Christ's Hospital's first century at Horsham. Its target is £5 million and it invites Old Blues and other supporters to share the excitement of the Masterplan (described on pages 78–81) for the renewal and expansion of the School and its facilities. It is a self-help Appeal, with the Steering Group strongly supported by an Appeal Team comprising representatives of all decades of Old Blues, the School and the City, and by regional networks overseas.

Prior to the public launch, members of the Appeal team had secured donations or pledges totalling £1.6 million from a carefully targeted list, including £500,000 from Almoners past and present and, in response to an energetic campaign by Donald Fox, over £300,000 from the 'Golden Oldies' who left the School prior to 1943. The Appeal Team continued their fund-raising efforts energetically through 2000, and Susan Mitchell hosted eleven weekend meetings at venues around the UK from Edinburgh to Exeter, appealing to Old Blues and clarifying the development plans with them.

Continuing her campaign, the Treasurer toured North America and Canada in September 2000. She reports:

'My aims were to narrow the gap between North America and Horsham for Old Blues, to raise money for The Appeal, and to find Old Blue co-ordinators for the territories where we did not already have them.

We visited San Francisco, Irvine and Menlo (California), Portland (Oregon) for lunch in honour of Guy Nevell and his fifteen years' work with the BSUF for Christ's Hospital; then to Vancouver and Toronto, re-crossing the border to Washington DC and New York.

In the course of nine meetings and presentations we met fifty Old Blues plus spouses, sweethearts and offspring, and my target of US$1 million for the Appeal was comfortably exceeded, significantly aided by the outstanding generosity of the Doyle family in California, and Michael Allen on the East Coast. Others, too, have been generous and gifts continue to arrive.

We found great enthusiasm for creating new links and renewing old ones and I had no difficulty in recruiting as co-ordinators Lance Reynolds for the West Coast of the USA; John Reynolds (no relation) for Toronto and Ontario; and Patricia Stockton for Washington DC.

My thanks go to my co-host and husband John; to Judy and John Doyle, who most generously gave us the marvellous experience of private flying, as pilot and co-pilot of their Cessna Citation jet, on the West Coast; to all those who organised our meetings at every venue and to all Old Blues and others we met who gave us an insight into the unswerving affection in which Christ's Hospital is held across the continent and across the generations.'

As this book goes to press, in May 2001, the Appeal has raised just over £4 million. It remains open and all gifts, large or small, continue to be gratefully received, but partic-

The presentations for The 100 Years On Appeal always devolved into enjoyable social gatherings. This is part of one in Washington DC, 27 September 2000. Clockwise from left: Kate Kerr, Alexandra Power, née Szantyr, Bill Band, Susan Mitchell, Kitt Band and Felix Edwards with his back to the camera.

Patricia Stockton, Old Blue co-ordinator in Washington DC and district, who very ably organised the meeting and dinner on 27 September 2000.

Jack Doyle, Old Blue and good benefactor, studying the Master Plan with the Head Master during a visit to the School.

ular thanks are recorded to those individuals who have pledged, donated or bequeathed a six-figure sum: John and Judy Doyle, Andrew Joanes, John and Susan Mitchell, Michael Allen, the late Mrs Eileen Attenborough and Michael Hiard.

THE WIDER COMMUNITY

For those who have an interest in Christ's Hospital but who are not members of these clubs or societies – as well as for those who are – there is the official Christ's Hospital website, www.christs-hospital.org.uk, and www.oldblues.com, funded by the Newgate Club and run by Steve Webb, publishing regular bulletins of news and events. *Housey!*, edited by Peter Bloomfield, and published twice a year by the Partnership Office free of charge to everybody on their database, contains current news and pictures. Highlights of the Christs' Hospital Annual Report will be published to the *Housey!* mailing list from March 2001 and the full Annual Report and Financial Statements are available from the Counting House.

Portraits in oils of many benefactors and
others who have served Christ's Hospital
over the generations hang in Dining Hall
and elsewhere at the School. Susan
Mitchell is continuing the tradition and
here she is sitting for a preliminary study
by Peter Edwards at his studio in
Oswestry, Shropshire. In the background
is the canvas for the eventual portrait,
which will be presented to Christ's
Hospital in 2002. The composition will
include the Treasurer's husband John, a
Donation Governor and familiar figure at
the School, who plays a full part in all
Susan's formal and social engagements
and in her fund-raising work on behalf of
Christ's Hospital.

Peter Edwards' numerous commissions
have included two other Old Blues –
Alderman Sir Richard Nichols for the
Salters' Company in his Mayoral year,
and Professor Sir Christopher Zeeman,
PhD, FRS, for Hertford College, Oxford,
where he was Principal, 1988–95.

EPILOGUE

BY
SUSAN MITCHELL
Treasurer and Chairman of the Council of Almoners

IN HIS PREFACE, the Head Master describes the year 2000 at Christ's Hospital as 'a delightfully ordinary year' and so it was; the chronicle of events recorded in this book is typical of a year at Housie as we approach our anniversary celebrations in 2002/3. As the year 2000 unfolds in these pages, it becomes increasingly evident that for pupils with ambition, commitment and the energy to grasp its opportunities there is a rich abundance of educational choice. There are also exciting chances for everybody to experience a wide range of musical, theatrical, sporting and community service activities outside the curriculum as well as within it, and exceptional opportunities to pursue other interests and hobbies and to participate in School excursions which put the gloss on many of the topics explored in term time.

Whilst this breadth of opportunity is facilitated by the financial support of the Foundation, it is, above all, the dedication and commitment of the staff, led by the Head Master and the Clerk, which is the true catalyst for the richness of the Christ's Hospital experience. That experience is designed to encourage each child to learn to take his or her place confidently in society and to fertilize that natural curiosity which, when developed with skilled teaching and pastoral care, can enable pupils to reach their individual maximum potential and to emerge as young adults equipped to cope with life in the twenty-first century.

Christ's Hospital's objective remains the same as it has been for nearly four hundred and fifty years – to provide for children with need. The nature of that provision has been and remains primarily educational but it has been modified at the edges over the years in response to social change and expectation. It is the firm intention and earnest aim of all those connected with the Foundation that it will continue to pursue the same objective and be similarly responsive for the foreseeable future.

For many of us there is also the vision that, with good financial management and the continuing generosity of all our benefactors the Foundation will be in a position to support more children than it is currently able to do before the next major milestone in our history is reached.

Susan Mitchell
Henfield, July 2001

195

APPENDICES: THE SCHOOL IN THE YEAR 1999–2000

APPENDIX I
A CODE OF CONDUCT FOR ALL MEMBERS OF CHRIST'S HOSPITAL

We are at school to learn to prepare for life in a demanding world.

THIS AIM DEMANDS THAT WE:
Master academic subjects and develop useful skills;
Establish effective working habits;
Discipline ourselves to be efficient and reliable;
Learn to live happily with other people.

An academic community cannot allow individual selfishness or thoughtlessness to get in the way of its broader interests – so there must be an agreed code of conduct which governs all we do.

Our many visitors often comment favourably about the impressive conduct, appearance and helpfulness of all they meet at Christ's Hospital.

Be proud of your School and of your part in it.

SCHOOL WORK

Academic progress is central to life in school. It is therefore vital that we are faultless in attending class, being on time, bringing all necessary materials and completing all tasks to the best of our ability. We should always be looking to raise the level of our performance and understanding by seeking to do more than the minimum to 'get by'. We must do nothing which may disrupt the learning of others, and we should encourage others at all times to develop to the limits of their potential. Commitments to teams, music lessons and practices, and to all school activities such as plays, CCF, Scouts, actives and clubs must be honoured as full parts of the school curriculum.

CHAPEL

Here, most especially, we must respect the feelings of others and help to build the atmosphere which serves the needs of the community. Positive involvement is a tonic to everyone's spirits.

DRESS AND APPEARANCE

The Housey uniform is one of our most cherished traditions. Wherever and whenever it is worn, it must be worn with pride and with care for its neatness and cleanliness. Pupils may wear their own clothes as and when the regulations currently posted in House allow.

Attention-seeking styles of dress, hair and personal ornamentation are not appropriate and the decisions of House staff must be complied with.

RESPECT

A community such as ours works happily only if everyone behaves with respect for the individuality of others and the interests of the whole community. People are different from one another and should be allowed to be so. Privacy is important but so is communal life. There will be many occasions when our individual impulses and wishes have to be seen as less important than the interests of the community. Being 'cheeky' is as serious as is an act of bullying, because the one often leads to the other. Instructions from an adult, School Monitor or House Monitor must be obeyed without delay or discussion and with good grace – if you believe there is something wrong in what you are told to do, take it up later with the person concerned, your tutor, HSM or through the complaints procedure.

HEALTH AND SAFETY

We must each take personal responsibility for adopting a healthy lifestyle. Above all, no action of ours must be allowed to bring danger, fear or unhappiness into the lives of others. Social life must be kept positive, avoiding excessively intimate or exclusive relationships, giving due regard to the law, as in all things.

HOME AND SCHOOL

Consideration for those who look after you at home and school must be paramount in all arrangements made for travelling, exeats and visits. Play your part in ensuring good communication between home and school.

The School's alcohol and drug policy and the anti-bullying policy are to be found on the following pages. Further detailed regulations on many matters from bed times to nail varnish are posted in Houses and on the School internet. It is neither possible nor desirable to seek to cover every situation in a comprehensive Rule Book. It is no defence to say something has not been ruled out so it must be acceptable!

If something is sensible and courteous, then it is unlikely to be wrong: behaviour which is inconsiderate, dangerous or bad-mannered is invariably wrong.

Dr Peter Southern
Head Master

Published in the CHRIST'S HOSPITAL CALENDAR *each term.*

APPENDIX II
CHRIST'S HOSPITAL ANTI-BULLYING CODE

BULLYING OF ANY KIND IS ALWAYS UNACCEPTABLE AND WILL NOT BE TOLERATED

DEFINITION

Bullying is behaviour which makes other people feel uncomfortable or threatened, whether this outcome is intended or not. Bullying includes harassment such as racist behaviour and sexual harassment. There are different sorts of bullying, but the three main types are:

Physical: hitting; kicking; pinching; taking, hiding or damaging belongings;

Verbal: name calling; teasing; insulting, "cussing";

Emotional: being unfriendly; excluding; blanking; tormenting; spreading rumours.

The term 'bullying' includes the following specific actions:

Hierarchical behaviour – greater age, superior year group or physical size bring no automatic privileges. They can never be used to justify such behaviour as pushing into queues at meal times, in the shop or hairdresser; sending someone on an errand (e.g. to fetch milk, toast, to take a message, or act as a 'servant'). Such actions are bullying and are never allowable. This may have been something we experienced in the past but this is never a reason for continuing something we found disagreeable when we were younger.

Initiation ceremonies – which involve degrading, humiliating or violent acts (including sleep disturbance) are bullying and are never allowable. This may have been something we experienced in the past but this is never a reason for continuing something we found disagreeable when we were younger.

People react differently and it is not always possible to tell if someone is hurt or upset. Apparent acceptance is never an excuse or justification for bullying.

AIMS

All members of the school community wish to develop and maintain an environment characterised by warmth, friendly contact across year groups, with a positive involvement from adults, where independence is respected and individuals can flourish without fear.

Every pupil has the right to be safe and happy in school and to be protected when feeling vulnerable.

POSSIBLE SIGNS

People who are being bullied may show changes in behaviour, such as becoming shy and nervous or feigning illness. They may show changes in their work patterns, seek to avoid prominence in performance or class contribution, may lack concentration, may keep to themselves in the House or stay away from certain activities or places in school.

PREVENTION

We hope to prevent harassment of any kind by:

a) sharing our concerns about those who may be suffering, confident that we can turn to House Captains, Monitors, House staff, Tutors or other teachers, Chaplains or Counsellor, knowing they will take any complaint seriously and sympathetically, and will always take active steps to support the victim. Those who receive such messages of concern must accept that failure to act appropriately will be seen as a serious misdemeanour;

b) supporting potential or actual victims – being positively friendly towards them, including them in group activities and helping to make them aware of tactics to avoid being the victim and to avoid potential bullying situations. We will make it clear to the victim that revenge is not appropriate, and to the bully that the behaviour is unacceptable and has caused distress.

ENCOURAGEMENT TO TELL

It is important that we all create an atmosphere in the school where people who are being harassed, or others who know about it, feel confident that they will be listened to and believed, and that action taken will be swift and effective and sensitive.

Keeping quiet protects the bully and implies that the harassment can continue.

Dr Peter Southern
Head Master

Published in the CHRIST'S HOSPITAL CALENDAR *each term.*

APPENDIX III
CHRIST'S HOSPITAL ALCOHOL AND DRUG ABUSE POLICY

PRINCIPLES OF OUR POLICY

Christ's Hospital strives to achieve a culture opposed to the misuse of alcohol or drugs; in order to do this, we need a partnership between home and school which requires trust and communication.

We seek to encourage this culture by education, guidance, warning and disciplinary sanctions. Welfare issues are quite as important as issues of school discipline and involve the good of others in the community as well as of an individual member of it.

Drunkenness, underage drinking and using illegal drugs at any time are incompatible with membership of the community of Christ's Hospital. The laws of the land must be observed regarding these issues, and any form of law-breaking, whenever or wherever committed, may endanger a pupil's place in the school.

The school is committed to working with those who make mistakes and keeping them within the community, unless they show that they are unable or unwilling to learn from their mistakes.

Initial testing for drug or alcohol misuse threatens no-one. It is used to clarify issues of concern and is seen as a useful and positive tool. In exploring areas of concern, the school will always keep an open mind about contributory causes.

Any pupil can seek help and support at any time on alcohol and drug related issues; such help would happen within the school's overall welfare programme, and testing may play a part in this.

Caring support can result in pupils being required to leave the school. This could occur: if mistakes are repeated; if the first mistake is so serious that proper punishment leaves no possibility other than leaving the school; if the mistake is so damaging to the individual concerned or to others that continued membership of the community poses an unacceptable risk; or if the most recent mistake follows a series of other serious disciplinary misdemeanours in other areas of school life.

APPLICATION

1. Specific education in alcohol and drug related issues comes via Education for Living and Biology teaching to pupils, and through specific training for all staff. Wherever possible, Christ's Hospital will provide general information for parents also.

2. General guidance comes via Housemasters and Housemistresses, House Tutors, Matrons, Personal Tutors and all pastoral contacts.

3. Counselling of those involved in alcohol or drug misuse will take place initially in school, but there may be referral outside school also.

4. Concern about an individual can originate from anybody, but would usually go via the Housemaster or Housemistress, who would always make it known to a Deputy Head or to the Head Master. Such concern will involve parents, and will result in a thorough and open-minded investigation.

5. Concern may result in searches of pupils' desks, studies or living areas; searches may involve the police. Such searches will always be carried out in the presence of a member of staff, and, wherever possible, in the presence of the pupil involved.

6. Interviews will be carried out with careful preparation, and with respect for the rights and needs of the pupils being interviewed.

7. If there is reasonable concern for an individual about drug or alcohol misuse, a test may be carried out under appropriate conditions.

8. On the pupil's entry to the school, all parents are asked to give permission for such testing. Parents will be informed when a test is to be administered and, if prior contact proves impossible, will be informed as soon as possible afterwards. Pupils will be asked to agree to the test before it is administered. Failure to agree to the testing process places an impossible obstacle in the way of the school's fulfilling its welfare obligations. In such an event, pupils will be sent home until the necessary permission is obtained and the test which has been missed will be deemed to have been positive.

9. If a test is positive, then the pupil will be involved in the school's programme of counselling, and will be randomly tested thereafter. A second positive test will almost certainly result in the pupil being required to leave the school.

10. A pupil involved in spreading the misuse of drugs or alcohol within the school, by selling or supplying, for example, will almost certainly be required to leave the school.

Published in the CHRIST'S HOSPITAL CALENDAR *each term.*

APPENDIX IV
CHRIST'S HOSPITAL TEACHING STAFF IN THE ACADEMIC YEAR 1999–2000

HEAD MASTER
Dr P C D Southern MA, Merton College, Oxford; PhD, Edinburgh

DEPUTY HEADS
Mrs E C Cairncross BA, Bedford College, London
R D T Sillett M/ETD, LCP, St Paul's College, Cheltenham

CHAPLAINS
Revd A Mitra MA, Keble College, Oxford (Senior Chaplain)
Revd G W Dobbie MA, BD, St Andrews
Revd N J Mitra MA, St Hugh's College, Oxford

SENIOR HOUSEMISTRESS
Mrs M A Fleming BA, University College, London, MA, Durham

BURSAR
Mrs E R A Adams FCA, ATII

HOUSEMASTERS AND HOUSEMISTRESSES

Peele A H P Holdsworth BA, Open University
Peele B I B Howard MA, Trinity College, Cambridge
Thornton A S J O'Boyle BSC, ARCS, Imperial College, London
Thornton B O K Marlow MA, Reading; MA, St Andrews
Middleton A Revd G W Dobbie MA, BD, St Andrews
Middleton B S H C Reid BA, Witwatersrand (S. Africa)
Coleridge A N M Fleming BA, Durham
Coleridge B Mrs A J Röhrs BSC, University of Natal
Lamb A Dr I C Hobson BSC, MSC, PHD, Manchester
Lamb B F McKenna BTech, Brunel
Barnes A Miss L A Helyar BA, Cardiff
Barnes B Mrs D J Stamp BED, Exeter
Maine A Dr R W Stuart BA, New Brunswick; MA, Dalhousie; PHD, Queen's College, Oxford
Maine B A R B Phillips BA, Kent
Leigh Hunt A Mrs V E Buckman BSC, Leeds
Leigh Hunt B Mrs E A Robinson BA, Queen Margaret College, Edinburgh
Hertford Miss L E A Thornton MA, St Andrews

DIRECTORS OF STUDIES

Dr R Q Hackett (Curriculum) MA, DPhil, St Peter's College, Oxford; CPhys, MInstP
P M J Slater (Options) MA, St Benet's Hall, Oxford

ARCHAEOLOGY

*N M Fleming BA, Durham; DipArch, LRPS

ART

*M A O'Connor MA, Goldsmiths' College, London
Miss Z Clifford MA, Norwich School of Art & Design
S A Cowley BA, Dundee
Miss S Daltry BA, Coventry; MA, Winchester
P A Deller BA
Mrs D LeBas MA, St Martin's

Mrs J S O'Connor Cert Ed Art and Design
Ms R Sier BA, Middlesex
S August BA

BIOLOGY

*M J Gladding BSC, Cardiff
Mrs V E Buckman BSC, Leeds
J B Callas BSC, University College, London
Mrs K L Callas BSC, University College of North Wales
Mrs A J Röhrs BSC, University of Natal (S. Africa)
R D T Sillett M/ETD, LCP, St Paul's College, Cheltenham

CAREERS

*J Endacott BA, Manchester
Dr K B Dillow MA, DPhil, Merton College, Oxford
Mrs V E Buckman BSC, Leeds
Miss L A Helyar BA, Cardiff
Dr P S Maddren BSC, PHD, Bristol
P M J Slater MA, St Benet's Hall, Oxford

CHEMISTRY

*Mrs J A Williams BSC, University College, London
Dr P S Maddren (Co-ord of Science) BSC, PHD, Bristol
Dr C R Lawrence MA, PHD, St Catharine's College, Cambridge
I H Torkington MA, Fitzwilliam College, Cambridge
W J M Yates BSC, Hull

CLASSICS

*Mrs M A Fleming BA, University College, London, MA, Durham
J E Denison MA, Trinity Hall, Cambridge
N M Fleming BA, Durham; Dip Arch LRPS
I B Howard MA, Trinity College, Cambridge
Revd A Mitra MA, Keble College, Oxford

DESIGN AND TECHNOLOGY

*K S Leadbeater DipAD, Newcastle; HDD, Leicester; MSIAD
P N Edwards BSc, Brunel
Miss B L Faulkner BA, De Montfort
V R Holme BEd, King Alfred's College, Winchester
A R Lewis BSc, Portsmouth
F McKenna BTech, Brunel

DRAMA & THEATRE STUDIES

*J Mayhew BA, MA, Durham
P T Ward BA, York; LRAM, ADB(Ed)
Miss J Wells BA, (Dance)
R del Pino (Assistant Theatre Manager)
Mr D Gibson (Theatre Technical Manager)
Miss L F Castleden BEd, Central School of Speech and
    Drama; MA, Kings College, London

ECONOMICS & BUSINESS STUDIES

*Miss J M Simmonds BSc, Southampton

ENGLISH

*A J Adlam MA, St Andrews
Mrs E C Cairncross BA, Bedford College, London
J Endacott BA, Manchester
Miss J E Everist BA, Reading
H P Holdsworth BA, Open University
O K Marlow MA, Reading; MA, St Andrews
S H C Reid BA, Witwatersrand (S. Africa)
Mrs V A M Simms BA, W. Sussex Inst. Higher Ed.; AMBDA
Dr R W Stuart BA, New Brunswick (Canada); MA,
    Dalhousie (Canada); PhD, Queen's College, Oxford
S W Walsh MA, University College, Oxford
P T Ward BA, York; LRAM, ADB(Ed)

FOOD TECHNOLOGY

*Mrs E A Robinson BA, Queen Margaret College,
    Edinburgh
Mrs R Hebblethwaite

GENERAL STUDIES

T J Jeffers MA, St Edmund Hall, Oxford; LGSM

GEOGRAPHY

*S Davey BSc, St Paul's College Cheltenham; MA, London
J Anderson BA, Queen's University, Belfast
W J Avenell BA, DipPE, University College, Durham
Mrs K N Newson BA, Sheffield;
    DipHE, St Paul's College, Cheltenham
J D Shippen MA, St Edmund Hall, Oxford; FRGS

HISTORY

*Dr J C Roberts MA, St Andrews;
    DPhil, University College, Oxford
T D Askew MA, University College, Oxford

Dr K B Dillow MA, DPhil, Merton College, Oxford
M J Potter MBE, BEd, Exeter
Dr P C D Southern MA, Merton College, Oxford;
    PhD Edinburgh
Miss E L Stead BEd, De Montfort
Miss L E A Thornton MA, St Andrews
Dr A R Wines MA, St Andrews; PhD, St John's College,
    Cambridge

INFORMATION & COMMUNICATION TECHNOLOGY

*Dr E J Wolstenholme BSc, PhD, Surrey

LEARNING SUPPORT

Mrs R Allwood DipEd, Homerton College, Cambridge
Mrs M Potter (ESL), BA, Bristol
Mrs V A M Simms BA, W. Sussex Inst. Higher Ed; AMBDA

LIBRARY

Mrs J B Jeffers (Librarian) ALA, Brighton
Mrs S Churchman (Library Assistant) BSc, Reading

MATHEMATICS

*A L Smith BSc, University College, London
D P C Blewitt BSc, Bristol
R M Castro BSc, Exeter
Miss L A Helyar BA, Cardiff
Mrs C M Hennock MA, Girton College, Cambridge
Dr I C Hobson BSc, MSc, PhD, Manchester
Mrs D D McCulloch BSc, MSc, Swansea
S J O'Boyle BSc, ARCS, Imperial College, London
D J O'Meara MA, St Catharine's College, Cambridge
Mrs D J Stamp BEd, Exeter

MODERN LANGUAGES

*M J Overend (French) MA, Sidney Sussex College,
    Cambridge
*F R Pattison (German) MA, New College, Oxford
*Mrs L Wyld (Russian & French) MA, St Andrews
Miss K E Biggs BA, (French and German) University
    College, London
G N Chandler (German & French) MA, Fitzwilliam College,
    Cambridge
Miss D W L Charbonnieras MA, Nanterre (Paris X)
Mrs C E Eason LesL, (French Assistante)
S T Eason (French & Italian) BA, Manchester; MIL
Herr M Ernst (German Assistant)
Mrs V Filonova-Jenkins (Russian Assistant)
I B Howard (French & German) MA, Trinity College,
    Cambridge
T J Jeffers (German & French) MA, St Edmund Hall,
    Oxford; LGSM
C H Kemp (Latin & French) BA, Queen's College,
    Cambridge
Mlle S Leocart (French Assistante)
K R A Nordgreen BA, Brasenose College, Oxford

A R B Phillips BA, Kent
R D T Sillett M/ETD, LCP, St Paul's College, Cheltenham
P M J Slater (French, Latin & Italian) MA, St Benet's Hall,
    Oxford
A M Williams BSC, (Spanish), Loughborough

MUSIC

*P A Allwood MA, King's College, Cambridge
P Brownlie GRNCM,
    PPRNCM, Royal Northern College of Music
T J Callaghan (Head of Strings) BMUS, Surrey; LRAM
Miss J B Marsh (Organist) MA, Sidney Sussex College,
    Cambridge; FRCO
T W Whittingham (Bandmaster) BA, London; LTCL
A J Thwaites (Head of Piano) BMUS, Manchester; GRNCM,
    PPRNCM, Royal Northern College of Music,
    dip GSMD Guildhall

PHYSICAL EDUCATION

*M J Potter MBE, BEd, Exeter
Mrs K L Newson BA, Sheffield;
    DipHE, St Paul's College, Cheltenham
Mrs H Rowland-Jones certEd, Chelsea College
Miss E L Stead BEd, De Montfort

PHYSICS

*S Mason BSC, Durham
N E Bailey BSC, Edinburgh
Mrs J M Barwise BSC, Manchester; MA, Chelsea College
Dr R Q Hackett MA, DPhil, St Peter's College, Oxford,
    CPhys, MInstP
A M Williams BSC, Loughborough

RELIGIOUS STUDIES

*Mrs S M Higgins BA, Manchester;
    certEd, Goldsmiths' College, London
Mrs E A Callaghan BEd, Sussex
Revd G W Dobbie MA, BD, St Andrews
Revd A Mitra MA, Keble College, Oxford
Revd N J Mitra MA, St Hugh's College, Oxford
I N Stannard BD, AKC, King's College, London; MA, Open
    University

STUDENT ASSISTANTS

Miss C Croft
R Massey-Hicks
Miss T Vaghi
N M Walsh BEd, Otago

WORD PROCESSING

Mrs V Kelly BA, Brighton

*Head of Department

MEDICAL STAFF AND MATRONS

MEDICAL OFFICERS

Dr S Fisher MB, BS, DRCOG, MRCGP
Dr K Noel-Paton MBBS, DOBST, OBST, RCOG

INFIRMARY

Mrs J Avenell RGN, (infirmary Manager)
Ms K Davidson RGN
Ms A M Gallagher RGN
Ms U Hall RGN, IHBCdip

DENTAL OFFICER

Mr V Wiffen BDS (London)

COUNSELLOR

Ms R Davies

MATRONS

Peele Mrs Y Sheppard-Burgess, Mrs H Breakwell
Thornton Mrs L Bassett, Mrs A Wilkinson
Middleton Mrs S Dyster, Mrs K Armour
Coleridge Miss H Sarstedt, Miss B Robinson
Lamb Mrs J Ingram, Mrs R Hunt
Barnes Mrs V Holliday, Mrs M Etherington
Maine Mrs K Grant, Mrs Y Siddle
Leigh Hunt Mrs N Chan, Miss S Faulkner

APPENDIX V
BUTTON GRECIANS IN THE ACADEMIC YEAR 1999–2000

SENIOR GRECIAN
Kate Atkinson (*Col A*)
SECOND MONITORS
George Busby (*Mid A*)
Sophie Naish (*LH A*)

PEELE A

Edward Marland* House Captain;
Adam Smith*

THORNTON A

Stephen Robson* House Captain;
Adrian Hill*

MIDDLETON A

James Busby* House Captain;
Ben Allwood*, George Busby*
Kasparas Jurgelionis Academic Buttons
Daniel Chandler Academic Buttons

MIDDLETON B

Tom Hurdman* House Captain, Academic Buttons;
Christian Ashby* Academic Buttons
Peter Gogalniceanu* Academic Buttons

COLERIDGE A

Bryony Passmore* House Captain
Rebecca Cook*
Jessica Daniell Academic Buttons
Clare Gladding Academic Buttons

COLERIDGE B

Sophie Channer* House Captain
Kate Atkinson* Academic Buttons
Katherine Crosse Academic Buttons
Nicola Batchelor Academic Buttons
Brigita Ziferman (Hertford) Academic Buttons

LAMB A

Adam Parmenter* House Captain, Academic Buttons
Peter Newman*
Andrew Saunders Academic Buttons

BARNES A

Alice Chubb* House Captain
Rejoice Amadi*

BARNES B

Vicky Bell* House Captain
Lucy Gwynn* (Hertford) Academic Buttons
Kim Miller Academic Buttons
Lucy Morgan* (Hertford) Band Captain,
  Academic Buttons

MAINE A

Tom Cairncross* House Captain, Academic Buttons
Leslie Lubwama*
Ryan Pickett Academic Buttons
In Tae Lee Academic Buttons

LEIGH HUNT A

Jo Tansley-Thomas* House Captain
Sophie Naish* Academic Buttons
Agnes Rothon* Academic Buttons

LEIGH HUNT B

Hannah Shaw* House Captain, Academic Buttons
Una Kosanovic*
Sarah Ginn Academic Buttons
Ellen Mayhew (Hertford) Academic Buttons

Buttons are awarded to Grecians, either for outstanding academic merit (ability, flair and rigour) or to those who are appointed School Monitors. House Captains are always School Monitors.

*School Monitor

APPENDIX VI
PUPILS IN THE SCHOOL IN THE ACADEMIC YEAR 1999–2000

Boys: 472   59%
Girls: 328   41%
Total: 800   100%

| HOME AREA | | | | | METHODS OF ENTRY | | |

	Number	%
Sussex	248	31
London & Middlesex	215	27
Surrey & Hampshire	95	12
Other home counties	89	11
West & South West	52	7
Kent	25	3
Anglia	18	2
North	18	2
Overseas	17	2
Midlands	11	1
Wales	9	1
Scotland	3 under	1
TOTALS	**800**	**100%**

METHODS OF ENTRY	Number	%
Presentation categories		
Governors' presentees	182	23
Wests' Gift	40	5
Distinguished service	24	3
Other presentees	86	11
Competitive categories		
Council of Almoners		
Nominees	228	28
London entry	137	17
New Foundationers	14	2
Other competitive	54	7
Non-Foundationers		
(children of full time staff)	35	4
TOTALS	**800**	**100%**

HOUSES AND YEARS GROUPS

Year group:	2	3	LE	UF	GE	Dep	GR	Total
SENIOR BOYS' HOUSES								
Peele A				12	10	11	12	45
Thornton A				10	8	12	9	39
Middleton A				13	11	9	13	46
Middleton B				13	12	11	11	47
Lamb A				13	11	13	8	45
Maine A				13	11	14	9	47
JUNIOR BOYS' HOUSES								
Peele B	16	17	18					51
Thornton B	17	18	18					53
Lamb B	16	17	17					50
Maine B	16	17	16					49
Boys total	65	69	69	74	63	70	62	472
GIRLS' HOUSES								
Coleridge A	8	8	8	8	6	8	7	53
Coleridge B	8	8	9	5	8	7	7	52
Barnes A	8	7	7	6	8	6	9	51
Barnes B	8	9	7	8	7	8	8	55
Leigh Hunt A	8	9	9	9	8	10	8	61
Leigh Hunt B	8	8	7	6	8	9	10	56
Girls total	48	49	47	42	45	48	49	328
Total, boys and girls	113	118	116	116	108	118	111	800

In July 2000 the separation of boys into junior and senior houses ceased. From September 2000 boys' houses followed the same arrangements as the girls, accommodating all pupils across the age range 11 to 17 years.

APPENDICES: HISTORICAL

APPENDIX I
CHRIST'S HOSPITAL AND THE MONARCHY

Edward VI, the Founder and Patron of the School, was in no doubt that, in signing the Charter on 26 June 1553, he was giving his supreme support to this fledgling charity. But after his death religious reforms had not been adopted by the School so the 'Blewe Boys' incurred the wrath of his successor, Mary, and she turned her face when they sought to make an oration to her from a platform at Aldgate on her accession in 1553.

The future of the School was put in jeopardy by her royal commission in 1554, which intended to shut it down; and it was only through the intervention of divine grace, in the form of Friar John's unexpected support, a position reinforced by powerful connections in the City of London, that the School did not close shortly after it had opened.

Elizabeth I appears to have been more favourably disposed towards the 'Blewe Boyes' for in January 1581 she received their Loyal Address at Temple Bar. To this day the Amicable Society of Blues mark her accession with a Dining Night. King James I received the Loyal Address at Barkingside, and Charles II was the first of a succession of monarchs to receive it in St Paul's, or more accurately in the churchyard, where he reined his horse while passing from the Tower of London to Whitehall on 22 April 1661, the day before his coronation. The pamphlet containing this address, given by senior pupil James Hewlett, is held at St Paul's Library. It states:

'We humbly beseech you (most dread SOVEREIGN) that as at first EDWARD VI who once sway'd the Sceptre of this kingdom, laid a Foundation for the Reception of poor Orphans, who have since been upheld by all Your Royall Ancestors, especially your late FATHER of blessed MEMORY, so you would shine upon us still by Your gracious Favour and Princely Indulgence. There are above eleven hundred of us, part whereof have, in the name of all, presented themselves this Day as lively Monuments of God's Mercy, and real objects of Christian Charity: for whom, through the pious care and faithful Industry of the Right Honourable the Lord Mayor, Aldermen, Governors, and liberal Benefactors, a Table hath been spread, and other necessaries both for Soul and Body afforded, even in the midst of those Exigencies that exposed others to Want and Penury.

'But I am afraid any longer (Most gracious SOVEREIGN) to detail your Royall Ears with Childish Smatterings. I have done.

'Heaven grant you long to live, and prosperously to reign over us: that when you have finished God's work, having Sate upon this Earthly Throne, Beloved, you may leave it Lamented. In the meantime let Orphans echo forth with Grateful Acclamations.'

A postscript has been added by an onlooker:
'Reader. Had you been there when this Speech was spoken, you would have been much affected with it, and admired at the Oratour's modest composedness in speaking, and HIS MAJESTY'S gracious Condescension in Casting an Eye upon the children there seated, and honouring them with his Royall Presence, reining up his horse near to the Sea Hold, to hear what the Youth was to present to him.

'The Youth that spoke this is now a Graduate of the University, and a hopefull Instrument of promoting God's glory, and the Honour and Credit of that Hospital where once he had his Education.'

Charles II, under the enthusiastic influence of Samuel Pepys, Secretary of the Admiralty, signed Letters Patent for the establishment of the Royal Mathematical School at Christ's Hospital on 19 August 1673, an act commemorated in the vast historical painting by Antonio Verrio, which hangs in Dining Hall. Charles II, whose thriftiness was renowned, did not commit royal funds to its establishment. That was due to a bequest by a Governor of Christ's Hospital, Richard Aldworth.

Subsequent monarchs received the Loyal Address at St Paul's churchyard – King William and Queen Mary on 29 October 1692, Queen Anne on 9 November 1702, King George I on 10 September 1714, King George II on 9 November 1727, King George III on 9 November 1761 and Queen Victoria on 9 November 1837. A bas-relief frieze, formerly housed at Temple Bar and now in the reception area of the School Office, shows a Senior Grecian, F G Nash, kneeling before the young Queen as she attends from the State coach on her way to Guildhall.

Queen Victoria was a real supporter of the School. As a Governor, she presented pupils to the School and instituted the practice of inviting pupils from the Royal Mathematical School to display their maritime paintings each year in the drawing room, either at Windsor or Buckingham Palace. Normally two paintings were selected to be hung in the royal collection, and their creators were rewarded with a golden pencil case. When the Queen celebrated her Diamond Jubilee in 1897 Christ's Hospital pupils lined the processional route, waving large white and pink handkerchiefs which had been provided especially for the occasion.

Her son, Edward VII, as Prince of Wales, laid the Foundation Stone on behalf of the Queen at Horsham on

23 October 1897, with full Masonic ceremonial. His statue is among those fronting the Old Science School. His son, George V, received the Loyal Address on the steps of St Paul's as he was entering the cathedral for a Thanksgiving Service after his coronation on 12 June 1911. He visited the School at Horsham shortly after becoming President in 1904; and his son, Edward VIII, visited the School to open the New Science Schools in 1930 subsequent to becoming President in 1919.

Edward VIII abdicated before his coronation and therefore received no Address, but his brother, George VI, received an oration on the steps of St Paul's on 24 May 1937, as did Queen Elizabeth II, our Patron, as she entered St Paul's on 9 June 1953. This oration was not read, just proffered, by the Senior Grecian, H B G Johnston, but its text, and the royal reply, have been preserved:

'May it please Your Majesty:

'Since Edward VI of Blessed Memory in 1553 granted his Royal Charter to the Religious, Royal and Ancient Foundation of Christ's Hospital, the children of Christ's Hospital have from time to time been granted the gracious privilege of presenting their humble duty on the occasion of their Sovereign's first visit to the City of London after the Coronation.

'In this four hundredth year of our Foundation, we offer our humble and loyal greetings to Your Majesty, deeply sensible of the honour which Your Majesty has bestowed upon us by becoming our Patron and the privilege we enjoy by virtue of the Presidency of His Royal Highness the Duke of Gloucester.

'That Your majesty may have a long, happy and prosperous Reign is the earnest prayer of the Sons and Daughters of this ancient House, who share the hope of all your Majesty's subjects that Your majesty and His Royal Highness the Duke of Edinburgh may be blessed with many years of health and happiness.'

9th June 1953.

Queen Elizabeth II replied:

'I thank you for your loyal and dutiful Address.

'It is with great pleasure that I receive your loyal greetings in the year when you are celebrating the four hundredth anniversary of your Foundation. By its work through the years your ancient House has won a high reputation and as your patron I share with you your happiness on this notable landmark in its history.

'I am confident that your fine tradition will continue to inspire all who pass through your Schools to give of their best in honourable and devoted endeavour and service, as their predecessors have in the past. May God bless the work of the Schools throughout the years that lie ahead.'

9th June 1953.

Richard, Duke of Gloucester, succeeded his father as President of Christ's Hospital in 1974. During that time he has maintained a keen interest in the life of the School, taking the Chair at Founders' Day dinner in 1977, opening the Counting House in 1985, laying the Foundation Stone for the newly-merged schools of Christ's Hospital Horsham, and Christ's Hospital Hertford, on 23 October 1985, in opening the Sports Centre in September 1990, and attending School functions on a regular basis.

This keen interest by His Royal Highness reflects an enduring truth – that the relationship between the Crown and Christ's Hospital is a real one, rich in affection and support – and that in conferring his patronage almost 450 years ago on this Religious, Royal and Ancient Foundation, Edward VI was opening a door which none could shut, of mutual, and valued, blessing.

APPENDIX II

THE BOYS' UNIFORM

When, in 1552, the City of London gathered up 'fatherless children and other poor children' and cared for them in the former premises of the Grey Friars in Newgate Street, there was a real imperative to follow the injunction of St Matthew 25, to 'clothe the naked', for indeed most of the children admitted to the School in November 1552 were filthy and ragged.

The citizens of London, from senior clerics and merchants to ordinary citizens, were so generous in their support that there were smart new clothes for the children who were the first occupants of the refurbished School. They were clothed in 'russet' cottons, a brown outer garment which was close fitting to the waist, with full skirts, made of a coarse napped wool. By the following Easter, however, in time for the Spital Sermon at Paules Cross, they were clothed in their splendid new uniform of a long outer coat of a dark blue plonket (a heavy woollen cloth, also known as 'blanket cloth'), covering an undercoat of yellow kersey (a coarse woollen cloth), with yellow hose, plum coloured girdle and a red cap. Underneath the outer 'Housey' coat and petticoat was a plain white shirt.

Hanging from the girdle was an ink-horn, a penner and a gypciere (a small bag for keeping coins), or a 'muck-ender', a long handkerchief, for wiping nose and eyes.

A cap completed the outfit. It was a 'thrum' cap, round, soft, woollen, with a small brim and a hat-band with a tuft on top. Originally red, within a few years it changed to black, though keeping the red hat-band. It was usually carried or tucked into the girdle, and only worn for ceremonial occasions, or for doffing. This uniform is shown in the putative Holbein which hangs above the fireplace in the Library. The caps had fallen into disuse by the 1860s perhaps because, according to informed sources, they were filled by pupils with water from the fountain in the quadrangle, and thrown at each other as water bombs.

The early uniform was, in accord with Tudor style, very colourful. The dye used for the coats was believed to be woad, which could be diluted to give a wide range of hues. The collar was in a shawl or roll design. There has been much speculation as to why blue was chosen. One view was that it was obtained by using a cheap dye. But Valentine Knapp, a nineteenth-century Old Blue, believes that blue was chosen to distinguish the children within the care of Christ's Hospital from those attending other charity schools, who would have worn a similar but a different coloured uniform.

It remained unchanged until the rise of Puritanism in the seventeenth century, when the light-blue shawl- or roll-collar was replaced by a small, stand-up one, to allow for a large, white, square, shirt-collar. The colour of the outer coat appears to have deepened to a dark navy, bordering on black, as was the cap.

By 1706, the coat was fastened with brass buttons, and by 1758 the buttons were of white metal and embossed with the head of Edward VI.

In 1638 the linings of the coats, as well as the petticoats and hose, were dyed yellow, 'to avoid vermin by reason the white cotton is held to breed the same'. The dye may have been saffron, or perhaps humbler onion skins. It was the smell of the dye which was believed to repel the rats and mice that gnawed at unguarded flesh, or overpowered the fleas and lice which were the scourge of many.

In 1736, instead of the yellow hose, breeches were provided for 'sick and weakly' children. Originally of brown leather, they were soon changed to moleskin (a coarse fustian typically used for working men's breeches), and by 1760 had replaced the hose. At first they had square falls for an opening, with a taped gusset at the back, side vents, with four buttons at the knee, and additional buttons to take braces. They were cut narrow and figure-hugging, with one fob pocket on the right hand side, and horn buttons. Over the next 150 years they metamorphosed through drab, brown drillings, to serge and the square falls were replaced by a button fly front. By the beginning of the twentieth century they were black, and as far as wartime restrictions allowed, made of wool, and wool-and-nylon mixtures.

Since their Puritan introduction the bands have changed their shape. From the eighteenth century, they became narrower and closer together, and by the middle of the last century they were no more than a collar band with two rectangular overlapping flaps attached, awkwardly, to the neck band of the shirt. Now they are simply two rectangles of starched white cotton, stitched together at the top, buttoned to the inside edge of the neck band, which fall off, too easily, in the wind, or when running.

Shoes are thought to have been black, low-heeled, with a narrow, squared-off toe. They have changed little over the centuries. In 1637 they were either in 'neats leather' (ox hide) for large sizes or smaller sizes in calves leather. Initially made by the school cobbler, by 1735 they were made in Northamptonshire. Later in the eighteenth century, in accord with current fashion trends, they sported a large buckle but by the middle of the nineteenth century were again tied with tapes, at least for the younger pupils. A buckled shoe reappears towards the end of the nineteenth century, and a fine calf-lined and buckled shoe was worn certainly until the first World War; possibly until much later. By the 1920s they were calf-lined, black, and laced. In Victorian times they were hob-nailed to increase durability, and even up to the 1950s all shoes were clamped (given a second sole and heel), with a steel quarter-tip added to the heel.

The stockings (never socks) which replaced the hose were always knee length and made of a worsted wool, dyed yellow, again a device for deterring vermin. There are stories that at night the stockings were alternatively worn on the feet, or wrapped around the head, whichever was deemed to need more protection.

The round metal badges which some pupils wear on the left breast of their Housey coat have their origins in the sixteenth century, when those in need were specifically supported by a particular body or company among the City's merchants, and the badge gave public expression to that fact. They perform the same function today – indicating the individual or corporate identity of the sponsor whose generosity, through the ancient right of 'presentation', has made possible the provision of a place at the School.

Button Grecians' or School Monitors' coats differ in several respects from the normal Housey coat and the sartorial distinctions of their special Housey coats are described in Chapter One.

The leather girdle, (never belt), is worn by Second Formers (11 to 12 year olds) with the 'narrowie' buckled at the front. Third Formers wear the buckle at the back. The LE (Little Erasmus, 13–14 year olds), have a 'broadie', and to that they add a special ornate silver, 'broadie' buckle. There is a practice, of plaiting their girdles by a process of slitting and folding. Worn properly, the girdle should sit naturally at the seam between the bodice and the skirt of the Housey coat.

There is no doubt that the ancient uniform of Christ's Hospital has been its most public and enduring feature. Most people know it as the School with a long dark blue coat and yellow stockings. It is remarkable, indeed, that in this age of rapidly-changing fashions and instant designer-wear, the outer coat of the uniform has remained virtually unchanged for 450 years.

APPENDIX III
THE HERTFORD SCHOOL AND THE MERGER WITH THE BOYS

Christ's Hospital's link with the county of Hertfordshire goes back to its foundation. For when, in November 1552, 380 children were admitted to the School in Newgate Street, 100 were immediately put out to nurse with families in Hertford and Ware, as well as in Essex. The rate for caring for these babies and toddlers was 8d. to 1s. per week, with a bonus for those who had had smallpox.

This link with Hertfordshire continued and, in 1666, was strengthened, when the Great Fire of London seriously damaged a number of buildings at the School, and pupils had to be evacuated to a safer environment. It is not known exactly how long this sojourn lasted, but it is recorded that in 1687 Broxbourne Church erected a gallery for the use of the Christ's Hospital pupils. During this time the Governors of the School had been considering the longer-term plans for the pupils, to which end Sir Henry Chauncy of Yardley Bury, a friend and prospective Governor of the School, negotiated the purchase of a plot of land at, 'an open and airy space at the end of the town next to London', on which a School-house, cottages to house 320 children, and two houses for Masters, were built.

In 1707 one of these cottages was reserved for the exclusive use of 'maiden children', and a Schoolmistress was appointed to serve them. In 1720 John and Frances West made their magnificent Gift to the School, with the stipulation that it should be used to educate both boys and girls, a stipulation which proved a lifeline for the education of girls at all at Christ's Hospital in later years; for there were times when the complete abolition of education for girls was seriously considered, and it was only the need to service this benefaction that ensured that at least 18 girls were retained on the Foundation.

By 1743 girls occupied four of the cottages at Hertford, and the establishment could, with justification, at that stage, be called a girls' school. The daily routine centred on the development of domestic skills, particularly on routine handcrafts, and discipline was often harsh – reinforced by the use of demeaning punishment bands indicating 'Gossip', or 'Beware the thief', which were tied on the arm or forehead – and backed up by severe beatings.

In 1750 'The Place' at Ware, which accommodated 200 junior boys, was closed down and the boys were transferred to Hertford, which necessitated the removal of the girls back to London. But this was only a temporary measure and, in 1778, the girls moved back to Hertford, this time occupying the new purpose-built school which had just been completed for them.

The major part of the girls' time was spent in sewing, mending and knitting: they sewed shirts and bands for the boys at Hertford and in London, as well as knitting their yellow stockings, and they sewed and mended for them-

selves. (In the Christ's Hospital Museum there are samplers produced by girls of twelve, which are of the highest standard.) In their last year they were taught household crafts in preparation for lives in domestic service. Weightier subjects were addressed, in writing, science and mathematics, but they were taught as catechisms, with no original thought desired or welcomed from the girls. It would be another hundred years, under the dynamic leadership of Miss M E Robertson, before the education of girls was seriously considered.

Through most of the nineteenth century the number of girls declined, until there were only the 18 pupils who had to be retained to comply with the conditions of the Wests' Gifts. This compared with over 1,000 boys on the Foundation. By this time the attractive green, brown and blue Tudor dress – which is so well depicted in the 'Charter painting' over the fireplace in the Library – had long been abandoned, and the girls wore coiffed caps and shoulder capes, or tippets, over a long dark blue dress.

In 1875 the School advertised for a Principal Mistress who must have, 'a thorough acquaintance with all subjects embraced in an ordinary English education, together with French, Drawing and Instrumental Music.' Mrs Susan Lyster was the successful candidate and, although she only stayed for three years, she was responsible for introducing a new style of dress. Now a plain blue serge dress was adopted, with a small upright white collar. The skirts were long and voluminous and worn with black button boots and coarse black woollen stockings.

In 1878 *The Blue* reported that Hertford had been increased to '70 little maidens', and that the Governors were looking to increase that by a further 130. Again in 1889 *The Blue* records that, 'The Girls' School at Christ's Hospital, Hertford, has passed a greater number of girls in honours than any other girls' school that entered for the Junior Cambridge Local last December.'

By 1891 the influence of The Scheme, which had been drawn up in response to the Endowed Schools Act of 1869, began to be felt in Hertford life; for the roll increased to 114, and History, Geography, Mathematics and some Natural Science were offered on the curriculum, as well as a choice between French and German. And instead of leaving in early teens to go into service, as most girls had done, they could stay until the age of 17, or even 19. The movement to liberate and empower women, which was beginning to touch upon so many areas of public life, was also having an effect upon the life of the girls at Hertford.

In 1902 the new School for boys at Horsham was finished, and the junior boys from Hertford joined the migration from London, to settle in their new Prep Houses, now known (since 1966) as Leigh Hunt A and B. Hertford had also been completely redeveloped to retain parity between the two Schools, and now there were eight new separate blocks, an Assembly Hall, Chapel, new classroom blocks, a swimming bath, gymnasium and a sanatorium. This redeveloped School was formally opened in 1906 by The Prince and Princess of Wales in a ceremony which was given added excitement when the horse drawing their carriage bolted. It was quickly restrained by a constable, and no harm was done. Later in the century an octagonal Library, an Art School, a new Science Block and a squash court were added.

This period, from 1902 to 1985, was – apart from two World Wars – a stable era for the girls, for they were able to cast off the sense of inferiority that had hounded them for years, and consolidate all that was good in their well-equipped School. Wards were run under a Ward Mistress who was not a member of the academic staff: initially the teaching Mistresses simply arrived on site to teach, but gradually greater integration of the teaching staff into non-teaching time was achieved. During this period the uniform changed rapidly, and photographs of the time show pupils in turn wearing gym slips, tunics, dresses, skirts, blouses, blazers and jackets; with a Tam o'Shanter, or a straw boater, or cloche, or felt hat.

Now the girls are fully integrated members of the community at Horsham and in the unfolding of the 450-year old story that is Christ's Hospital, the years that they spent at Hertford can only be viewed as a sojourn.

APPENDIX IV
A HISTORY OF THE CURRICULUM

In the early days of Christ's Hospital it was considered that the basics of reading, writing, arithmetic and learning a musical instrument were the most profitable subjects to teach children whose aim in life was to secure employment.

The classics were to be taught in Grammar Schools to children who were destined for the universities of Oxford or Cambridge. The fact that some Christ's Hospital pupils, too, were taught classics appears to have come as something of a surprise, but John Priestman is recorded as having gone from Christ's Hospital to Cambridge in 1566, and he was not necessarily the first to do so.

The list of officers appointed on 6 October 1552 to serve the children makes no difference in status between masters and ancillary staff: indeed there was a case in 1573 where a teacher was promoted to the post of porter!. Three hundred and eighty children were admitted to the School in November 1552; of these 80 were girls and put in the charge of matrons and sisters. The boys were taught by six masters – an Upper Grammar Master, and Grammar Usher; The Clarke, who also taught writing; two School Masters for the 'Petties ABCs'; and a 'Teacher of Pricksonge'. Subjects were taught by rote and children were expected to remain passive. Punishments were summary and harsh.

In the 16th and 17th centuries, as benefactions permitted, various 'Schools' were founded at Christ's Hospital to teach the different subjects. The Grammar School was part of the original foundation of 1552. The Writing School had first been established through the generosity of Lady Mary Ramsey in 1596. This fine school was destroyed in the Great Fire of 1666 and its replacement, designed by Christopher Wren and Nicholas Hawksmoor, was completed in 1695 through the generosity of Sir John Moore, at a cost of over £5,000. Sir John's statue, by Grinling Gibbons, now stands in a niche on the exterior wall of Big School at Horsham.

The Mathematical School, for training pupils in navigational skills, was established in 1673 through the good offices of Samuel Pepys. The Drawing School was set up in 1693 to teach Technical Drawing to the 'Mathemats', and the celebrated illustrator Bernard Lens joined its staff in 1705. The Reading School was established by Sir Robert Clayton in 1778. The Science Schools are a feature of Horsham life. The Old Science School, which aimed at teaching according to 'self-discovery' or heuristic methods, was built in 1902. The New Science Schools were completed in 1930.

This system of separate Schools is still, to some extent, in operation. There is still a Music School and Big School (now largely used as an assembly hall), and a Design and Technology (formerly Manual) School. They are now viewed more as 'departments', as in most other schools, but there is still a measure of independence, which can make timetabling a complex puzzle for Dr Roger Hackett, the School's Director of Studies.

The curriculum was modified over the years to include Hebrew and, in 1837, the teaching of French was begun. Chemistry was added in 1869; German and Natural Philosophy – the forerunner of Physics, were introduced in 1871. That year also witnessed the first public display of marching and playing by the School Band. The merger with Hertford in 1985 brought new skills, when Food and Nutrition were introduced to the curriculum; and also, since the 1980s, Information Technology has gained in importance – both as a subject in its own right, and as a useful tool in the development of all other learning skills – in the lives of both pupils and staff.

APPENDIX V
ST MATTHEW'S DAY

There are many theories about the adoption of St Matthew's Day as one of the high days in Christ's Hospital's calendar. The most likely is that it was on that day that – falling as it does in September, which originally would have been just under a year since the School was opened – the Governors of the three Royal Hospitals were first called to give an account to their masters in the City of London of how their affairs were being handled.

In November 1552, 380 people – men, women and children – moved into the newly-refurbished premises of the Greyfriars in Newgate Street. Careful accounts had been kept during this first year thanks to the work of Richard Grafton, the School's Treasurer, and it was decided that these accounts should be presented to the Aldermen of the City of London for their approval on 21 September 1553.

Initially the three Hospitals – Bridewell, St Thomas and Christ's – presented joint accounts to their City scrutineers. But over the next 100 years they developed separate systems of government, and each Hospital appointed officers to keep accounts and oversee their own affairs. They also, regretfully, became less careful in keeping accurate accounts, and in keeping their business open to public scrutiny; so much so that Samuel Pepys, when investigating the affairs of Christ's Hospital in the 1680s, found many instances of inefficiency, malpractice and downright corruption.

After a great deal of dispute with the City of London it was agreed that, every year, on St Matthew's Day, those men who carried the responsibility for the management of Christ's Hospital – the Governors – should present themselves, carrying their green staves of office, to the Lord Mayor and Aldermen of the City of London. This practice has continued through the centuries but now only a token number of Governors actually present themselves to the Lord Mayor and his Officers. However, a complete list of the Governors of Christ's Hospital and Bridewell Royal Hospital (King Edward's School, Witley) is presented to him by the Clerk of Christ's Hospital for his inspection.

When Christ's Hospital was based in Newgate Street, this formality took place in The Great Hall. It now takes place in St Paul's Cathedral, where the whole School, together with teaching staff, and some support staff, Old Blues and parents, assemble. At one time the list of Governors was hand-written and richly embellished; now it is computer-generated, and has just a plain blue cover.

This solemn occasion was, in the course of time, enriched by orations from Senior pupils. Following the tradition of the Scholars' Disputations, which formerly took place in the cloisters of Newgate Street, the Senior Grecian would have given an oration to the assembled group of officers and dignitaries. Under the careful and lengthy tutelage of the Upper Grammar Master, he would have been rehearsed in his oration, which touched on the benefits he had received at the School and the prospects before him. The Second Monitor would deliver his oration in Latin. Collections would then be taken up after the orations, whose purpose was to support these pupils in their further studies at the universities. Since the move out of London in 1902 the oration has become part of the Horsham tradition of Speech Day, which takes place in May or June and is attended by the Lord Mayor, Sheriffs and household officers.

In the days when beadles assisted in the oversight of pupils it was also customary, on St Matthew's Day, for the City Marshal to give a report of their work. Those considered to be effective were approved by the Court of Aldermen to continue in office.

The actual St Matthew's Day service was, for many years, held in Christ Church, Newgate Street, the former conventual church of the Greyfriars, which the School attended on Sundays. When it was bombed during the Second World War the service was transferred to St Sepulchre's, Holborn. From 1902 until 1996 only a representative number of pupils joined the Marching Band in processing through the City and attending the service. However in 1997, in recognition of that special year in which the anniversary of the laying of the Foundation Stone for the Horsham site was celebrated, all the pupils took part in the St Matthew's Day service at St Paul's Cathedral and this practice is being followed until 2002.

APPENDIX VI
THE SPITAL SERMON

The origins of the Spital Sermon are uncertain, but it is known to have been an established tradition some two hundred years before Christ's Hospital began its great work of charity in 1552. Certainly in the reign, and under the instruction, of Richard II in 1398 sermons were being preached at Paules Cross and St Mary Spittle. And in John Stow's Survey of London, vol. 1 (Kingsford ed. 1910) it states that Philip Malpas, one of the City Sheriffs, gave £20 in 1439 'to preachers at the Spittle the three Easter Holidays'. The Sermon takes its name from the Priory or

Hospital of St Mary Without Bishopsgate, better known as St Mary Spital, which was founded in 1197. The term 'Spital', or 'Spittle', as it is also known, derives from 'Hospital', which means a charitable institution: over time the aspirant was dropped from usage, being too cumbersome for the forbears of cockney dialect and culture.

The aim of the Sermon was to attract attention, and so alms and bequests, to the Hospital. The Sermon was usually preached by a bishop, invited by the Lord Mayor, the Court of Aldermen and the Governors of the Royal Hospitals, namely St Bartholomew's, Bethlem, Bridewell, Christ's and St Thomas's. The City's links with Barts, Bethlem and St Thomas's were severed by the National Health Act of 1946, and now the Sermon is attended only by the Lord Mayor, the Court of Aldermen, Common Councilmen, and the Head Masters and Governors of Bridewell (now King Edward's School, Witley), and Christ's Hospital. The lesson is read each year by a senior pupil from one of the Schools, while the other School provides the Choir. Each year the rôles are reversed.

Stow describes how, in 1439, sermons were preached at Paule's Cross on the three Easter holidays; these were reduced to two when the services were moved to Christ Church, Newgate Street. Since the 1880s only one has been preached, usually on the Thursday of the week of the meeting of the Common Council after Easter.

It became customary for the pupils and governors of Christ's Hospital to attend these sermons and Stow records that: 'In the year 1594, the pulpit being old was taken down and a new set up; also a large house . . . for the governors and pupils of Christ's Hospital to sit in'. But it apparently quickly fell into disrepair.

The theme for contemporary bishops, who are invited to preach by The Mansion House, is 'To spread the Truth'. The venue for the sermon has changed over the centuries. Pearce tells us that, in 1641, when Richard Vines of the Westminster Assembly was the preacher, the service was held in Christ Church, at which he preached on 'The Impostures of Seducing Teachers'. The original pulpit in Spital Square was destroyed in the Civil War (1642–46): after that the service was held at St Paul's Cross, St Mary Spittle or at St Bride's in Fleet Street. According to Pearce, it removed to Christ Church in 1797 and remained there until that church was bombed in the Second World War.

Since then it has been preached in the beautiful church of St Lawrence Jewry next Guildhall. The word 'Jewry' in its title refers to the fact that this part of London was the Jewish quarter, before the Jews were expelled in the 14th century.

The Spital Sermon has always been considered one of the high days in the Christ's Hospital calendar. It was at the Spital Sermon in 1553 that the children, according to Stow, first appeared in their 'blew' coats.

The smart appearance of the pupils was commented upon by Samuel Pepys in his diary entry for 2 April 1662 in which he comments, 'Mr Moore came to me and he and I walked to the Spittle an houre or two before my Lord Mayor and the blew-coat boys come, which at last they did, and a fine sight of charity it is indeed.' In 1670 their sartorial elegance was given greater impetus by the will of Edward Arris in which he left £100 for the School, the interest from which was to 'bee laid out for ever in gloves for the Children to be worn euery Easter when they wait upon the Lord Maior to St Maries Spittle.' The intention was not only to supply gloves, but that, according to the Court Book of 5 July 1670, 'every child may have upon his gloves, a paper with these words printed in legible characters (He is Risen).' Obviously difficulties arose from the execution of these instructions and within a short space of time the paper was transferred to the left breast. The legend was variously corrupted into 'He is risen, he is risen, All the Jews must go to prison', to 'He is a Rifleman', so perhaps it is as well that the custom came to an end in 1877.

Another custom associated with the Spital Sermon is that, by a Court Order of 24 March 1681, 'The Mathematicall children' are, 'to carry a Ruler & Compasse, the Writing children to have a red pen in their eare, and the Reading Scholars to have a Bible or Testament in their hands'. This practice continued until the first quarter of the nineteenth century. Pearce notes that it was the custom at one time to give the boys wine with their buns; this may have had something to do with a complaint made by the Court of Aldermen in 1693 'of great rudeness and disorders lately committed by the boys of Christ's and Bridewell Hospitals at Church time in Easter last.'

Another tradition, dating from 1625, was that of asking a pupil to compose a short poem which would be set to music by the School's Music Master. This would be used both as an anthem at the services, and – by careful wording on the reverse of the order of service – as a plea, to encourage observance to the injunction to give alms to the poor, and in particular those in the care of Christ's Hospital. They were florid rather than subtle in their sentiments, as the following example shows:

'Low on the Dunghill and the Dust, Naked and Poor we lay
Our clothing Rags, our Food a Crust, our Beauty Filth and Clay:
May length of Days, and Wealth, and Peace, and Virtue's brighter
   Crown,
King William and Queen Mary Grace, as they Grace England's
   Throne.'

Now that it is shorter and only attended by the choir, some staff and a few senior pupils, today's observance seems altogether understated, and poorer, by comparison.

APPENDIX VII
THE MARCHING BAND

It is so much part of the essential life of the School that it is hard to believe that, in Christ's Hospital terms, the Marching Band is a relatively late arrival on to our corporate scene. For it was only in 1868 that some pupils, finding drill dull, asked if instruments could be bought, and a small band formed, to enliven their marching.

Mr Foster White, the Treasurer of the time, warmly assented and, at his own cost, purchased a few instruments. He also paid the salary of Mr Richard Hopkins, the first Band Master, and thus the first Christ's Hospital Band was formed.

Within three years Mr Foster White became ill and had to relinquish his post as Treasurer. He had been held in high regard, not only for the prizes which he instituted, the lectures that he arranged and the geological expeditions that he championed, but also because of the Suppers he laid on for the Band. With his departure the Governors were faced with a decision: would they take over the commitment of financing and resourcing the Band?

The Head Master was strong in urging this, a decision which was supported by the Sub-Committee of Education. He estimated that it would cost between £100 and £125 a year; which was, perhaps, optimistic, if he was including the salary of a Band Master. In the event the Almoners decided to keep the Band and Mr Hopkins was confirmed in his post of Band Master. From his sickbed Mr Foster White conveyed the news that he had made a gift to the School of the instruments which he had purchased. It was now, in name and in fact, the Christ's Hospital Band.

Over the years it has grown from a small, static group to the dynamic 100-strong, highly-trained corps that we enjoy today. Earliest reports from *The Blue* suggest that initial performances excelled more in volume than in finesse, as J H White's contribution in the 1870s recounts: 'Easter

Tuesday was a great day at our School. We were proud of our band which, with its big drum, kettle drums, cornets, trombones and other instruments of torture, could make more noise for less money, the musicians not being paid, than any other band in the Metropolis.'

By the 1920s it had grown to some 30–35 members, who played the whole School into lunch each day. The smaller Bugle Band then accompanied the march into tea. Only breakfast passed without the Band to herald it, though Sunday always remained a day of rest for the musicians.

The celebrated display of Beating Retreat, which takes place in the evening of the last day of the Summer Term, is an amalgam of three different ceremonies. It blends together the medieval tradition of beating a drum half an hour before sunset to warn all visitors to leave the town; it encompasses the naval practice of the lowering of the Royal Ensign at sunset; and it was the beating of a drum which signalled the time for malingering soldiers to return to their barracks. These three practices are now combined into an hour of faultless marching and countermarching; a fitting tribute to those who are leaving. It is believed to have started during the Second World War, in support of the War Effort appeal in Horsham, and to salute those leaving Christ's Hospital to train for active service.

The Marching Band is one of the brightest jewels in the crown of Christ's Hospital, a symbol of hope and encouragement to all who experience that breathtaking, spine-tingling moment when, in full cry, it skirts Big School and appears under the arch of the Quad. It is 132 years since Treasurer Foster White purchased those first instruments. We thank him for his generosity and vision, and thank the Band for the glorious, unique and irreplaceable contribution it makes to the life of Christ's Hospital.

APPENDIX VIII
FOOD AND DIET

When the Governors of Christ's Hospital met on 6 October 1552 to appoint officers to serve the children, the first appointment they made was that of Thomas Cleaton who was not only a Sheriff of London, but also a baker, and it was for those services that he was chosen. They also appointed Anthonye Ideson as Cooke, and John Wasse as Bruer. As the School was situated literally next to the meat market it is presumed that they had easy, if not always safe, access to supplies of meat. The earliest menus not only mention milk, butter, bread and beer, they also talk of mutton and beef; and fish – plaice, whiting and herring.

The menu changed over the centuries, to include pud-

ding pies, water gruel with currants, old pease and pottage and furmity, (wheat boiled in milk with sweetener and spices). Beer continued to be provided at mealtimes, but was of inferior quality and known as the 'washings of the brewers' aprons'. It was only the Grecians who were permitted good beer.

In the late 18th century a physician to the School, Richard Budd, insisted that potatoes be included in the diet. In 1874 the matter became more pressing when over seventy children at Hertford suffered from an outbreak of ringworm, which was shortly followed by scarlet fever. In response the accommodation of the children was improved and the Steward ensured that larger quantities of vegetables were supplied to the children; he also announced that he had introduced rhubarb jam and baked apples to the menu once a week.

G A T Allan records that, 'Revolutionary changes were made in 1893, and a meat breakfast was served four days a week; pudding twice a week, on other days cheese; variety of dishes was introduced, such as haricot, stew, hash, steaks, mince; and the evening drink was strengthened into tea. When "fish and duff" was served the pudding came first; the plates were then scoured with bread – thrown under the table – and the same plates were used for fish.' (The bread on the floor may account for the hundreds of rats which appeared from various holes and swarmed over the Great Hall in London as soon as the pupils had vacated it.) 'Boys had the option of a piece of bread and cheese, or a mug of milk instead of cheese, served in the Wards at 8.00pm.'

In the 1920s Head Master Hamilton Fyfe urged the provision of more fresh fruit, but knowing that it would be too expensive for Dining Hall to supply, he asked that it should be sold in the Tuck Shop at cost price, to a maximum value of £50 a year.

Dr G E Friend, who was Medical Officer at Christ's Hospital from 1913–1947 noted, 'The average quantity of food given is insufficient. The daily supply of milk is too small. Anti-ascorbic elements are dangerously short. There is deterioration of health going on amongst the boys, and the index of vitality is being lowered.' In consequence it was agreed that the boys should be provided alternately with butter and margarine at meals. It was Dr Friend who also insisted that pupils be supplied with forti-fied biscuits during the second World War; these were made by the Horsham firm of Prewett's. It is noteworthy that in those early days a cartload of bread was brought to the School each day from Horsham, drawn by labouring horses.

Dr Friend was assiduous in weighing and measuring each pupil and it could therefore be noted that under his careful supervision the average Blue of 1953 had become ten pounds heavier and one and a half inches taller than his counterpart of the 1920s.

The second World War brought shortages and spectacular improvisation to the diet of the children. Robin Hull, an Old Blue, recalls: 'The food, by tradition, was execrable, and wartime shortage made it worse. . . . Leftovers on plates were 'skiffage', destined for the School pigsties. One celebrated but extremely unpopular dish was nicknamed Skiffage Pie; Housey Stew consisted of tough gristle floating in a sea of fat; fish came steamed, unappetisingly, in a thin milky fluid, and then there were the horrors of macaroni cheese and "worms in carbolic", as the boys called the spaghetti they were offered.'

Apart from 'skiff', the other slang terms commonly in use were crug (or krug) for bread; 'flab' for butter, and 'kiff' for tea, which was drunk, one-handedly, from a kiff-bowl. Some of these beautiful blue and white china bowls still exist, and can be seen, along with wooden spoons, piggins, trenchers and candlesticks, in the Christ's Hospital Museum. And several Old Blues still treasure them, as the Treasurer found out when she visted Portland, Oregon in the Summer of 2000.

APPENDIX IX

OLD BLUES CLUBS AND SOCIETIES

There could be no challenge to a claim by **The Amicable Society of Blues** to be the oldest of the seventy-two Old Blue associations, clubs and societies in existence in the year 2000. On 15 September 1629 one hundred and nine 'such Persons as weare Children brought up in Christ's Hospital met there, and went to a service in Christchurch to give God thanks, and afterwards dyned together . . . in the greate hall.' This is the first recorded occasion that the community of Blues met, in its Greyfriars home, to commemorate its foundation with prayer, psalm, sermon and thanksgiving, and afterwards to dine in the friars' refectory. The contemporary list of this congregation records no city, livery company or clerical grandees in attendance. Those present in 1629, the eve of the great struggle between king and parliament, were for the most part comparatively young – the preacher, Thomas Salisburie, who heads the list, was admitted in 1596, at the age of nine – but they were truly representative of their Foundation: egalitarian brothers in the community of Blues whose purpose was, first, to give due thanks for their heritage, and then to dine. These twin aims have remained constant over the centuries, and they are demonstrated by the Amicable Society of Blues.

The minutes of the Society's Audit night 1895 describe it as 'the oldest society of gentlemen educated in Christ's Hospital'. Some claim it is the oldest dining society in Great Britain or even the world. These latter claims may be difficult to prove but what is indisputable is that the Society has met continuously since 1629.

Membership of 'the oldest dining Society in the world' is not, however, solely concerned with dining. Amicables have been, and are, concerned to give practical expression to their gratitude for the great benefits they have received 'in this place' living up to their motto 'Let brotherly love continue'. In 1824 the Society founded the Benevolent Society of Blues; in 1826 it spawned the Founder's Day Dinner; at the end of the nineteenth century Amicables promoted and sustained the Christ's Hospital Club, and the Amicable Foundation was the Amicables' response to the Quatercentenary Appeal, making regular contributions to the European Tour Fund for pupils planning educational visits to Europe.

The Amicable Society is an example of the unique traditions of Christ's Hospital which survive the passage of time, encouraging Old Blues to continue to take a keen interest and play a part in the life of Christ's Hospital and above all to support financially various aspects of School life while acting as custodians of the Christ's Hospital ethos.

The Christ's Hospital Club was founded in 1891 and, as noted above, received support and encouragement from the Amicables in its early days. Until 1987 the Club was based in the Counting House at 26 Great Tower Street, where the Club rooms had comfortable facilities. For ninety-four years the Club provided a lunch-time meeting place for Old Blues living and working in London, as well as a venue for its office and committee meetings. When the Counting House moved to Horsham in 1987, Mrs Wendy Killner joined the staff and settled the Club's library, Club room and office in a suite of rooms behind Dining Hall.

The link between Christ's Hospital and **Freemasonry** goes back to the mid-nineteenth century when the Treasurer, Head Master and other Newgate Street notables were members of the Aldersgate Lodge No. 1657. The occasion of the Diamond Jubilee in 1897 was seen as a fitting opportunity to create a Christ's Hospital Lodge, which was duly consecrated on 25 February that year. Later the same year the President, HRH The Prince of Wales and also Grand Master of the United Kingdom Lodge of England, laid the foundation stone for the new School at Horsham with full Masonic ritual.

In the field of Old Blue sport, the **Old Blues Rugby Football Club** enjoys a particularly long and distinguished history. The Club was founded in 1873, only two years after the Rugby Football Union itself, making it one of the oldest rugby clubs in the world. In 1897, a proposal that its name should be changed to Christ's Hospital Old Boys was defeated: Scholars of the Foundation had been 'Blues' for 320 years. As Old Blues they had banded together in loyal and convivial societies and as Old Blues they would continue to play their 'rugger'. An early fixture, on 8 November 1873, was between the Club and the School, a tradition which was to continue until more recent years when it was considered necessary to protect school boys from the perceived risks of playing young men only a few years older than themselves.

As rugby developed at Christ's Hospital, greatly helped by the move to Horsham, so did the strength of Old Blues. Consequently, in the decade before 1914, the OBRFC established its reputation as a first-class club and this continued until the 1950's. In 1922 the Club bought a 13 acre ground at Fairlop in Essex and until the 1950s, Bath, Bristol, Gloucester and Leicester were regular opponents and on one occasion the 1st XV played Harlequins on Bigside.

For a variety of reasons, numbers and standards fell dramatically during the 1960's and 70's and it became necessary to open membership of the Club to non-Old Blues in 1968. Thanks largely to Jack Watt, a pre-war player and by then President of the Club, Blues survived these difficult years and in 1982 sold the Fairlop ground and bought the 19 acre ground at Motspur Park, half of which was later sold to King's College School. Since moving to Motspur Park, playing strength, enthusiasm, standards and match results have improved enormously, co-operation with the School has been enhanced and the Club is now getting a steady flow of talented young players.

APPENDIX X
PRESIDENTS, TREASURERS, HEAD MASTERS, AND CLERKS

PRESIDENTS

1553	Sir George Barnes[1]
1556	Sir Martin Bowes[2]
1557	Sir Thomas White[3]
1559	Sir Thomas Offley
1582	Sir Thomas Ramsey
1590	Sir Wolstan Dixie
1594	Sir Richard Martin
1602	Sir Stephen Slaney
1609	Sir Humphrey Weld
1611	Sir William Craven
1618	Sir John Leman
1632	Sir Martin Lumley
1634	Sir Hugh Hammersley
1636	Sir Chris Clitherow
1641	Sir Richard Gurney
1643	Sir John Cordall
1648	Sir John Gayer
1649	Sir John Wollaston
1658	Sir Thomas Vyne
1660	Sir Thomas Atkins
1661	John Fowke
1662	Sir John Frederick
1683	Sir Robert Vyner
1684	Sir John Moore[4]
1687	Sir John Peake
1688	Sir William Ashurst
1702	Sir Francis Child
1713	Sir Richard Hoare
1718	Sir Robert Child
1721	Robert Heysham
1722	Sir Francis Forbes
1727	Sir George Merttins[5]
1727	Francis Child
1740	Sir John Barnard
1758	Sir Robert Ladbroke
1773	Sir Henry Bankes
1774	Robert Alsop
1785	Richard Clarke
1798	Sir John W Anderson
1813	Sir William Curtis
1829	William Thompson
1854	HRH George Duke of Cambridge
1904	HRH George Prince of Wales
1919	HRH Edward Prince of Wales
1936	HRH Albert Duke of York
1937	HRH Henry Duke of Gloucester
1975	HRH Richard Duke of Gloucester

TREASURERS

1552	Richard Grafton[6]
1557	Richard Buckland
1559	Anthony Cage[7]
1561	John Jackson
1573	William Leonard
1573	Thomas Hall[8]
1582	William Norton
1593	Robert Cogan
1614	William Dale
1614	Richard Heath
1624	John Harper
1633	John Hawes
1638	John Babington
1652	Richard Glyd
1662	William Gibbon
1679	Charles Doyly
1683	Nathaniel Hawes
1699	Robert Oxwick
1700	Francis Brerewood
1707	Thomas Lockington
1717	Sir George Merttins
1727	Richard Cheeks[9]
1735	Robert Gay
1737	Philip Scarth
1758	Daniel Webb
1770	Thomas Burfoot
1785	William Gill
1798	James Palmer Jnr.
1824	Thomas Poynder
1835	Richard Otham Pigeon[10]
1849	William Gilpin
1867	William Foster White[11]
1873	John Derby Alcroft
1891	Sir Walter Vaughan Morgan
1910	Septimus Croft
1920	Frederick Augustus White
1922	Mervyn Bowcher Davie
1930	Joseph James Brown
1938	C Wilfred Thompson
1945	Reginald E Oldfield

TREASURERS AND CHAIRMEN OF COUNCIL

1957	Sir Barnes Wallis
1970	Sir Eric Riches
1976	Alan Alistair Ross
1984	Edward John Kenney
1987	James Forbes
1996	Susan Mary Mitchell

---

[1] Sir George Barnes and Sir Martin Bowes were referred to as 'comptroller generalls', not Presidents.
[2] Sir Andrew Jud and Sir Rowland Hill each served for several months between Sir Martin Bowes and Sir Thomas Offey.
[3] Sir Thomas White was actually President in 1563 (MS12812) but the inscription in Big School reads 1557.
[4] Sir John Moore served as President several times, in 1687 and 1688, due to the deaths of Sir John Peake and Sir William Ashurst.
[5] Referred to as Sir R Martine (MS12812 and Court Minutes).

[6] Richard Grafton officially became Treasurer after the Charter of 1553.
[7] 'Anthony' Cage is actually Robert or Richard Cage (MS12812, etc).
[8] Thomas Hall approved as Treasurer in 1574.
[9] Richard Cheek referred to as Cheeke (MS12812 and Court Minutes).
[10] Richard Hotham Pigeon: a spelling mistake by the wood carver.
[11] Due to severe illness White was replaced by two Governors and an Almoner in 1872 until a new Treasurer could be appointed in 1873.

UPPER GRAMMAR OR HEAD MASTERS

1552	John Robynson
1564	Ralph Waddington MA, King's, Cambridge
1612	Revd Thomas Haynes MA, Lincoln, Oxford
1630	Thomas Walters MA, Magdalen, Oxford
1651	*George Perkins
1662	*Shadrach Helmes, St John's, Cambridge
1678	Revd James Mansfield MA, Trinity, Cambridge
1682	Revd Samuel Mountford MA, Hart Hall, Oxford
1719	*Revd Matthew Audley MA, Trinity, Oxford
1725	*Revd Peter Selby MA, Trinity, Cambridge
1737	*Revd Seawell Heatherley MA, Pembroke Hall, Cambridge
1753	Revd James Townley MA, St John's, Oxford
1760	Revd Peter Whalley BCL, St John's, Oxford
1776	*Revd James Boyer MA, Balliol, Oxford
1799	*Revd Arthur William Trollope DD, Pembroke, Cambridge
1827	*Revd John Greenwood DD, Pembroke and Peterhouse, Cambridge
1836	*Revd Edward Rice DD, Trinity, Cambridge
1853	Revd George Andrew Jacob DD, Worcester, Oxford
1868	*Revd George Charles Bell MA, Lincoln and Worcester, Oxford
1876	*Revd Richard Lee MA, Jesus, Cambridge
1902	Revd Arthur William Upcott DD, Exeter, Oxford
1919	William Hamilton Fyfe MA, Merton, Oxford
1930	Henry Lael Oswald Flecker, MA, CBE
1955	Clarence M E Seaman, MA
1970	Dr David Hay Newsome MA, DLitt
1979	*L G Derek Baker, MA, BLitt, FRHists, Oriel, Oxford
1985	*John Talbot Hansford, MA, St John's, Cambridge
1987	Richard Christopher Poulton, MA, Pembroke, Cambridge
1996	Dr Peter Campbell David Southern, MA, Merton, Oxford, PhD, Edinburgh

*Educated at Christ's Hospital.

HEAD MISTRESSES OF GIRLS IN LONDON[1]

1553	Mrs Smoothing
	Mrs Saepsched
1626	Mrs Dorothy Ffarrant
1642	Mrs Katherine Ducker
1651	Miss Benedict[2] Ducker
1652	Mrs Gutter
1658	Mrs Price
1684	Mrs Muriall Allbright
1691	Mrs Bennett Price
1707	Miss Sarah Parry[3]
1715	Mrs Susan Ditton
1717	Mrs Susanna Brown
1743	Mrs Susanna Lucas
1767	Mrs Elizabeth Duncombe

[1] The Girls' School moved to Hertford in 1778.
[2] Sometimes written Bennett.
[3] In 1708 she married and became Mrs Lorrain.

HEAD MISTRESSES AT HERTFORD

1778	Mrs Elizabeth Duncomb
1787	Miss Susannah Richardson
1793	Miss Ann Sparrow
1826	Miss Elizabeth Thompson
1852	Miss Sarah Ann Peacock
1875	Mrs Susan Lyster
1878	Miss Alice Elizabeth King
1893	Miss Margaret Ethel Robertson, MA
1921	Miss Norah Cecily Craig, MA
1942	Miss Dorothy Ruth West, MA, Newnham, Cambridge
1972	Miss Elizabeth M Tucker, MA, Newnham, Cambridge
1984	Miss Jean Morrison, MA, St Andrews
1985	*Closure of the Hertford School*

CLERKS

1553	John Watson[1]
1562	James Peele
1586	*Richard Wilson
1592	Lawrence Coachman
1597	*John Bannister
1623	*Thomas Stephenson
1690	*William Parry
1703	*George Yeo
1711	William Brocket
1745	John Yeo
1749	*John Bowden
1760	Joseph Eyre
1790	*Richard Corp
1819	*Thomas Wilby
1836	*George Trollop[2]
1864	Mathias S S Dipnall
1889	*Richard Leigh Franks
1920	*Thomas Edward Limmer
1932	*George A T Allan
1946	*Roger Courtenay Evans
1958	*Alan Evan Allison
1966	*Albert Wilson Robinson
1971	*Roy Fortesque Salisbury
1986	*Michael Alan Pearey
1998	Michael Lloyd Simpkin

[1] John Watson was also appointed Writing Master.
[2] George Trollop (1836–1863) was the son of the Head Master.
* Educated at Christ's Hospital.

APPENDICES: GOVERNANCE AND FINANCE

APPENDIX I
GOVERNANCE

STATUS

Christ's Hospital is a Charitable Foundation established by King Edward VI by a Royal Charter dated 1553, and privileged to enjoy the patronage of Her Majesty the Queen.

OBJECTS

Christ's Hospital is a Christian institution dedicated to providing a stable background and boarding education of high standard to boys and girls, having regard especially to children of those families in social, financial or other particular need.

The assets and endowments of Christ's Hospital are managed to ensure that this prime purpose is maintained both for the benefit of present and future generations.

MISSION STATEMENT

The Mission Statement appears on page 17.

STRATEGIC AIMS

To have the highest quality of teaching, administration and support staff delivering top class care and education for its pupils in a boarding environment.

To have all-round educational facilities and accommodation in a good state of repair to meet contemporary needs.

To achieve widespread awareness of the *raison d'être* and values of Christ's Hospital to the extent that the School will attract children who are in need, who have high academic and all round potential and who will benefit from the style of education offered.

To build up resources to a level where options can be considered for increasing the number of pupils or the range of education offered with the knowledge that any new policies decided upon could be funded.

THE SCHEME OF ADMINISTRATION

The arrangements for the governance of Christ's Hospital are laid down in the Scheme of Administration (the equivalent of a Trust Deed). The Scheme and its associated Articles of Governance runs to 99 pages and were last revised and approved by the Charity Commissioners in 1990 and became effective on 1 January 1991.

The Scheme defines the two principal bodies: the Council of Almoners and the Court of Governors.

The Council of Almoners

The trustee body of the charitable Foundation and the governing body of the School is the Council of Almoners.

It is responsible for formulating and monitoring the policies and administration of Christ's Hospital and the endowments; it has full authority to do this except where this rests specifically with the Court of Governors.

The Council is responsible for ensuring that the assets of the Foundation are properly managed; allocating funds to the School and approving expenditure priorities; ensuring that the processes for admitting and discharging of pupils are appropriate to the ethos of the Foundation; and for long-term planning.

The Council carries out these responsibilities through a Committee structure and, of course, through the Head Master, the Clerk and the executive officers. The principal Committees are concerned with Education and Finance and other Committees deal with Planning, Investments (Property and Securities), the Horsham School Estate, Remuneration, Disciplinary matters, the Hospital's Treasures, and Audit matters. From time to time, the Council appoints Working Parties, which are usually of a temporary nature, to examine and make recommendations to it on specific matters.

Standing Orders for the Council of Almoners define the number of meetings that shall be held annually, the procedures to be adopted at meetings, and for the election of the Treasurer and Deputy Chairman of Council and their duties. They define the powers of investment and give details of the constitution and powers of the Committees and the rights of Almoners. The Council of Almoners regularly reviews Standing Orders to ensure that they permit its duties to be carried out efficiently.

The Head Master and the Clerk are entitled to attend all meetings of the Council and its Committees.

MEMBERSHIP OF THE COUNCIL OF ALMONERS
Trustees

President: HRH The Duke of Gloucester, GCVO (ex officio)
Vice President: The Rt. Hon. The Lord Mayor of the City of London (ex officio)
Treasurer and Chairman of the Council of Almoners: Mrs S M Mitchell (1)
Deputy Chairman: Mr C Bruce-Jones, FCIB (1)

Mr P J Attenborough, MA (5)
    Chairman Education Committee
Mr D K Bawtree, CB, CEng, FIEE, FIMechE, DL (3)
    Chairman Remuneration Sub-Committee
Mr T J Binnington, FRICS (1)
    Chairman Property Sub-Committee

216

Mr P Bloomfield, FIMgt (1)

Alderman D W Brewer, CMG (2)

Mr D Farrington, LLB, FCIArb (1)

Mr I B Flanagan, FRICS (10)

Miss M P Gilbertson, OBE, FCSP, MRSM (1)
    Chairman Treasures Committee

The Revd Canon G Greenwood, BA, MSc (8)

Alderman J S Hughesdon, FCA, FRSA (2)
    Chairman Finance Committee

Mr S E B Kasozimusoke (9) Retired December 1999

Professor L E Lanyon, MRCVS, PhD, DSC (6)

Mr G C H Lawson (2)
    Chairman Securities Sub-Committee

Alderman Sir Richard Nichols (1)

Professor A Ryan, MA, DLitt, FBA (4)

Lord Simon of Highbury, CBE, MA, MBA (1)
    Appointed June 2000

Mr G D Shelley, BA, MSc (1) Retired June 2000

Councillor Eleanor Stanier, MA (9)
    Appointed January 2000

Mrs C A Stevens, BSc, MPhil (1)

Alderman Sir Alan Traill, GBE, QSO, MA, DMus (2)
    Chairman Disciplinary Committee

The Rt Revd F V Weston, MA (1)

Mr D W Willis, MA, CEng, FIEE, FBCS (10)
    Chairman Estates Sub-Committee

Professor L Wolpert, CBE, FRS (7)

The bracketed numbers signify the various bodies by which the Almoners are nominated:
(1) The Court of Governors
(2) Court Of Aldermen
(3) Ministry of Defence (Royal Navy)
(4) Oxford University
(5) Cambridge University
(6) London University
(7) The Royal Society
(8) London Schools
(9) Wests' Areas (Reading, Newbury, Twickenham)
(10) Co-opted

Almoners are elected or nominated for a term of six years, with the exception of the Wests' Gift nominee, who is appointed for four years, and co-opted members, whose term of appointment is at the discretion of the Council, for up to six years. Almoners may, if they wish, stand for re-election, or be re-nominated, for a second term. Almoners normally stand down after two terms (12 years), but may seek re-election or nomination again after an interval of at least one year.

The lower age limit is 18. Almoners must retire from the Council at the end of the year in which their 75th birthday falls, and candidates may not normally stand for election or re-election after the age of seventy-two.

The Treasurer, who is the Chairman of the Council, is elected annually by the Council in June from the current

Council membership, and normally serves for not more than six years. The Deputy Chairman of the Council is also elected annually in June and the Chairmen of all the Committees are elected annually by the Council in November.

Almoners normally serve on one, or sometimes two, Committees or Working Parties. Almoners are consulted each year as to their Committee preferences. The Council may also co-opt non-Almoners to serve on Committees and most Committees have one or two such members.

The Council meets four times a year and most of the main Committees each meet three or four times a year; the Disciplinary Committee meets only when required and the Working Parties arrange their own meetings to meet their specific objectives. Approximately half the meetings of Council and Committees are held in London and half at Horsham, with the exception of the Property and Securities Committees which usually meet in London, and the Estates Committee which meets at Horsham.

The majority of Almoners attend an average of 75% or more of meetings of the Council and any Committee on which they serve. If an Almoner were to fail to attend for a year without explanation, he or she could be asked to resign from the Council.

THE PRINCIPAL DUTIES OF THE TREASURER AND DEPUTY CHAIRMAN

The Scheme requires the Treasurer to preside at meetings of the Council and the Court of Governors in the absence of the President and Vice President; to represent Christ's Hospital on civic and social occasions and on or to other appropriate bodies such as the Governing Bodies Association, the Charity Commissioners, etc.; and to be a member of the Audit Committee, but not its chairman.

Standing Orders allow the Treasurer a second or casting vote in the event of equality of votes when presiding at a meeting and to be an ex-officio member of all committees. The Treasurer is expected to work closely with the Clerk and the Head Master, as the Almoner to whom they report.

The Treasurer is accountable to Council for taking such action as she considers necessary between Council meetings; initiating and progressing medium and long-term planning; ensuring, in liaison with the Clerk and the Head Master, effective communication with staff, parents, Governors and the wider CH community – and such other matters as may be requested by, or agreed with, Council from time to time.

The Deputy Chairman presides at meetings of the Council and the Court of Governors in the absence of the President, Vice President and Treasurer; deputises for the Treasurer in her absence; liaises with and supports the Treasurer and performs such duties as may be delegated to him by agreement with the Treasurer, and as Council may request.

THE COURT OF GOVERNORS

In addition to the President (HRH The Duke of Gloucester) and the Vice-President (the Lord Mayor of London for his year of office), membership of the Court comprises 24 Aldermen and 12 Common Councilmen of the City of London, up to 10 Special Vote Governors, and an unlimited number of Donation Govenors elected by the Court on the recommendation of the Council of Almoners after making an unconditional donation (see page 220) to Christ's Hospital. Every Almoner for the time being is a Right of Almonership Governor. On 31 July 2000 the total number of Governors was 618. Thirty nine new Donation Governors were elected in the previous twelve months and twenty-six made further donations under the Centenaries Governors scheme (see page 85). The Court elects ten members of the Council and confirms the appointment of all other Almoners. In addition, it is responsible for the election of the President from time to time; the election of Special Vote Governors; the appointment of professional auditors and the Governor Auditor; the election and re-election of pensioners to charities administered by Christ's Hospital; the disbursement of the Governors' Discretionary Fund; the election, nomination and presentation to vacant ecclesiastical Benefices within the gift of the Governors; and is entitled to receive and consider the accounts presented by the Council of Almoners.

Upon election to the Court, new Governors are invited to an induction day at the School. This provides an opportunity to meet the Head Master, Clerk, other senior staff, some of the current pupils and the Treasurer and Deputy Chairman. Presentations, followed by discussions and questions, are given about the governance, finances, current issues of importance and longer-term plans for the School. The majority of Donation Governors undertake the duty of searching for and selecting a suitable candidate for entry to the School at Year 7 (age 11) and to help them in that task A Handbook for Donation Governors is given to each new Governor, and the Admissions Officer and the Head of a local primary school each give a short talk and answer questions. The Handbook provides guidance on the selection of a candidate for admission to the School and on relationships with the chosen child and his or her family (see also pages 81–5).

In accordance with current legislation, no Governor or Almoner may receive any remuneration, in cash or in kind, for service as a Governor or Almoner.

APPENDIX II
FINANCES

FUNDING

All operational costs of the Charity, including capital expenditure, are funded from income.

Most of the income to meet this expenditure comprises rents, dividends and interest earned on the charity's Endowment and Restricted Fund investments. This income on its own is insufficient to meet all of the annual expenditure and it is supplemented by grants received from outside sources, parental contributions and income from the trading subsidiary, Christ's Hospital Enterprises Limited.

The Charity also depends upon, and is always grateful for, legacies and donations. Unless otherwise specified by the donor, or in response to a specific appeal, unconditional donations are added to Endowment Funds.

In 1999–2000, the cost of providing a boarding education for each of the School's 800 children was £13,130. All pupils' families are means-tested annually. In that year nearly 40% of pupils attended the School at no cost to their parents; full cost was payable by only 24 pupils' parents; the other 57% contributed smaller amounts, according to their income, on a sliding scale.

Under the terms of the Scheme, the Endowment and Restricted Funds, including any capital appreciation arising on them, may not be spent. Only the income arising from the investment of those Funds is available. The securities and property assets which represent the majority of the Endowment and Restricted Funds are managed prudently to ensure that the overall value of the Funds is maintained and enhanced in real terms and a sensible balance achieved between income yield and capital growth.

GLOSSARY OF TERMS

This glossary defines the terms used in the financial statements for the year ended 31 July 2000 on pages 221–2. It also explains the legal position with regard to the various Christ's Hospital funds, the restrictions applying to their use and the implications this has for the way in which the funds must be accounted.

Charity

This is the legal entity which comprises all the endowments and accumulated income and liabilities of Christ's Hospital.

Consolidated Balance Sheet

This details all the assets of Christ's Hospital and its subsidiary, Christ's Hospital Enterprises Limited, which are used to achieve the Foundation's objectives.

Consolidated Statement of Financial Activities

This single accounting statement analyses, for the year, all incoming resources, expenditure and other movements on all the funds of Christ's Hospital and its subsidiary company, Christ's Hospital Enterprises Limited.

Designated Funds

These are funds created by the Council of Almoners for specific purposes. There is no legal restriction on the way in which the funds may be applied. They comprise:

Annual Fund Established to attract donations which provide additional resources for the direct benefit of every child in the School, through the establishment and improvement of facilities which might not other wise be provided.

Capital Fund Represents the net book value of fixed assets used for operational purposes.

Education Fund Established to maintain and enhance the quality and standards of education for the children in the School's care.

Investment Property Fund Established to provide for the refurbishment/redevelopment of investment properties.

School Fund Instigated to provide funding for major capital and revenue expenditure planned for the School over the next few years. To the extent that such funds are used for capital, a transfer to the Capital Fund will be made; revenue costs will be charged directly to this fund.

Treasures Fund Established to provide and maintain artefacts relevant to Christ's Hospital.

Endowment Funds

The endowment funds are permanent funds and must be held indefinitely. They are not expendable. However, assets in the fund can be exchanged; for instance the funds arising from the sale of a property may be reinvested in some other form of suitable investment such as securities.

Only the income arising from the investment of such assets may be spent.

Gains or Losses on Fixed Assets and Current Asset Securities

A gain or loss made on the disposal of an asset of either of the above classes will become part of the balance of the fund in which it is held, thus increasing or decreasing the value of the fund. This is defined as a Realised Gain or Loss.

A gain or loss made on the revaluation of an asset of either of the above classes will become part of the balance of the fund in which it is held, thus increasing or decreasing the value of the fund. This is defined as an Unrealised Gain or Loss.

General Fund

This comprises all the endowments and accumulated income of Christ's Hospital, except for those held as Restricted Funds.

Restricted Funds

These funds are subject to specific trusts generally declared by the donor and are under the same management and control as Christ's Hospital. These funds may only be utilised for the specific purposes for which they were donated. These funds are largely permanent funds and it is only the income arising from the investment of the funds which is expendable, subject to any restrictions placed on the use of such funds. The funds comprise: Wests' Gift for Children, The Governors' Discretionary Fund, The RAF Foundationers' Trust, The Stubbings Memorial Fund, The Ewart Kingsley Read Trust, The 617 Squadron Association, The Brodribb Trust, The Medical Foundation, The Engineers' Foundation, The Master Mariners' Company.

Unrestricted Funds

Funds which are expendable at the discretion of the Council of Almoners. The income arises from the investment of the endowment funds, grants receivable, parental contributions, income from Christ's Hospital Enterprises Limited and other sundry income. These funds provide the major part of the expenditure required to run the School.

Trading subsidiary

Christ's Hospital Enterprises Limited.

PARENTAL CONTRIBUTIONS

Christ's Hospital is not a conventional fee-paying school. In accordance with the Mission Statement and charitable objectives, the majority of pupils are selected on the basis of their need for an academic boarding education of the highest quality, coupled with their potential to benefit from it. All families are means-tested annually and in 1999–2000 parents or guardians were asked to contribute on a sliding scale.

Child benefit, mobility and attendance allowance and housing benefit were disregarded in the calculation of income. No contribution was payable if income was £10,791 or less.

A discount of 50% of the assessed contribution was granted for a second sibling, and 66% for each additional sibling in the School at the same time.

In the year ended 31 July 2000 the application of this scale resulted in nearly 40% of pupils paying no contributions and the remainder contributing, between them, £1,719,000, equal to just 14.2% of the cost of running the School. Just under 3% of pupils paid the maximum contribution of £13,067.

DONATION GOVERNORSHIP RATES

For those wishing to seek election as a Donation Governor, the minimum qualifying rates for unconditional gifts to Christ's Hospital are based on the cost of educating a child in the School for one year. The rates approved by the Council of Almoners for the year beginning 1 September 2000, entitling Donation Governors to one presentation, were:

Category of Donor	Basic rate	Rate if made under Gift Aid*
Old Blue†	£13,861	£10,812
Other individual	£17,323	£13,512
Corporate	£41,580	Not applicable

*these figures assume a basic rate of UK income tax of 22% and apply to UK taxpayers only.
†including immediate family and former members of staff with at least seven years service.

Existing individual Donation Governors were able to seek a second or further presentation upon payment of £5,000 under Gift Aid.

Sixth Form Donation Governorship

Available to corporate donors only:
3 successive pupils each for the 2 year
A-Level course: £39,870
5 successive pupils each for the 2 year
A-Level course: £56,980

The gross family income limit for admission in September 2000 as a Donation Governor's presentee, or other presentee category (except Wests' Gift), was £34,083, equivalent to one and a half times National Average Family Income (NAFI). (See also pages 81–5 for more information about methods of admission).

FINANCIAL SUPPORT FOR CHRIST'S HOSPITAL

Christ's Hospital is heavily dependent on donations and legacies from its former pupils and from other supporters, and is most grateful for all of them, whether large or small. The extent of this benevolence varies from year to year and the summary given here is a snapshot relating just to the year 1999/2000. Many other donors have supported Christ's Hospital in earlier years and we regret it is not possible to mention all our valued benefactors here by name.

In the year ended 31 July 2000, we received £1.4 million in donations from around one thousand individuals and corporate bodies, as well as 11 legacies from Old Blues and 3 from other individuals totalling £742,000.

Grants totalling £116,000 supporting 74 pupils in whole or in part were received from: Canon Holmes Memorial Trust, Chamberlain Trust, Finsbury Educational Foundation, Worshipful Company of Mercers, Mitchell City of London Charity and Educational Foundation, Oliver Whitby Foundation, RAF Benevolent Fund, Reeve's Foundation, Royal Wanstead Foundation, Sue Thomson Foundation, Worshipful Company of Wax Chandlers, and Worshipful Company of Carpenters.

Further generous support was provided by the Corporation of London and the Worshipful Company of Ironmongers as Corporate Donation Governors, the Worshipful Society of Apothecaries as Sixth Form Donation Governors, the CH Countryside Club as a Donation Governor. Contributions to The 100 Years On Appeal were gratefully received from the Worshipful Company of Actuaries, the Worshipful Company of Insurers, the Ian Allan Group and the Artists General Benevolent Institute. The Miller Family Foundation generously funded the Hugh Olson Bursary Fund in memory of Hugh Olson, a former Common Council Governor.

The Government Assisted Places Scheme contributed £388,000 towards 52 pupils' education in 1999/2000; due to the abolition of the scheme this will taper off to nil by 2004.

Christ's Hospital Enterprises Limited (see pages 178–9) earned a net profit of £124,000 in 1999/2000, all of which is covenanted to Christ's Hospital.

FINANCIAL SUPPORT FOR PUPILS AND OLD BLUES

Aside from the provisions for means-testing parents annually so that contributions are asked only of those who can afford to pay, grants are available from the Foundation and the Necessitous Children's Fund to support children from families suffering the greatest financial hardship. These grants meet a wide a range of needs including, for example, pocket money, travel to or from School, foreign educational trips, music lessons and sports clothing.

The Advancement in Life Fund allocates around £20,000 a year to assist leavers and young Old Blues, usually through support for further education.

The Benevolent Society of Blues (BSB) supports members of the Old Blue community from all generations, in addition to current pupils who benefit from BSB donations to the School through the Necessitous Children's Fund. The Society received 75 applications for assistance during the year ended 31 July 2000, which resulted in £94,720 being provided as grants or loans. Many more continue to benefit from a further £250,000 of loans granted in earlier years. The Society had 13 presentees in the School and 14 Old Blues in receipt of pensions at 31 July 2000. Additionally the sporting feats of five pupils were supported from the fund established in memory of Michael Pearey.

The Amicable Foundation contributes regularly to help pupils making educational trips in Europe; in 1999/2000 the School was very grateful to receive £7,000 for the European Tour Fund and Highbury Fund. A number of designated annual prizes and awards are available to pupils.

Individual pupils and young Old Blues are, in many cases, supported by their Donation Governors with amounts ranging from pocket money to more substantial contributions to university costs.

CONSOLIDATED STATEMENT OF FINANCIAL ACTIVITIES FOR THE YEAR ENDED 31 JULY 2000

£ 000s	Notes	Endowment Fund	Restricted Funds	Designated Funds	Unrestricted Funds	Total 2000	Total 1999
		2	3	4	5		
INCOMING RESOURCES							
Income from Property			50		4,266	4,316	4,278
Income from Securities	6		272		4,365	4,637	4,676
Income from Cash Deposits			655	1,087	309	2,051	1,681
Legacies and Donations	7	949		1,193		2,142	1,782
Income from Trading Subsidiary					35	35	70
Grants Receivable – Assisted Places					388	388	447
– Other					162	162	278
Parental Contributions					1,719	1,719	1,630
Sundry			14		74	88	197
Total Incoming Resources		949	991	2,280	11,318	15,538	15,039
RESOURCES EXPENDED							
Direct Charitable Expenses							
Christ's Hospital School:							
Normal expenditure	8		477		10,027	10,504	9,587
Exceptional expenditure	8			1,543	79	1,622	1,964
Grants Payable			34			34	144
Support Costs			2			2	3
		0	513	1,543	10,106	12,162	11,698
Management Expenses							
Fund Raising					150	150	118
Investment Property and Securities	9	334	32		356	722	589
Administration					577	577	528
		334	32	0	1,083	1,449	1,235
Total Resources Expended		334	545	1,543	11,189	13,611	12,933
NET INCOMING RESOURCES BEFORE TRANSFERS		615	446	737	129	1,927	2,106
Transfers between Funds	2, 4 & 5	63		278	(341)	0	0
Net Incoming Resources for the Year		678	446	1,015	(212)	1,927	2,106
GAINS ON INVESTMENT ASSETS AND CURRENT ASSET SECURITIES							
Realised	10	41	124	(152)	(147)	(134)	4,877
Unrealised	11	12,994	490		257	13,741	13,971
Net Movement In Funds		13,713	1,060	863	(102)	15,534	20,954
Balances brought forward 1 August		191,733	20,811	28,044	5,137	245,725	224,771
FUND BALANCES AT 31 JULY		205,446	21,871	28,907	5,035	261,259	245,725

The notes which form part of these Financial Statements may be found in the full Annual Report.

CONSOLIDATED BALANCE SHEET AT 31 JULY 2000

£ 000s	NOTES	ENDOWMENT FUND 2	RESTRICTED FUNDS 3	DESIGNATED FUNDS 4	UNRESTRICTED FUNDS 5	TOTAL 2000	TOTAL 1999
FIXED ASSETS							
Investments: Properties	12	102,794	720			103,514	86,236
Securities	13	87,037	13,396		4,569	105,002	106,242
Cash Deposits	14	6,009	6,252	16,559	311	29,131	30,809
Properties used for Charitable Purposes	15			10,308		10,308	3,124
Chattels		5,074				5,074	5,074
Other	16(a)			1,157	151	1,308	880
		200,914	20,368	28,024	5,031	254,337	232,365
CURRENT ASSETS							
Securities	17				390	390	7,761
Stocks	18				255	255	263
Debtors	19	1,192	26	65	1,089	2,372	4,642
Cash at bank and in hand		3,340	1,506	818	1,351	7,015	3,172
		4,532	1,532	883	3,085	10,032	15,838
Creditors: amounts falling due within one year	20		29		3,081	3,110	2,478
NET CURRENT ASSETS		4,532	1,503	883	4	6,922	13,360
NET ASSETS 31 JULY		205,446	21,871	28,907	5,035	261,259	245,725

These financial statements were approved by the Council of Almoners on 15 November 2000 and signed on its behalf by

Mrs Susan Mitchell
Treasurer and Chairman of
the Council of Almoners

The notes which form part of these Financial Statements may be found in the full Annual Report.

FIVE YEAR SUMMARY

£000S	1999/00	1998/99	1997/98	1996/97	1995/96
Net Assets 1 August	245,725	224,771	193,302	165,941	151,431
Income from Property	4,266	3,755	3,832	3,939	4,323
Income from Securities & Cash	5,761	5,933	5,085	4,669	4,981
Wests' Gift for Children	847	803	781	753	628
Other Endowment Funds	144	164	162	148	137
Total Investment Income	11,018	10,655	9,860	9,509	10,069
Legacies & Donations	2,142	1,782	1,151	834	766
Parental Contributions	1,719	1,630	1,406	1,307	1,359
Grants	550	581	707	580	466
Christ's Hospital Enterprises Limited	35	70	219	86	125
Other	74	321	205	151	144
TOTAL INCOME	**15,538**	**15,039**	**13,548**	**12,467**	**12,929**

DIRECT CHARITABLE EXPENSES

	1999/00	1998/99	1997/98	1996/97	1995/96
Christ's Hospital School	12,126	11,594	10,341	9,098	8,310
Grants payable	34	144			
Support costs	2	3	16	38	36
TOTAL	**12,162**	**11,741**	**10,357**	**9,136**	**8,346**

MANAGEMENT EXPENDITURE

	1999/00	1998/99	1997/98	1996/97	1995/96
Fund raising	150	118	100	74	72
Property	447	318	514	542	632
Securities	275	271	270	201	182
Administration	577	485	86	84	81
TOTAL	**1,449**	**1,192**	**970**	**901**	**967**
TOTAL EXPENDITURE	**13,611**	**12,933**	**11,327**	**10,037**	**9,313**
Excess of income over expenditure	1,927	2,106	2,221	2,430	3,616

GAINS ON FIXED ASSETS AND CURRENT ASSET SECURITIES

	1999/00	1998/99	1997/98	1996/97	1995/96
Realised	(134)	4,877	7,717	4,246	1,597
Unrealised	13,741	13,971	21,531	20,685	9,297
Movement in funds	15,534	20,954	31,469	27,361	14,510
NET ASSETS AT 31 JULY	**261,259**	**245,725**	**224,771**	**193,302**	**165,941**

The accounting policies and full notes to the Statement of Financial Activities and the Balance Sheet can be found in the Annual Report and Financial Statements 2000, obtainable from the Counting House, Christ's Hospital, Horsham, West Sussex, RH13 7YP.

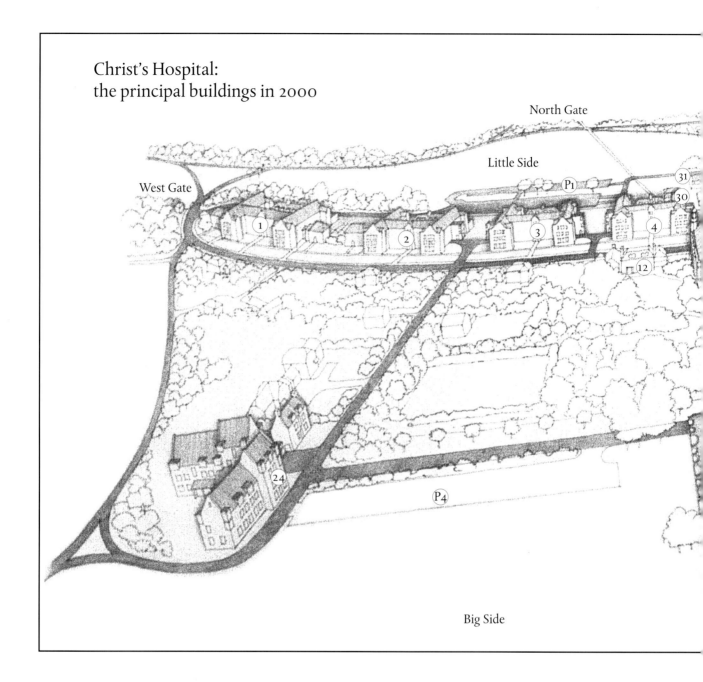

Christ's Hospital:
the principal buildings in 2000

North Gate

Little Side

West Gate

P1

31

30

1

2

3

4

12

24

P4

Big Side

1	Peele	13	Chapel
2	Thornton	14	School Offices
3	Middleton	15	West classrooms
4	Coleridge	16	Big School
5	Lamb	17	East classrooms
6	Barnes	18	Art School
7	Maine	19	Science School
8	Leigh Hunt	20	Library
9	Common Room	21	Dominions Library
10	Dining Hall and kitchens	22	Temporary classrooms in The Arts Quad
11	Court Room	23	New Science School
12	Head Master's House		

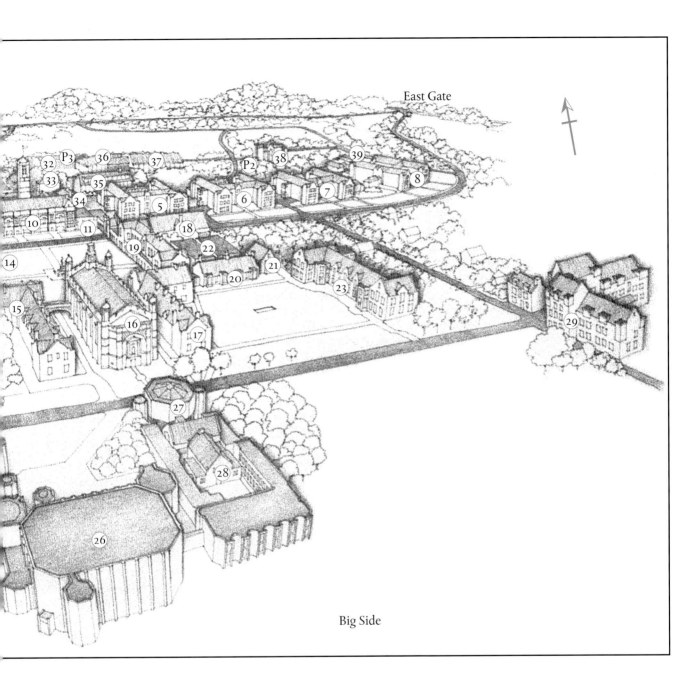

East Gate

Big Side

BIBLIOGRAPHY

G A T Allan (CH 1897–1902) *Christ's Hospital*, Ian Allan Ltd, London, 1949.

G A T Allan, revised J E Morpurgo, *Christ's Hospital*, Town & County Books, 1984.

William Harnett Blanch *The Bluecoat Boys; or School Life in Christ's Hospital*, E W Allen, 1877.

Edmund Blunden *Christ's Hospital, a Retrospect*, The Whitefriars Press.

Hester W Chapman *The Last Tudor King*, Jonathan Cape, London 1961.

Christ's Hospital Four Hundred Years Old, Christ's Hospital, 1953.

Christ's Hospital MS 12815.1. *Register of Wills, Gifts and Grants* 1552–1702, pp 497–8.

Cunnington and Lucas, *Charity Costumes*, A & C Black, 1978.

Antonia Fraser (ed) *The Lives of the Kings and Queens of England*, The Orion Publishing Group, London, 1999.

John Guy *Tudor England*, Oxford University Press, 1988

John Howes *Contemporaneous Account in Dialogue-Form of the Foundation and Early History of Christ's Hospital and of Bridewell and St Thomas' Hospitals*, 1582, 1587.

Robin Hull *A Schoolboy's War*, Limited Edition Press, 1994.

David Jesson-Dibley *The Foundation of Christ's Hospital*, Christ's Hospital, 1953.

R Brimley Johnson (ed) *Christ's Hospital: Recollections of Lamb, Coleridge and Leigh Hunt*, George Allen, 1896.

W K Jordan (ed) *The Chronicle and Political Papers of Edward VI*, George Allen and Unwin Ltd, London, 1966.

Valentine Knapp (CH 1868–1876) *Blewe Clothes of Christ's Hospital*, Knapp, Drewitt & Sons Ltd, 1928.

C S Knighton (ed) *Calendar of State Papers: Domestic Series, Edward VI 1547–1553*, Public Record Office, HMSO, 1992.

David Loades (gen ed) *Chronicles of the Tudor Kings*, Bramley Books, 1997.

Carol K Manzione *Christ's Hospital of London 1552–1598*, Associated University Press, London, 1995.

Bertie Mawer *Bridewell to Witley, 1553–2000, King Edward's School*, Ian Allan Ltd, Shepperton, 2000.

J E Morpurgo (CH 1929–36) *Barnes Wallis: a Biography*, Longman, London, 1972.

J G Nichols (ed) *The Literary Remains of Edward VI*, Burt Franklin, New York for the Roxburghe Club.

Frances M Page, PhD. *Christ's Hospital Hertford*, G Bell & Sons Ltd, 1953.

E H Pearce *The Annals of Christ's Hospital*, Hugh Rees Ltd, London, 1908.

C M E Seaman *Christ's Hospital: the Last Years in London*, Ian Allan Ltd, London, 1977.

Alison Sim *Pleasures and Pastimes in Tudor England*, Sutton Publishing Ltd, 1999.

John Stow *Survey of London*, vol 1 Kingsford ed 1910.

Simon Thurley *The Lost Palace of Whitehall*, Royal Institute of British Architects, 1998

Revd William Trollope *A History of the Royal Foundation of Christ's Hospital*, William Pickering, London, 1834.

J I Wilson *A Brief History of Christ's Hospital*, John van Voorst, London, 1838.

PHOTOGRAPHIC ACKNOWLEDGEMENTS

Photographs on the pages indicated supplied by: Christ's Hospital Museum and Archive, photographed by David Billings 2, 5, 8, 9, 10; John Gale 182 (top); David Graham Photography 101; Richard McGregor 191 (real tennis); Michael Pickard 86 (three Masters); Gerald Sharp Photographers 97 (Drapers' Hall).

Photographs on the pages indicated taken by: Judith Avenell 52; Harald Bauer 124; Ann Bawtree 190 (fives); Richard Beale 78; Peter Bloomfield 21, 149 (tea time) 151 (Toowomba Grammar School); Neil Fleming 11, 12, 32, 43, 59 (Bandmaster), 64 (fives), 67, 87 (Senior Grecian and Head Master), 93, 94, 95, 96, 97 (Senior Grecian and Old Blues), 99, 100, 119 (Nicola McCabe, 'doughty also-rans' and timekeeper), 120 (1st netball), 131, 132, 133, 134, 135, 139 (Lord Mayor on walk about), 148 (Band), 153, 154, 160 (Band) 161 (Kaeran MacDonald), 162–3, 180; Dominic Gibson 27, 56, 115, 144; Tim Graham viii (President); Bryan Hall 186; Vaughan Holme 169; Pam Legate 128, 148 (mini-bus tours); Susan Mitchell 37, 109; Nicola Owen, CH parent 98; Frank Pattison 168; Ken Pattison 63; Muir John Potter 66, Andrea Sarlo 155; J D Shippen 69, 143; Dick Tyler 189; 'Topper' Warrington 187; Chrissy Williams 146 (Kerren Simmonds); David Williams 64 (pony riding), 102. All other photographs taken by John Mitchell.

SUBSCRIBERS

The publishing team thanks all those who have subscribed for one or more copies of this book prior to publication:

Brian E Adams, ThB 1931–39
Matthew Adams
Rachel Adams
Sharon Alce
Arnold J Allen
Peter and Ros Allwood
Mr Stanley A Amey
Alexander Gordon Anderson
Bill Annett OBE
David Arnold
C S C Ashby
Edwina Ashton *née* Taylor, 5s
Gerald Ashton
Piers Ashworth
The Revd Ian Atkinson
The Revd P G and Mrs E M Atkinson
Peter Attenborough
Brian L Attwood
Nora Aveston MA
Richard Ayres, ThA 1975–82
The Revd John M Bacon
Teresa Bagnall
Doreen Baker
Elliot Stephen Baker
Ian Baker, LaA 1952–58
Mrs Barbara Clio Fawcett Ballantyne
Michael Bamford
Edward G U Band
Sam Banner, LaB, PeA 1993–2000
Mr and Mrs Eric Barber
John Barker
Michael M Barker
Terry Bate
Miss I F Bates
David Bawtree
Ianthe Baxter
R D Baynes
Eric T Beauchamp
Dr John Vincent Beer
C G Bell
Ann Bennett *née* Stephens
Christopher J Bennett
Mrs Jean Best *née* Haughan, Hertford
    1951–59
Oliver Maurice Bevan
D H S Biggs, PeA 1935–42
T J Binnington
Susan K Birch
J D Bird
Peter Birkett
A F Bishop
Iain Bisset
Peter Bisset
Nicolette Bitschi
Dorothy Blincoe
Nigel L Blood

Peter Bloomfield
Jayne Blower
Eric A Bond
Alexa Jane Borchardt-Scheibe
Vera Boulding *née* Scamans, 3s 1934–42
Chris and Katharina Bradfield
George J Brazier
Alderman David Brewer CMG
Cyril and Eleanor Bridgland
Elizabeth and Michael Brierley
Alan H Brown, LaA 1942–49
Robert Browne
J A F Bruce, MA 1936–44
Chris Bruce-Jones
Royston Brunst
Barbara Buchanan
Elizabeth Anne Buddle
Humphrey Bunyan
Duncan McQueen Burns
Lucie Burns, student 2000–02
The Revd Michael J Burns
Adrian Buxton
Elizabeth Cairncross
Mr and Mrs J B Callas
Robin V Carey
Mrs Christina Casement
Mr B A Castle
Dr Michael F Challis
John S C Chandler
Paula Chandler
P Charles
David Chase
Mr and Mrs P J Chauhan
The Revd Simon Chevill
G C C Chivers
The Christ's Hospital Club
S W Chubb
Mr and Mrs John Clare
Kathleen Judith Clark *née* Mulvany
Marjory J Clark
Margaret Clayton
Gillian A Clenshaw
Michael A Clenshaw
Mr and Mrs S P Cleverdon
Miss Sasha Coates and Mr Simon Bell
R Cameron Cochrane
Frank A Collinson, LaA 1936–43
Jim Cook
Rachel Cooke
Bryan W Cooper
Roger George Corbett
Geoffrey Corbin
A G Cork
Helen Cosslett *née* Osborne, CH 1967–73
Richard Courtney
Dr I Coward

Evelyn E Cowie
G M Cox
Steven Cox
Elizabeth Coxon-Taylor, CH 1928–36
F D Cran
Mr and Mrs R J Cremona
Martin V Crick, LHB, LaA 1978–85
David R H Crockford
John H Crockford
Mrs M S Culshaw, wife of the late
    Laurence Culshaw, MidB 1920–24
Susan Curtin – grateful parent
Paul M Cutting OBE, DFC
J H Daglish
Mrs Rohan Dale
Michael Darke
Brenda Davidson
Peter Drummond Davies, Old Blue
Mrs Susan Davies-Jenkins *née* Wilson,
    CH Hertford 1957–65
Susannah Davis
P H de Grunchy
H J de Nordwall
John Delight
O A (Denny) Denly MBE, ThB 1935–42
Simon Denly, LHA, LaB 1970–77
Andrew James Dickinson
Roger H V Dixon
Katharine M Dobson *née* Hills, 6s 1959–65
Judy and John Doyle
Anthony G Duncan
Kathleen Duncan
Mr and Mrs Russell Dunn
Jess Dunsdon
Mrs Mary Dupoy *née* Proctor, 3s 1951–58
Lucinda Dye
Mrs Jennifer Dyer
David Eastburn, MidA 1947–55
Pat Edwards *née* Stewart, CH 1944–53
Tim and Ben Edwards
Russell W Emptage
D J V Evans
Mrs Valerie Exall
John and Ann Eyles
Reginald Fairfax
Canon Hugh Farlie
David Farrington
Robert Alfred Fennell
Lucy Figgis
Mr John Chadwick Finlay
Shirley L Finnel
Roger FitzGerald, Architects Design
    Partnership
Ian B Flanagan
Kevin Fletcher
James Forbes

D Alan Foster
Donald Fox
Mrs P M W Frankland OBE
Joe and Helen Freeman
Sarah Freeman
Sarah J Freeman
Wg Cdr T J French RAF (Rtd)
G F Gainsborough
John and Lisel Gale
Chantal Geall
Simon T B Gibbs
Moyna P Gilbertson
Mr and Mrs Oliver Gilchrist
John M Gillham MC, KCSG, FCIOB
Michael and Christine Gimber
Penny Glass née Hollingsworth, 3s
    1971–78
Chris Godfrey
David Goodman
Catherine Goodyear
Brian Gould
Diana Gould née Robinson
Alderman Sir Alexander Graham GBE
Mrs Cherril Graham
Christopher John Grant
Fred Grant
Mr A G Gray
M Barry S Gray
General Sir Michael Gray KCB OBE DL
Audrey Gregory
Marcus Greig, CH 1992–99
M de G Gribble
Kay Griffiths
Elisabeth Gwynn
M A Hall
Pamela Hall née Morris, 4s 1937–44
Ann Hallerman
J B Hambling
Peter R J Hambrook
Eileen Hammond née Maycock
Barclay Hankin, ThA, LaB 1927–36
Dr Peter Hansell FRCP
John T Hansford
Jeremy P K Harland
Iris Harris née Joel, 4s 1933–39
Mary Harris
Leslie Harrison
Nigel Harrison
Patrick F Hawkins
Ms Jules Hayman
Barbara Head
Brian Head
Peter J Hebben
The Hon Mrs A Henderson née Alexia
    Hedley
Amanda Herries
Caroline Hewitt
Peter Hexter, LaA 1945–51
Mrs M F Hildrew
Janice Hill née Edwards, CH 1952–59
Kiko Hill

Nicholas Hill, ThB 1940–48
Peter and Valerie Hill
Sally Hill
Geoffrey Hines
Georgina and Raymond Hockaday
Rosalind S Hodgson, LHB
Mr and Mrs Philip Hodson and Luke
Phyllis Hoffman
Tony Hogarth-Smith
Matthew Hoggarth
Paul Holdway
Miss Sally Holland
P B Hooper
Spencer Hudson
Trevor and Maggie Hughes
John Hughesdon
Nancy Holbrook Hunter
R D Hunter
Mr and Mrs E P Hutton
D Fergus Ireland
Robert Ireson, LaB 1940–46
Yasmin Ismail
Meredith Jackson
G W Jacobs
Christian Beresford Jarrett
Mike Jefferies
Ken Jenkins
General Sir Garry Johnson KCB, OBE, MC
Paul Malcolm Johnson
Mrs J M Johnston
David Jones
Ms Linda C Jones
Jane Holbrook Jukes
John Hunter Jukes
S E B Kasozimusoke
David and Jane Keating
Edward John Kenney
David M Kenworthy
Beryl Kingdon née Brown, 5's 1936–41
Mr Surendra Kotecha
Gregory M S Lauder-Frost FSA (Scot)
Stephen Launchbury
R Alan Leach
Karen Lebon
Ms Erin Lettis
Mrs Helen Lewis
Lt Col R G Lewis TD
Shona Lewis
Sidney Lightman
M Lloyd
Felicity Long, CH 1936–43
Keith Lugton
Hugh M Macfarlane
Keith and Pam Mackness
Andrew Mallows
Mr and Mrs B L Mann
Ken Mansell
Richard T March, PeA
Derek Marriott
K P and J L Martin and India, BaB
John Marvin

David F Mason
Shaun Mason
R J Massen
Mrs A M Masters
Ian Matthews
Nathan Matthews, CH 1994–2001
Anthony Max
Gordon McAllister
Heather McDermid née Denly, 1s 1964–73
James Kenneth McDonald
Richard McGregor
Mr and Mrs P McMullen
Gill Meason née Kirkman, CH Hertford
    1940–48
Mary and Eddie Meeks
Mr Sebastian A Mercer MBE
Emma Millicheap
K J Mills
John Mitchell
Richard Mitchell
Susan Mitchell née Hamilton
A Mitra
Dr S and Mrs C Mockford
Mr B M Monaghan
David Monaghan
Sarah Moon
James Morford
Nicholas Morgan
Stanley George Morgan
Margaret Morris née Oxford, 5s, 7s
    1939–46
M Motyer
Dr Yemi Mshelia
Constance Mullick née Tolley, CH 1921–28
Mr J P A Mullinger
Nicki Murray
Fiona Nairn
Sophie Naish
Anthony T Napier
Philip D Naylor
J M W Nelson, ThB 1950–56
Colin Nesbeth
Valerie Nesbitt née Richings, 3s 1956–63
Susan New
The Revd Simon and Mrs Gina Newham
M Nicholas
Sir Richard Nichols
Laura Nightingale
Ian A Norman
Betty Northcote née Adams
Beth O'Connell, BaA
Kathleen Olaofe née Dowse
Alan A M Onslow
Fiona Orger
G O'Ryan-Roeder
Neville Osmond
Valerie Ovenden
Thomas Peter Overington
William N G Owen, Gr 2000–01
Ivy Stella Page née Peachey, CH 1924–29
Andrew Palmer

Roger Parker
Wyn Parry
Frank Pattison
Richard Paulin
Carol Payne *née* Merrett, 8s 1966–71
Richard P Pearey
Thelma Pearey
Bill Pearson, ColA 1932–40
Christopher Pearson
Diana Pelly
Jane Phelan
G J Phipps Jones, MaB 1924–33
M J Pickard
Hazel Picking *née* Roberts, 3s 1936–42
Michael Pinsker
Lorraine Pitt
Dr and Mrs F S F Poon
Mrs Jean Pope
Mr and Mrs C Porcheron
Derrick G Porter
Janet Porter
Peter F Portwood
Tim and Kate Postlethwaite
Eve Potter
Susan Presley *née* Cotton, 2s 1952–57
Gordon Prince
Martin J Prowse
Dennis Quinn
John Rapp
Nigel Redman
P B Rendle
Philippa and Joshua Reveley
John R Reynolds, ThB 1942–49
Ken Reynolds, New Hamburg, Ontario
Lance Reynolds
Bruce M Richards
Geoffrey C Richards CEng MIEE, ThA
    1939–47
Catherine Richmond *née* Buttery
Candy Rider
Paul Rider
Irene Rigold
Lucien Rivière
G W Robinson, ColB 1941–46
The Revd John P Robson LVO
Stephen Robson
Edward Rosoman
G C Rothwell
Hugh Rudkin
Nicholas J Rumball
Sally Rutty
R F Salisbury
Gavin Neil Salvage
A W Samuel
Rob Sanders
Richard Saunders
Adam and Amy Scott
Rosemary Scott *née* Breen
Ann E Seekins
Robert Seeley, ThA 1934–40

Dr Dennis F Shaw
Geoffrey Shelley
Gemma and Ricky Sherlock
Michael Short
G J M Shrive
Dr Paul E C Sibley
R D T Sillett
Kerren Simmonds
Peter Simmonds
Marion Simpson *née* Bridges, CH 1936–41
Mr M A Smallwood
J M Smart
Mrs P M Smeed
Judith Smith *née* Points
Margaret Smith *née* Stephenson, 8s
    1939–45
Dr Pauline M Smith
David A Smyth
Jill Sowter *née* Palmer
David Spackman
Peter Sparks, ColB 1924–33
Mrs K Speers
R H Spencer, LaB 1924–31
Patrick Spens
Dr Gordon Spink
The Revd Patrick F A Springford
A W Squibb
L M Stacey
Angela Stamp
Debbie Stamp
Eleanor Stanier
Ian Stannard
Eric Staunton
Esther Stead
L T T Steel
James Stenning
The Revd Basil Stephens
Bernard and Rhoda Stevens
Carol Stevens *née* Rayson
David M Stevens
Paul W Stevens
Mrs Kathleen Stewart-Smith
Gwendoline Mary Stillman *née* Taylor, 1s
    1932–38
Ralph and Katharine Stockbridge
Patricia Stockton
Janet Stone
Titus Stott
W A R Strickland
Mary Stroud, BaA 1990–97
Amanda J Stubbs
John Sutherell
Lynne Swatton
Richard Sydenham
Dennis and Heidrun Tambe
Jo Tansley Thomas
James Tasker
Dr Alan Taylor
Julian F Taylor
Patrick T B Ternan

Hazel Thackston *née* Craig
Geoffrey Thomas, MidA 1949–57
Nick Thompson
Roydon Thompson
Lucinda Thomson
Tim Titchmarsh
Steve Treharne
Christopher Tremayne
Mrs E D Tresham
Richard Tully
Group Captain J B Veal CBE, AFC
Ben Vickery
Lieut Col R M A Wade, MaA 1938–45
Nathan Foster Waites, LaA 1988–95
Alderman Sir Christopher Walford
Mr and Mrs S A Walker
Dr John R Waring
David L Warner
John L Watkinson, grandfather of John C
    & Sarah L Keyes
Mrs K M Watts
H W T Webb
Robin Webb BRD, PrepA, LHA, ColA
    1964–70
Steve Webb
Emily S Webster
John Wells
The Right Revd Frank V Weston
Geoffrey Wheeler
Melissa Whichelow
Alan Whipp
Emma Louise White
Susan White
Sheila Whitfeld *née* James
Mr Victor Wiffen, Dental Officer 1981–
Dr Derek Wiggins
Peter R Wildey
Rima Jono Wilkinson
Mrs Cornelia Williams
Jenny Williams
Mathieu R Williams
Thomas G Williams
Audrey Willis
Donald Willis
Mr E F H Willis, CH 1925–31
Gordon Scott F Wise
Alexander Wodzianski
Sarah Woodall, 7s, ColB 1978–87
Robert L Woolley
Deborah M Wright *née* Stone
N E Wyncoll
Audrey Yates *née* Martin, 4s 1924–30
Isabel Yeats
Virginia Youdale *née* James
Mr R M Young

and 29 others who prefer to remain
    anonymous.

INDEX

References in *italic* indicate that the subject is illustrated and those in **bold** signify the principal entry.